Greece Against Rome

Greece Against Rome

The Fall of the Hellenistic Kingdoms 250–31 BC

Philip Matyszak

Pen & Sword
MILITARY

First published in Great Britain in 2020 by
Pen & Sword Military
An imprint of
Pen & Sword Books Ltd
Yorkshire – Philadelphia

ISBN 978 1 47387 480 0

A CIP catalogue record for this book is
available from the British Library.

Typeset by Mac Style
Printed and bound in the UK by TJ International Ltd,
Padstow, Cornwall.

Pen & Sword Books Limited incorporates the imprints of Atlas,
Archaeology, Aviation, Discovery, Family History, Fiction, History,
Maritime, Military, Military Classics, Politics, Select, Transport,
True Crime, Air World, Frontline Publishing, Leo Cooper, Remember
When, Seaforth Publishing, The Praetorian Press, Wharncliffe
Local History, Wharncliffe Transport, Wharncliffe True Crime
and White Owl.

For a complete list of Pen & Sword titles please contact

PEN & SWORD BOOKS LIMITED
47 Church Street, Barnsley, South Yorkshire, S70 2AS, England
E-mail: enquiries@pen-and-sword.co.uk
Website: www.pen-and-sword.co.uk

Or

PEN AND SWORD BOOKS
1950 Lawrence Rd, Havertown, PA 19083, USA
E-mail: Uspen-and-sword@casematepublishers.com
Website: www.penandswordbooks.com

Contents

List of Plates

1. Marble head possibly depicting a Ptolemaic queen of the period 270–250 BC. (*Picture from the Metropolitan Museum, NY*)
2. The god Osiris depicted in classical Egyptian style from the Ptolemaic era. (*Picture from the Metropolitan Museum, NY*)
3. War elephants as depicted in a nineteenth century woodcut. (*Public domain picture*)
4. Antiochus III the Great. (*From a bust in the Louvre, Paris*)
5. Parthian coin of the Hellenistic era. (*Public domain picture*)
6. Apamea on the Orontes. Named after the wife of Seleucus I, this became a major city under later Seleucid kings. (*Creative commons license 1.2 Bernard Gagnon*)
7. Head of an 'Ethiopian' showing how both the Egyptian and Greek elements of the upper classes in Egypt subscribed to Hellenistic conventions of sculpture.
8. Ptolemy IV Philopater 221–204 BC. (*Contemporary coin*)
9. Bronze statuette of a veiled dancer from the Hellenistic era. (*Picture from the Metropolitan Museum NY*)
10. Hellenistic portrayal of a Bactrian camel. (*Picture from the Metropolitan Museum, NY*)
11. Part of the Rosetta Stone, with hieroglyphics at the top. (*Public domain photograph*)
12. Nabis, last king of Sparta 207–192 BC. (*From a coin of c.200 BC*)
13. The tomb of Archimedes in Syracuse as imagined by the German artist Carl Rottmann (1797–1850).
14. The goddess Cybele on her chariot. (*P. Matyszak*)
15. The theatre in Syracuse. (*Jeremy Day*)
16. Merchant ship of the classical era. (*P. Matyszak*)
17. Cornelius Sulla, 138–78 BC. (*P. Matyszak*)
18. Gnaeus Pompeius Magnus 'Pompey the Great'. (*P. Matyszak*)

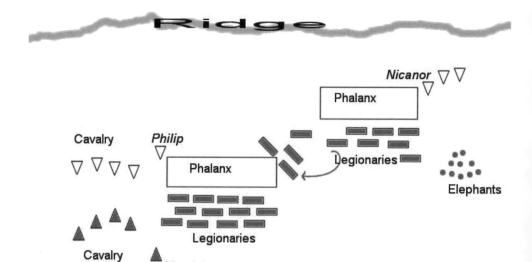

Cynoscephalae 197 BC, at the moment the advancing Romans were able to attack the more rigid Macedonian phalanx.

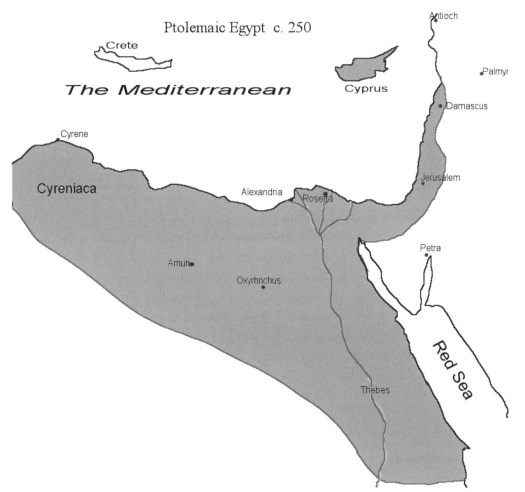

Map of Ptolemaic Egypt including disputed territories.

Anatolia and the Levant.

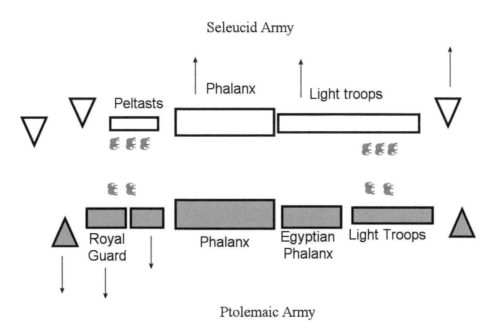

The Battle of Raphia 217 BC showing lines of retreat.

Introduction: Three Rivals Unalike

Civilization and sophistication were no match for brute force. No matter that the Persians felt themselves culturally superior to the Macedonian army of Alexander. No matter that their cities were larger, their lands more extensive and their science more advanced in fields such as astronomy. What mattered was fighting ability, heavy armour and the Macedonian pike phalanx. Against these, Persian sophistication had no answer. The heirs of Sumeria and Babylon were slaughtered on the plains of Gaugamela and Issus, and their capital of Persepolis was first pillaged and then burned to the ground.

Alexander of Macedon took over the Persian empire, and in the process became the conqueror of the largest empire the world had ever known. His rule extended from the town of Elephantine on the Nile to Kandahar in Afghanistan, south to the Ganges river in India and west to the shores of the Adriatic Sea. Small wonder that it is said that, when he realized the extent of his domains, Alexander sat and wept, because he had no worlds left to conquer.

Yet it is one thing to be a conqueror and quite another to be a ruler. Even before Alexander fell ill and died in Babylon in 323 BC, his empire was starting to unravel. It was simply too big. A messenger travelling from Athens, if he made good speed and covered 40 kilometres a day every day, might hope to reach Alexander in India within four months of departure. A reply sent post-haste would arrive at the earliest in Athens eight months after the original message was sent, and if that message informed Alexander that he and his army were urgently needed, the reply would read, 'Hold on, I'll be with you next year.'

Corrupt governors, rebellious tribesmen natural disasters – all of these issues happened far from the seat of government, and the ruler would only hear of them long after the issue had, one way or another, been resolved. Added to which, Alexander was no Solomon. If he had talent as a ruler, he kept it to himself. His one major initiative – integrating Persian and Macedonian culture – was adopted wholesale from his father's plans and failed in the implementation. Apart from that, Alexander never showed that he had what it would take to hold his massive empire together.

It may be that the Persians were right. Relatively speaking Alexander *was* a barbarian, albeit one with a very good army. Certainly, what happened to his empire after Alexander died did little to impress anyone with Macedonian sophistication. Alexander had not named a successor, mainly because in the fine tradition of Macedonian royalty, that heir would promptly have started scheming to assassinate Alexander before he changed his mind.

With no undisputed heir, Alexander's generals set about dividing up the empire almost before his corpse had cooled. It was agreed that (nominally) the new rulers were Alexander's children, with Alexander's half-brother as acting king. However, the half-brother was simple-minded and the children were still infants. Therefore it fell to Alexander's senior general – a man called Perdiccas – to actually take charge. Unlike Alexander the conqueror, Perdiccas had to be a ruler, and he quickly discovered that his new empire was basically ungovernable even for a superb politician, which he was not.

Things fell apart rather swiftly. Perdiccas quarrelled with and alienated Alexander's other senior generals, though in truth it is hard to see how he could have satisfied all their ambitions. Rather like Alexander himself, these generals were as single-mindedly ambitious, unscrupulous and amoral as sharks. Aficionados of Macedonian politics might have laid bets as to who would be first to stab Perdiccas in the back, and those who put their money on Ptolemy would have scooped the pool.

Ptolemy I Soter (367–283 BC) had decided early that he fancied Egypt, and he lobbied hard for the job of governor. He was granted his wish, partly because Egypt in any case needed a new governor to replace the current incumbent who was both disloyal and corrupt. In this regard Ptolemy was a definite improvement, since he was merely disloyal. Perdiccas discovered this fact when he received word that the remains of Alexander had been hi-jacked en route to his planned tomb in Macedonia. As a result of this intervention, with great ceremony, Alexander was interred first in central Egypt, and later in Alexandria, the Egyptian city he founded in 331 BC.

This act of disobedience was rightly construed as a unilateral declaration of independence. Perdiccas had little choice but to try to bring his mutinous subordinate to heel, lest the generals commanding the rest of the empire quickly follow Ptolemy's example and launch a series of secessions.

Ptolemy knew what he wanted, and also the limits of his ambition. When Perdiccas proved unable to force his way into Egypt to quash the rebellion, he was assassinated by his own officers who offered Ptolemy rule of the entire Macedonian empire. Ptolemy politely refused. Egypt was enough for him, and the land was to remain in the possession of his family and descendants for the next three centuries.

Once Perdiccas was dead, all pretence that the Macedonian empire was a united entity was abandoned. Secure behind the natural defences of sea and desert, Ptolemy doubtless watched with interest as Alexander's remaining generals fell upon one another in round after round of brutal warfare punctuated by shifting alliances, brutal double-crosses and faithless truces.

For a while it seemed that a general called Antigonus Monophthalmus and his son Demetrios would end up on top. However, that threatened supremacy caused all his rivals to unite against Antigonus. In 301 BC the confederation forced Antigonus to battle at Ipsus in Asia Minor. Antigonus lost the battle and his life. The mercurial Demetrios tried to keep going without his father but the tide of war had turned against him.

As the world moved into the third century BC, the fate of Alexander's empire was becoming apparent. Egypt was Ptolemaic, and the opportunistic Ptolemy would try to expand into Libya in the west and as far into Syria as possible while using his navy to dominate the islands of the eastern Mediterranean. At the same time, Ptolemy tried hard to be a pharaoh to his Egyptian subjects and a Hellenistic king to the many Greeks who began emigrating to his domains. This split Egyptian/Greek personality was to remain a standard feature as long as the Ptolemaic dynasty endured.

Macedonia, where it had all started, quickly became less relevant to the affairs of the rest of the empire. The kingdom had its own problems close to hand, and while they were coping with invaders from Epirus or across the Danube, Macedon's rulers had little interest in affairs in Bactria or India and little ability to interfere there even if they had wanted to, which they didn't.

The main preoccupation of the Macedonians was fighting off barbarian invasions of their kingdom. The second priority was to keep a grip on those parts of Alexander's empire which they regarded as 'theirs'. This included Thrace, rich in minerals and manpower, and the rest of Greece, rich in little other than trouble. Nevertheless, Greece came with a cultural heritage which strengthened the Macedonians' claim to be Greeks, and anyway, Greece would be even more trouble if it became independent or was conquered by another of the Hellenistic powers.

The Macedonian rulers also ended up as the guardians of the surviving family of Alexander the Great. This was not a happy situation for those family members because Macedon's rulers saw them as, at best, political pawns and, at worse, rivals for power. One by one they were assassinated, executed or perished in vain bids for power. Alexander's heirs never made it to a third generation, and power passed to the family of that Antipater who was left as regent in Macedonia when Alexander began his Persian adventure. This dynasty was swiftly replaced in turn by kings descended from the defeated Antigonus Monophthalmus.

Finally there was Seleucia, which might be thought of as all the rest of Alexander's empire once Egypt and Macedonia had been subtracted. (The kings of India also reckoned that the Greeks had no business ruling there, and almost as soon as Alexander had left the sub-continent, they did some subtraction of their own.)

Even with these losses taken into account, there was a very substantial amount of empire left. It was not immediately clear who was going to rule it, for the eventual winner, Seleucus, was not in the first rank of Alexander's generals.

Seleucus endured several perilous years as a rival of the more powerful Antigonus, and managed (just) to hang on to Babylon and Mesopotamia. From this power base Seleucus gradually and opportunistically expanded his power. He recognized the inevitable loss of parts of the eastern empire in India and made the best of the situation by trading land for elephants. It was these war elephants that made the crucial difference at the battle of Ipsus and resulted in Antigonus exiting the stage – doubtless to the considerable satisfaction of Seleucus.

In the settlement after Ipsus, that central, largest part of the empire went to Seleucus. This was something of a mixed blessing, for it left him with the predatory Ptolemy to the south, independent-minded states to the east (and the always-truculent Jews on the Mediterranean seaboard), and the constant threat of Macedon to the west.

Relations with the Ptolemies were off to a particularly fraught start because, after Ipsus, Ptolemy calmly helped himself to a large part of the Levant simply because he knew that Seleucus would not be able to stop him. This region, especially the part called Coele-Syria remained a bone of contention between the Ptolemies and the Seleucids, and it was the venue for at least four major wars in the next hundred years.

The response of Seleucus to his invidious situation was to build. He founded a number of major cities at strategic locations and encouraged hordes of settlers from Greece to emigrate and populate them. One such city – Seleucia on the Tigris – was founded because Babylon was poorly located for defence, and because the priests of Babylon claimed too great a role in running matters in Mesopotamia. Unable to compete with this newer rival, Babylon went into an irreversible decline that eventually saw the end of its thousands of years of history as one of the world's greatest cities.

Seleucus also made the conscious decision to move the heartland of his empire from Mesopotamia to Syria. It was in Syria that he built up his greatest cities such as Antioch and Aleppo, and where he concentrated his military efforts, both against the threat of Ptolemy in the south and the constant risk of another round of Macedonian-sponsored anarchy in Asia Minor. As a result, almost from the start, Bactria became an afterthought of empire. Over the following decades, that most easterly of Greek states started to drift away and, by 250 BC, it declared an independence which in practical terms it had long possessed.

This loss was not seen by the Seleucids as a total disaster as it left the Seleucid kings greater freedom to worry about the numerous problems closer to home. It would be fair to say that the job of a Seleucid king was a non-stop exercise in crisis management which had the king and his army rushing from one region to another in a constant struggle to contain a series of military emergencies. Any time left over from dealing with these problems was usefully spent fighting the Ptolemies.

It seems never to have occurred to the Hellenistic kingdoms that they might do better by co-operating, rather than being locked in a permanent rivalry. As it was, the only times that any two of these states joined forces was so that they could gang up on the third. As a result, war between the Hellenistic kingdoms was endemic. Even when it was not a hot, stabbing war, then it was cold war by which the rivals tried to sabotage one another by diplomatic deals or by nefarious plots, organizing or subsidizing rebellions, or encouraging an aggressive neighbouring state or tribe to be as troublesome as possible.

Yet while its leaders were militarily and politically at loggerheads, the Greek part of the Hellenistic world was an integrated cultural unit. (Many parts were non-Greek and Egyptian priests, Macedonian peasants and Persian aristocrats never felt that they had anything in common – mainly because they didn't – apart from being ruled by Greek kings.)

The Hellenistic kings might have schemed and warred against each other but they looked to one another's royal families for marriage partners to maintain the legitimacy of their line. (The Ptolemies stayed ahead of the game by practising strict incest, and were therefore primarily exporters of marriage material, mainly in the form of spare nubile daughters.)

At a lower level, trade between the Hellenistic states seems to have developed and continued even while the national armies were at each other's throats. Likewise, it does not seem to have occurred to anyone to stop people in Macedon-controlled Greece from freely emigrating to Seleucid-controlled Syria and Egypt, and Greeks did so, in the tens of thousands. This movement to literally greener pastures (Greece is mostly mountains, and the remaining bits are none too fertile) led to the depopulation of the peninsula. For the remainder of antiquity, Greece was never more than a quiet backwater.

Athens, Pergamon and Alexandria openly competed for the best intellectual talent, and no-one prevented the movement of playwrights, poets and philosophers as they went to take up residence in the nation of their chosen sponsor. As a result of this academic freedom, the Hellenistic world saw a flowering of intellectual accomplishment in both the arts and the sciences.

To a Greek of the late third century BC, the world was his oyster. Outside the great Hellenistic kingdoms, there were Greek settlements around the Mediterranean from Spain to the Crimea. Greeks shared a common culture and language which was common even to the aristocracies of non–Greek states such as Etruria.

Across several thousand kilometres of the planet's surface, a Greek was never far from a city where he could discuss trade or philosophy with fellow Greeks. There were temples to the Greek gods where he could sacrifice in traditional ways before settling down to a Greek symposium with new friends after watching a production by the same playwrights who were enjoyed on the other side of the Hellenistic world. At that time, the Hellenistic world seemed unshakeable and permanent.

Chapter 1

The Limits of Hellenism

Since we are dealing with entities called the 'Hellenistic kingdoms', it is only reasonable to ask how 'Hellenistic' those kingdoms were, once the dynastic struggles had ended, and a century after the death of Alexander. By this point, Hellenism had become an established fact across much of the ancient world. Was Hellenism a philosophy, a culture or a term defining a particular ethnic group? Was it similar to the process known today as 'westernisation', and if so, was the uptake of Hellenic ways something which the Greek rulers of the Hellenistic kingdoms tried to foist upon their subjects?

'Hellenism' certainly had much in common with the modern process of 'westernisation' and can be thought of as a somewhat analogous process. Hellenism is defined as the spread of Greek language and the culture of the classical era to nations which were not themselves Greek. Unlike many similar expressions, the term 'Hellenism' is not an invention of modern academia. It was actually used to describe the process by those people to whom it was happening. Thus, for example, the Jewish people of 150 BC could complain, 'the adoption of foreign customs had led to extreme Hellenization'. (2 Maccabees 4)

In later years the most 'extreme Hellenization' happened to the Romans who became thoroughly *Greekified* in the process of conquering Greece. ('Greece captured her rough captor', remarked the Roman poet Horace, *Epistles* 2.210.) This happened to the extent that today historians refer to the 'Graeco-Roman civilization'. If a conqueror could be seduced by Greek ways to such an extent, how much more vulnerable might be the peoples whom the Greeks had conquered? Also, was there a conscious effort by Greek rulers to Hellenize their subjects – and if not, why not?

It should be pointed out that the Greeks were refreshingly non-racist in their outlook. They never referred to themselves as 'Greeks' but as 'Hellenes', and it was clear that they regarded being Hellenic as resulting from the adoption of Greek language and Greek ways, rather than being a genetic condition. As Thucydides explains:

> Before the Trojan war the name was not widespread, nor is there any sign that the people acted together as Hellenes. … It was not till [the mythical ruler] Hellen and his sons grew strong in Phthiotis, and other cities offered to come into alliance with them, that those cities in the alliance one by one started to call themselves Hellenic. Nevertheless it was a long time before that name became common to all.
>
> … Homer, born long after the Trojan War, never calls the Greeks by that name…nor does he ever use the term 'barbarian'. This is probably because the Hellenes had not yet chosen that distinctive name by which they separated themselves from the rest of the world. Thus it seems several communities first called themselves 'Hellenic' as they came to recognize that quality in each other, and others assumed the name afterwards.
>
> Thucydides *History of the Peloponnesian War* 1.3ff

In other words, Hellenism was not something one inherently was – it was something one became and which those who had so become 'recognized' in others. Being born a Greek certainly did the job, but adopting Greek ways worked also. This could be done by an individual or a community.

A good example is the city-state of Pergamon in Asia Minor, which became one of the leading cities of the Hellenistic world. Pergamon was largely the creation of a man called Philetaerus who found the place barely worth the appellation of 'city' – when he arrived it was merely a scattering of houses around a hilltop fort. Neither the population nor Philetaerus were particularly Greek in their origins. Philetaerus was born in the city of Tium on the coast of the Euxine (Black Sea). His father was Macedonian and his mother was an Anatolian woman with the very non-Greek name of Boa.

Yet no-one, including Philetaerus himself, considered him as anything but one hundred per cent Hellene. He was a loyal supporter of the house of Seleucus and received favour accordingly. The population of the city was a mix of Greek immigrants and the native peoples of Asia Minor, yet all eventually thought of themselves as Hellenes. Even today, surviving relics of Pergamon such as the Great Altar (now reconstructed in a museum in Berlin) are regarded as masterpieces of Hellenic culture.

Pergamon shows that Hellenism was not an ethnic or racial definition but a process that turned 'barbarians' into 'Greeks'. While the Greeks, especially those of the classical era, were very firm about the exclusively heritable nature of citizenship of individual cities, they were much looser in their definition of what constituted a 'Hellene'. This definition became even looser in the Hellenistic era.

It is at this point that we need to separate 'Hellenism' and 'westernisation'. Not because of any great dissimilarity between the two processes when they did occur but because 'westernisation' carries with it substantial baggage. In the colonial past, many western powers made a deliberate attempt to replace the cultures of indigenous peoples with their own.

For example, within the British empire, 'westernisation' sometimes included the forcible removal of indigenous children from their parents and their placement in either European homes or residential schools, where the children were trained to become little replicas of their colonial masters. Unsurprisingly those who conflate Hellenism with westernisation see in Hellenism similar attempts by the Greek kings and their servants to destroy and replace native culture.

Yet if there was an ideological push to make the peoples of Syria, Mesopotamia and Egypt into Greeks, the evidence is completely lacking from the records. Admittedly, those records are remarkably scant in any case, but even this does not fully explain the absence of any comment. Where we have evidence of Hellenism taking place it is almost incidental, and in no cases was it to become as deep-rooted as the process of Romanization was to be in that later empire.

Certainly, within the Hellenistic kingdoms some local aristocrats and other elites quickly decided that the shortest route to power and preference within a Greek administration was to become Greek themselves – and in terms of the desired objective, this decision appears largely to have been correct. Also, Greek art and the Greek language made substantial gains in the Hellenistic kingdoms.

In places like Bactria the influence of the Seleucid kings was relatively transitory, yet the influence of Greek art is clearly evident centuries later – by which time Greek art had also influenced the art of northern India. One should note though, that Greek art was not influential because of other aspects of Greek culture. It was – and is – influential simply because it was extremely good art. Even today Greek painting, sculpture and vases are capable of touching and inspiring viewers, no matter what their origins.

Greek as a language certainly was a means of spreading Greek culture, but its adoption was pragmatic rather than ideological. Greek served as a unifying force throughout the Hellenistic kingdoms. When we consider that there were at least a hundred languages spoken – some were not written – in Anatolia alone, the necessity for a common tongue in an international community becomes self-evident.

It helped that Greek is a remarkably expressive language (in later years we see Cicero, who was one of the greatest speakers of Latin who ever lived, frequently reaching for a Greek term to express something that he was unable to say in his native tongue). Also the version of Greek used throughout the Hellenistic kingdoms was more straightforward than the often elided and elegantly convoluted Greek of classical writers. The version of Greek common to the people of the Hellenistic kingdoms has exactly that name; 'koine' which means 'common'.

And yet ...

There was only one Hellenistic kingdom where any but the ruling class were Hellenic, and that was Macedon and its Greek dependency, mainly because these people started the era as Hellenic anyway. Hellenism as a means of converting the Seleucid and Ptolemaic kingdoms into replicas of Greece was a miserable failure – if that was ever the intention in the first place.

To see why this was so we have only to look at the peoples over whom the Hellenic kings ruled.

The Mesopotamians had a history going back over 5,000 years to the Sumerians and Hurrians. They had seen the arrival of Akkadians, Amorites, Arameans and Assyrians (even before we come to 'B' with 'Babylonians'). All of these peoples had risen to prominence in Mesopotamia and, after a period of ascendancy, had merged with and vanished into the local population. No-one was particularly impressed by the Greeks, and the locals (correctly) assumed that these latest arrivals also would be gone within a century or two. This was also the case in Syria, where cities such as Damascus were already a few thousand years old and well accustomed to dealing with conquerors who assumed that their rule would last forever.

Then there were the Jews and Phoenicians. The Phoenicians had a particularly rough ride under Alexander, who wiped out the Phoenician city of Tyre (the city did recover and remains a going concern still today). In resisting the charms of Hellenism, the Phoenicians had centuries of their own culture to draw upon. It was hard for Phoenicians to feel inferior to the culture of the people whom they had taught to write and build ships. (The Greek script is adapted from the Phoenician, notably by the addition of vowels, and several shipbuilding innovations which made the Greeks such famous seafarers were adopted from Phoenician inventions.)

The Jews were a small but remarkably truculent nation. Like most states in the Levant they had a long tradition of dealing with invaders, the preferred Jewish technique being to wear them down by repeated rebellions.

Numerous experiments had been tried by a succession of rulers of different nationalities to determine the best way of ruling the Jews (most of which have been documented in the Bible).

By the time of the Seleucids, there was a sort of consensus that the best way of ruling the sons of Judah was to leave them mostly to their own devices. With no-one to unite against, the Jews would do a remarkable job of falling out among themselves. However, a people with so strong a self-identity were unlikely victims for cultural assimilation, and as will be seen, they reacted violently when that self-image was challenged.

Finally, there were the Egyptians. No-one needed to point out that the Egyptians had been civilized for thousands of years while the barbarians on the Greek side of the Mediterranean were still figuring out how to get lice out of their beards. (While there was no need to point this out, the Egyptians nevertheless frequently did so). The response of the Ptolemaic kings was not to attempt to foist Hellenistic ways upon a proud and conservative people, but to pretend to them that actually the Ptolemies were Egyptians also, albeit Egyptians from elsewhere.

Thus we have several imposing sculptures of Ptolemy I, former general of Alexander, in full Egyptian regalia as he presents himself to his Egyptian subjects as indistinguishable from the Pharaohs who had preceded him. There was no attempt to interfere with Egyptian religion, other than to point out where syncretism might usefully be accomplished. (Syncretism is the merging of religions with similar belief systems.) Some of the most impressive Egyptian temples that have survived into the modern era were built by the Ptolemies.

In other words, when comparing westernisation in the British empire and Hellenism in the Seleucid empire we are not comparing like with like. With the British, native peoples who had not progressed far beyond the dug-out canoe might be excused for being impressed by an ocean-going steamship. Oral tradition, however rich, has difficulty keeping pace with large libraries, and maxim guns were a convincing advance on clubs and spears.

On the other hand, the Mesopotamians, Egyptians and Syrians were well aware that they had been civilized long before the Greeks, and that much of Greek civilization was built upon their accomplishments. Furthermore, the Greeks also were well aware of this. Therefore the Greeks had none of the smug sense of superiority which early modern westerners felt over the rest of the world. They were well aware that theirs was but one culture among many, and those other cultures were at least equally ancient and well-established.

Where the Greeks did feel that their culture was superior, as with politics and religion, they simply lacked the urge to foist their culture upon others who did not feel the same way about it. Proselytizing, be it of religion or culture, was a trend which developed later. In the Greek view, if you had a superior political system, why share it with potential enemies and so make their society more efficient? If yours were the true gods, why have them share their beneficence with strangers?

If you had a superior culture, then keeping it to yourself made you a superior people. Call it selfishness, or call it tolerance, but the ancient Greeks simply did not feel the modern urge to draw others into their own way of life. That included their culture. One reason that the Greek kings did not actively attempt to Hellenize their subjects was because they lacked the ideological drive to do so and well understood the difficulties of trying.

The Hellenes of the Hellenistic kingdoms

The one reason why Hellenistic kings might have wanted to Hellenize their subjects was because their kingdoms were always short of Greeks. Greeks were useful to the Hellenistic kings because they were skilled craftsmen, merchants and artists. However, there was no shortage of people elsewhere in their kingdoms with the same talents. What the Hellenistic kings really needed were soldiers.

The Greeks had a low opinion of the military abilities of the people whom they had conquered, because after all, the Greeks had conquered them. However, the Greeks were neither arrogant enough, nor stupid enough to believe that they had done so through some divine right. (Naturally there were exceptions to this generalization. The Greeks were human after all.) The Romans may later have sneered at the 'servile Asiatic character' (Aristotle *Politics* Bk3 1285a), but the Greeks had often enough been perforated by Persian arrows and ridden down by Iranian cavalry to respect their former enemies.

Therefore, by and large, the difference between Greek and eastern warfare came down to different military systems and the willingness of the soldiers to die while part of those systems. Given the resistance of most subject peoples to being Hellenized, it followed that their commitment to Hellenistic kings had its limits. They were generally willing to give the king taxes, but not their lives. Furthermore – as experiments by the Ptolemies demonstrated – training non-Hellenized troops in Greek military systems meant that one ended up fighting against more competent rebels.

Therefore, in Hellenizing their kingdoms, the Hellenistic kings took the two inter-related options which gave the most return for the least investment. (They did, after all have a great deal else to do.) The first option for a king in need of Hellenes was to import them wholesale. This was done enthusiastically. In this same era the Greeks of Greece were disillusioned with Macedonian rule, and where Greeks still had a degree of political freedom this led to the sort of violent political infighting which had always been a Greek speciality. This infighting produced an abundance of exiles who, after being welcomed into the eastern kingdoms, frequently decided that being thrown out of Greece was the best thing that could have happened to them.

Peasants who struggled to make a living on stony Greek fields were assured by family and friends who had gone abroad that fertile fields waited for their arrival. Even today, at oracular sites such as Dodona, archaeologists have found requests written to the gods for advice as to whether it was better to emigrate or stay home. In the case of tens of thousands of Greeks, the advice was evidently that they should go.

The Hellenistic kings did their best to make this good advice. The Seleucids particularly were enthusiastic followers of Alexander's habit of founding cities wherever he discovered a suitable site. A suitable site was not merely one with excellent agricultural prospects, for most of these already had cities located there. Ideally a city should also be on a good trade route, or where there was a potential for such, and above all, it should serve as a military bastion and a reservoir of potential recruits for the army.

It is uncertain what happened to the locals when Greek engineers appeared and started laying city grids across what had once been their farmland. The general opinion among modern historians is that the locals were incorporated into the citizenry of the new city. Often land was underworked, because local populations remained at suboptimal levels (mortality was high in the ancient world), and sometimes the agricultural potential of land was boosted by irrigation projects. At other times the locals may have adapted to alternative professions within the city.

Quite certainly, living side by side with immigrants from Greece, many of these locals became Greek themselves through marriage and assimilation. Others, especially those outside the cities simply accepted the Greek presence with varying degrees of resentment. It is said that 'a rising tide lifts all boats' and certainly the economic effect of a new city on a regional backwater created new markets and opportunities, even for those whom the Greeks regarded as second-class citizens. Looking at both the Ptolemaic and Seleucid kingdoms it is possible to discern a correlation between military success, economic growth and the prevalence or otherwise of rebellions.

Nevertheless, in a world where ninety per cent or more of the population was dedicated to agriculture, city-dwellers were necessarily a minority. Since the Greek immigrants were often city-dwellers, this meant that Hellenes were also a minority in the east and doomed to remain so. Hellenization in the Hellenistic world was largely an urban phenomenon. Doubtless there were large tracts of Anatolia and the Iranian highlands where farming populations hardly knew that they were ruled by Greek overlords and cared little for the knowledge anyway. For them, village life continued as it always had, the works of Euripides and Plato remained as foreign as they always had been, and their rulers made little attempt to change this.

Chapter 2

Rome and the Greek World in 250 BC

The year 250 BC was the year of the 132nd Olympiad as the Greek world measured time (starting with the first Olympic games of 776 BC) and 504 AUC as the Romans did. (That is, 504 years since the founding of the city of Rome.) This point saw the Hellenistic kingdoms at the height of their strength, and the Romans struggling to maintain their position as a rising power. Even at this early point, Romans and Greeks had a history of almost continuous interaction.

Egypt was under the rule of Ptolemy II the son of the general who had founded Ptolemaic rule as that ancient country's thirty-third dynasty. Ptolemy II was known as Philadelphos, 'Loving Brother', to the Greeks while for his Egyptian subjects he took the name Mer y'amun Setepen're, 'Loved by Amon, the Chosen of Ra.' (Amun was an Egyptian creator deity, and Ra was the sun god. Between them they comprised the most important gods in the Egyptian pantheon.) This multiplicity of names was typical of Ptolemy II and his successors as they struggled to keep a balance between keeping the kingdom a power in the Hellenistic world while remaining relevant to the Egyptian peoples whom they ruled.

Ptolemy II's designation as a 'loving brother' would certainly have been disputed by his rather unstable sibling Ptolemy Keraunos who, under Ptolemy I, had been exiled and later killed after usurping the throne of Macedon. (See *Rise of the Hellenistic Kingdoms* for the full story.) On the other hand, Arsinoe, Ptolemy II's older sister, certainly understood the title, for it was originally attached to her with the meaning of 'Brother Loving'. Which 'loving' Arsinoe comprehensively did, as she was both Ptolemy's sister and his second wife. (The first wife was exiled to southern Egypt and Arsinoe took over – and apparently did a good job of rearing the children from that first marriage.)

As a boy, Ptolemy II had the best education available, and he seems to have been completely at home in his environment. This was quite an achievement, as this environment included a toxic mixture of greed, intrigue and treachery at the royal court. Abroad, things were little better with the main theme of international relations being brutal realpolitik, shifting alliances and a complex web of diplomacy and espionage punctuated by periods of outright warfare. Added to this was Ptolemy's personal lifestyle of luxurious debauchery – in all, a combination of circumstances quite sufficient to destroy any normal mortal.

Yet in 250 BC Ptolemy II was not only coping, he was thriving. Under his rule, Egypt grew ever more prosperous as Egyptian merchants were encouraged by their king to explore and develop trade routes reaching deep into the Middle East and India. One enduring testament to this mercantile outreach was the introduction of camels to Egypt for the first time. (While often considered native to North Africa, camels are actually American animals which migrated across the Siberian land bridge to thereafter be domesticated by the peoples of central Asia.)

Ptolemy also gained kudos from his Egyptian subjects by completing a canal from the Red Sea to the Nile, a project originally started by the Pharaoh Necho four hundred years previously. The project had been abandoned when it was discovered that the Red Sea was higher than the Nile, and a completed link might cause disastrous flooding. However, Ptolemy applied Greek engineering skill to Egyptian circumstances and came up with the first lock system to ever be applied to a major canal.

Ruling Egypt was a difficult job for a non-Egyptian. While they occupied Egypt, the Persians had to deal with a series of rebellions. Ptolemy I originally had the opportunity to take over Egypt because his Macedonian predecessor was making a mess of the job. Yet Ptolemy I and his son made the task look relatively easy. This suggests that both put considerable thought into how they identified themselves to their new subjects.

The first aspect of this approach we have discussed – that the Ptolemies presented themselves to the Egyptian people as Egyptian pharaohs. The actual Pharaoh might have been a debauched, wine-swilling Macedonian, but that was not what his people were told. For them the Pharaoh was, as he had ever been, the sun-god's representative on Earth, and a semi-divine being in himself. There was no change from previous dynasties in how the Ptolemies were depicted in religious iconography, and little change in the religious rites which they celebrated and in which they were celebrated. Ptolemaic rule was about continuity with the pre-Persian past, not radical change.

This was also the case with the administrative machinery which the Ptolemies inherited. By and large, Egypt was a theocracy. That is, the kingdom's bureaucrats were also its priests. Rather, as with Europe in the early medieval period, the clergy did much of the administrative work of local communities, recording births, marriages and deaths, and sorting out personal and property disputes. Egypt's had an administrative machine refined through centuries of use, and the Ptolemies by and large let the priests get on with running it.

There was of course also the fact that Ptolemy was king to a large and growing Greek population in Egypt, and that Greek population needed to live alongside the Egyptian one. Note 'live alongside' for it was not in Ptolemy's interest to integrate the two. Ptolemy needed the Egyptian peasantry to produce Egypt's abundant grain and harvest its papyrus and other products. He needed Greeks as merchants to export these products abroad, and to man his very extensive navy. (Like his fellow Hellenistic kings, Ptolemy dreamed of naval domination of the Aegean. It was even more important for him, because Egypt had a claim to Cyprus and several other Aegean islands, including the island of Cos, where he was born.)

Greek militias were needed to hold down the native population should it get restive, and to provide soldiers for the army, since in times of internal peace Ptolemaic kings liked go abroad and create problems for the Seleucids and Macedonians. In most instances, the Egyptian Greeks were accommodated in new city foundations. Of these Alexandria was the largest, but far from the oldest. Greek merchants had maintained a presence in Egypt at least since the end of the Bronze Age and possibly before.

The Greek city of Naucratis was founded in the seventh century BC, and this city became something of a role model for later settlements. (It has recently been discovered that there was another city, Heraclion, on the coast. The changing Mediterranean coastline led to this city being submerged and lost in antiquity, but it has recently been re-discovered by archaeologists and is proving a veritable treasure trove of artefacts.)

Further inland, archaeologists have found that many cities were a fascinating mix of Egyptian and Greek culture, with Greek amphitheatres sharing civic space with temples to Horus and Ra. The best model we have is naturally Alexandria, which was shared between the native Egyptians, the Greeks and a very substantial population of Jews. In Alexandria the three communities each kept to their own parts of the city, with the Egyptians uneasy mediators between the Greek and Jewish populations which generally loathed each other, though the Egyptians were prone to outbreaks of nationalist sentiment of their own.

Macedon in 250 BC, the kingdom where it had all started was now settling down after a period of dynastic upsets which had seen rulers come and go in a game of thrones every bit as lethal as any medieval fantasy. The family of Alexander had been one of the first casualties of this brutal struggle. Not holding power, but capable of doing so through the evocative power of their famous name, Alexander's heirs were quickly disposed of by the ambitious and ruthless men who took control of Macedon after his death.

The thoroughly unpleasant Kassander was replaced by the murderous but short-lived Ptolemy Keraunos, then by Antigonus Gonatas, Pyrrhus of Epirus (of whom more later), Antigonus Gonatas again, Alexander II of Epirus, and then once again by the remarkably resilient Antigonus Gonatas. Even when Antigonus finally wedged himself on the Macedonian throne for good, his rule was far from secure.

Agents of the interfering Ptolemy II provoked a war in Greece by stirring the Athenians into a rebellion which took years to suppress (known to historians as the Chremonidian War of 267–261 BC after the Athenian demagogue who led the rebels). As soon as this rebellion was quashed, Ptolemy promptly instigated another revolt in Corinth and continually urged the Spartans to make an attempt to regain their ancient greatness.

It is quite possible that Antigonus would have been a happy man if a fortuitous earthquake had taken out the entire Greek peninsula and left nothing but placid waters over that troublesome possession. However, Macedon needed control of Greece for no other reason that if the

Macedonians did not control Greece then some other unfriendly power would quickly do so. This in itself would be no problem, if not that the best way to invade Macedon's heartlands was from the south. Therefore the best way to protect Macedon from invasion was to be the power which occupied the south in the first place.

Unlike the sprawling and impossibly diverse empire of the Seleucids or the split personality of the Graeco-Egyptian kingdom, the Macedonians were an integrated nation state. They were Macedonians who lived in Macedon under Macedonian laws and a Macedonian king. This made the place a lot easier to rule once Antigonus had got on top of the country's murderous palace politics.

We hear of little internal dissent within Macedon itself, which was just as well for the Macedonians could ill afford civil strife. The Macedonian perception of their state as struggling alone against a hostile world was well-founded. To the north and west were tribes of Dardanians and Illyrians, and to the east and north were Thracians and Danubian tribes. All of these kept a keen eye on Macedon, and at the first indication that the Macedonian army might be otherwise engaged these tribes would swoop southwards in massive raids which they often co-ordinated among themselves.

The main thing keeping the Macedonian army busy was, as we have seen, southern Greece. Apart from Thebes, which an angry Alexander had pounded into insignificance after a failed rebellion in 335 BC, the Greek states kept yearning for their lost independence. That the era of the city-state had passed did not stop the Athenians, Corinthians and Spartans – among others – from wanting the glory days to return. Because the southern Greek states were unable to agree on anything (other than they wanted to regain their independence) they never presented a united front to their enemies. Consequently, southern Greece was always doomed to be occupied by larger kingdoms. The southern Greeks never seemed to grasp that fact and were pathetically eager to ally themselves with whatever power cynically offered them their 'freedom'.

Between fighting barbarians and the southern Greeks the Macedonians always had a skilled veteran army. Even with the Spartan nation severely diminished, keeping just the Spartans down required a highly-competent army, as the Macedonians were forced to prove during the Chremonidian war. Fortunately for Antigonus, in 250 BC the Spartans were having internal political problems which removed them as a military threat – though as it later proved, only temporarily.

Instead of the Spartans, Antigonus was currently vexed in Greece by the Achaean League, a federation of states in central Greece led by the very competent Aratus of Sicyon. Naturally the league was supported by Ptolemy II who never missed a chance to stir up trouble.

Antigonus always had a preference for diplomacy rather than warfare, partly because he was a very good diplomat, and partly because warfare meant deploying the Macedonian army, which was already needed in several different places at once. Instead of going to war in Greece, Antigonus cultivated the rivalry between the Achaeans and the Aetolian League of states to the north-west of the Achaeans. There was reasonable hope that the two leagues would cancel each other out, especially as the Spartans loathed the League for reasons of their own and would happily join in any Aetolian attack on the Achaeans.

Despite being necessarily on a semi-permanent war footing, Macedon was also a participant in the intellectual flowering of the Hellenistic era. Pella boasted a fine library at which leading scholars of the day were invited to study. Antigonus himself was keenly interested in philosophy and corresponded frequently with Zeno, the founder of the Stoic school in Athens. After Zeno's death in 262 BC, Antigonus became patron of the philosopher's successors. Patronage of the arts and philosophers was to become a hallmark of the Antigonid dynasty. But then, given their difficult circumstances, the Macedonian kings had much to be philosophical about.

Seleucia The year 250 BC saw the birth of the longest-lasting, and in some ways the most influential of the Hellenistic kingdoms. This was Bactria, on the far eastern fringe of the Hellenistic world. Conquered by Alexander and ruled by Seleucus, Bactria nevertheless took third place in the minds of later kings preoccupied firstly with events in Syria and secondly with those in Mesopotamia.

Bactria was merely distant, for in no other way was it a negligible part of the empire. True, it was relatively thinly populated, especially compared to the teeming Indian kingdoms to the south. Nevertheless, Bactria possessed a large number of cities, fertile lands and a well-developed economy. In short it was a prosperous, thriving state that needed more than the occasional attention of a foreign ruler over a thousand miles away.

Certainly, this was the opinion of one Diodotus, the Seleucid governor of Bactria and of the several minor provinces attached to his satrapy. He was of the opinion that Bactria needed home rule under its own king, and he was the ideal man for the job. Perhaps Diodotus was also encouraged to declare himself king following the birth of his daughter in that fateful year of 250 BC. A monarch can certainly do better by his family in marriage than can a satrap subject to recall and demotion at the whim of a distant master.

It also helped that Diodotus was probably in close contact with his neighbour, Andragoras, satrap of the province of Parthia. Andragoras was also inclined to independence, partly because he was a native son of the area (his name as given appears to be the Greek version of the Persian original). The other reason was because Parthia and the affiliated state of Hycarnia were struggling to cope with waves of invaders from central Asia. Since the Seleucid kings had problems of their own further west, Andragoras received very little help. Eventually the exasperated satrap decided that since he was on his own anyway, he might as well formalize the fact and declare independence.

Diodotus in Bactria was thus aware that even in the unlikely event that a Seleucid king was prepared to take the time off from major problems in Anatolia and Syria, that king would still have to struggle through a hostile Parthia to get to him. Overall, becoming ruler of an independent kingdom seemed a very safe bet, and Diodotus accordingly became Diodotus I of Bactria and surrounding states.

As usual with events in Bactria, the rest of the Hellenistic world took little notice. The historian Gnaeus Trogus made a passing comment, summarized by his epitomater, Justin who says that 'Theodotus, governor of the thousand cities of Bactria, rebelled and took the title of king; and other people of the east [i.e. Andragoras of Parthia] followed his example.'

We note that Justin appears to have got Diodotus' name wrong, which indicates his level of concern. Hereafter, the Bactrian kingdom drifts slowly out of the orbit of the Hellenistic world, but (unlike most historians of the time) we shall continue to follow the fortunes of this outpost of the Greek world as it grew and changed over the centuries.

Meanwhile back in Syria … In 250 BC, the Seleucid empire was ruled by Antiochus II, and when we study the sea of (partly self-inflicted) troubles faced by that king, his lack of action with regard to the Bactrian and Parthian secessions becomes more understandable.

Antiochus II got his job because his father Antiochus I had sent Antiochus' older brother to govern the eastern part of the empire. When it became clear that the brother was exploring the same path to independence that Diodotus and Andragoras were later to take, Antiochus had his son executed. This promoted the next in line – the future Antiochus II – to the status of royal heir.

His father's career would have given Antiochus II some idea of what to expect of ruling the empire. Antiochus I had become king when his father was assassinated (few Seleucid kings were ever to die in bed). Immediately Antiochus became embroiled in war with Macedon while simultaneously having to suppress rebellions in Syria and Anatolia. Barely had he got on top of these conflicts when the Galatians arrived in Asia Minor and became a public menace. As soon as the rampaging tribesmen had been slapped down, war broke out with Egypt.

After almost a decade of inconclusive warfare, fighting had declined to the point where Antiochus I could charge north again to deal with the kingdom of Pergamon. This city-state not only rejected Seleucid suzerainty but was doing so well despite that rejection that it was proving a dangerously bad example to other minor kingdoms nearby, such as Cappadocia and Bithynia. The attempt to bring Pergamon to heel failed disastrously. Antiochus I was defeated in battle in 262 BC and died soon thereafter, bringing Antiochus II to the throne.

One issue of Hellenistic diplomacy was that it was largely personal. For example, Seleucia did not make a treaty with Egypt. Instead Antiochus I struck an agreement with Ptolemy II. Therefore, when either king died, that agreement died with him. It was up to the successor to make new deals on whatever terms he could. Such agreements affected not only external relations, but internal ones also. Subject kings in the Seleucid empire swore fealty to the person of the king, not to the office. Therefore, when the king died, it was again up to his successor to extract new oaths of loyalty – often by armed force, since subject kings felt no loyalty to someone they had not sworn to serve.

Therefore, the death of Antiochus I voided the deal he had made with Ptolemy II to end the Syrian War. The opportunistic Ptolemy decided that he might as well test the new king's mettle by resuming the conflict with a series of maritime raids. Ptolemy quickly discovered that Antiochus II was a pretty good commander. The new king kicked the Ptolemaic puppet Timarchus out of the strategic city of Miletus in 259 BC, and the grateful Milesians hailed him as a god for doing so. (Hence the usual epithet for this king, who is distinguished from the many Antiochi to come by the epithet 'Theos' – 'Antiochus II, the god'.)

Rather like his counterpart Antigonus Gonatas of Macedon, Antiochus preferred diplomacy to warfare. Therefore it surprised no-one that the cordial ties between these two kings (united by a mutual loathing for Ptolemy) were formalized by the marriage of Antiochus' daughter to the son of Antigonus. Another daughter of Antiochus had already been married to a Persian nobleman who had become king in Cappadocia in exchange for a – largely nominal – pledge of loyalty.

Ptolemy II recognized that the new Seleucid king could keep up his end of a fight, and decided to cut his losses before they became significant. In 253 BC Antiochus II and Ptolemy made peace, with Ptolemy ceding to Antiochus the gains he had made in the recent war. This concession came at a price – Antiochus had to divorce his wife Laodice and marry Ptolemy II's daughter Berenice. Any children of the union would get precedence over the offspring from the previous marriage when Antiochus died.

(For all their wealth in other areas, the Hellenistic kings suffered appalling poverty in the names of royal princesses. There were basically five, which everyone had to share – Berenice, Laodice, Arsinoe, Eurydice, and Cleopatra. Berenice – 'Bearer of victory' was also the name of the wife of Ptolemy I, and that of the future queen of Ptolemy III. Since these queens were often strong-willed and historically significant figures, keeping track of which one was whom is an ongoing challenge.)

With Berenice replacing Laodice as Seleucid queen, Ptolemy's grandchildren stood to inherit the Seleucid empire. Given the – literally – cut-throat nature of Hellenistic succession, this also meant that when

Antiochus II died, Laodice and her children would die also. No new king would tolerate the dynastic threat posed by a viable alternative to himself. Anyone opposed to the current king would quickly become a supporter of a possible replacement, so the king would eliminate that threat at the first opportunity. Unsurprisingly therefore, Antiochus' Laodice was even more bitter about her divorce than most estranged spouses.

The deadly palace diplomacy of the Seleucid empire was echoed down through the lower levels of government. A Seleucid king had to stay on top of the palace intrigues, poisonings and power struggles in the courts of the dozen or so major kings and satraps over whom he was suzerain. (The consequences of failing to do this were demonstrated by the secessions of Anagoras of Parthia and Diodotus of Bactria.)

As well as these major kingdoms and satrapies, the Seleucid empire was a patchwork of minor kingdoms some of which were barely more than hilltop fortresses dominated by local warlords. Then there were the great temples of Asia Minor and Mesopotamia, theocratic city-states ruled by priests, and the pirate nests of Caria which could be usefully directed at Ptolemaic shipping. On top of this there were barbarian tribes, some resident and others visiting for trade and plunder, and the merchant cities along the Silk Road – golden geese that required careful handling if one was to extract the maximum revenue without harming trade.

From the deserts around the Red Sea to the lush valleys of Pontus, from the mountains of Iran to the seacoast of Phoenicia, the Seleucid empire was geographically and ethnically diverse. Bactrian camels loaded with exotic spices from India and silks from China moved along the trade routes, accompanied by war-elephants from India destined for the breeding-pens of Syria.

Seleucia had tragic princesses in abundance, an exasperating surplus of pirates, magic-users from Mesopotamia (whose Chaldean people have given the modern word 'magic' from their wise men called 'magi'), a host of strange and exotic religions, and ruined palaces and lost cities aplenty. In short, to the modern imagination Seleucia was a fantastically diverse, wild and romantic place that had everything but dragons. Sadly, Antiochus II probably regarded his kingdom as more of an exasperating mess.

Part II. Rome

It is not as if the Greeks were unaware that Rome existed. Almost from the start they were aware that a tribe of barbarian bandits had fortified a hilltop in central Italy on the border between Latium and Etruria. However, on the scale of exciting things that were happening in their world, this event ranked very low. The most exciting event of the decade in Italy was probably the foundation of Naples as a Greek colony, while in Greece the growing diplomatic tension between Sparta and Messenia was rapidly escalating towards war. When news filtering from the east involved the potential clash of the mighty armies of Assyria and Babylon, a hillside squabble between Romans and Sabines could safely be ignored. In fact, until the third century BC, it could be said that, though the Greeks were aware that Rome existed, by and large, they simply did not care that it did.

The opposite was not true. If the Greeks paid little attention to Rome, the Romans certainly paid attention to Greece. How could they not when one of their kings had a Greek father? This was Tarquin I (king of Rome 616–579 BC), whose father was one Demaratus of Corinth. It was also later alleged that Numa, the second king of Rome was on good terms with the Greek philosopher Pythagoras. No-one was surprised when those from a later era discovered the supposed tomb of Numa and books within written in Greek. Right from the start, Roman leaders were expected to be familiar with Greek culture.

When Rome became a republic in 509 BC, the Greeks were partly responsible. The family of the last Etruscan king, the tyrannical Tarquinus Superbus, had travelled to consult the Oracle at Delphi in central Greece. While there, they asked who would be the next ruler of Rome. The Oracle replied that power would pass to whomever was the first to kiss his mother.

In the royal retinue was an aristocrat who had escaped execution because the suspicious Tarquin believed him to be simple-minded. Yet this 'simple-minded' brute was the first to realize that the Earth is the mother of all. He pretended to stumble and planted a smacking kiss on the ground. In due course, the brute (Marcus Iunius Brutus) went on to become the leading consul in the Roman Republic.

Relations between Greece and Rome remained generally cordial for the next two centuries, mainly because Rome had nothing that the Greeks wanted, and Rome was too preoccupied with local wars to covet any Greek possessions. This changed early in the third century BC, mainly because Rome was highly successful in these local wars. In consequence, Roman power had expanded to the borders of Greek territory in southern Italy, and the Romans showed no signs of stopping.

If the Romans would not stop voluntarily, then they would have to be stopped. The Italian Greeks sent to the motherland for help, and Pyrrhus of Epirus (prompted by ambition and the Oracle at Delphi) stepped up.

By 280 BC an Epirot army had landed in Italy. Again, in the Hellenistic world, this event received less attention than it deserved. Antiochus I of Seleucia was embroiled in military and political strife with Macedon and Bithynia, and Ptolemy II was busy wrapping up a successful war against Antiochus in the Levant. Antigonus of Macedon was preoccupied with the reformation in Greece of the Achaean League which he (correctly) diagnosed as a future headache.

If there was a reaction to the Epirot invasion of Italy, it was that Antigonus and everyone else were simply relieved that the headstrong Pyrrhus and his powerful army had gone off on a western adventure and were consequently no longer a public menace in western Greece. Yet in embarking on his apparently madcap adventure, Pyrrhus had a plan (allegedly explained in Plutarch *Pyrrhus* 14 by the man himself). First he would conquer the west, including Sicily and Carthage. Then with Rome also conquered, Pyrrhus would have the money and manpower to turn east and defeat Macedon and Greece.

With this mini-empire now powering his ambitions, Pyrrhus could then, if he desired, subdue the Seleucids, and Ptolemaic Egypt. Then driving on to reconquer Bactria, he would restore the empire of Alexander. As masterplans go, this was somewhat over-ambitious. However, that does not mean that the plan was fundamentally flawed. As it turned out, the plan needed several generations to execute, and when it was executed, the people who did the job were not the Epirots but the Romans. Pyrrhus himself failed at Step A, the conquest of Italy.

The war with Rome was a brutal clash between the irresistible force of the Greek pike phalanx (plus elephants) and the immovable object of the

Roman legions. Pyrrhus won battles at Heraclea in 280 BC and Asculum in 279 BC, but lost much of his army in the process. Pyrrhus complained that while his men were irreplaceable, Rome's legions refilled with men 'like a room being filled by an indoor fountain' (Plutarch *Life of Pyrrhus* 21). Another victory like Heraclea, Pyrrhus complained, and he would be ruined. (This complaint has given ages later the term 'Pyrrhic victory' for a success that defeats the purpose of trying to succeed in the first place.)

Eventually Pyrrhus decided to put step A of his plan for world domination on the back burner and proceed instead to Step B, the conquest of Sicily and Carthage. This also did not go according to plan. The Greek cities were originally welcoming, but this welcome soured when Pyrrhus started seriously to squeeze them for the resources he needed to defeat the Carthaginians. With the Greeks turning against him and the Carthaginians putting up a vigorous fight, Pyrrhus turned back to Italy. He was encouraged by a new alliance with the warlike Samnites, a powerful mountain people who were stubbornly resisting Roman expansion.

A final battle was fought near Beneventum in 275 BC, where it appears that Pyrrhus was defeated by his own elephants. Our reports of the battle are scant and contradictory, but it seems that Pyrrhus tried advancing by night along mountain passes in the hope of defeating two Roman consular armies one after the other before they could unite. Regrettably the passes were too difficult and Pyrrhus arrived too late to prevent the Romans from joining forces. Nevertheless, he threw his elephants as shock troops against the combined Roman army.

These elephants were already edgy from their overnight mountain excursion and, once they started taking casualties from the Romans, they basically went berserk. They rampaged back through the Epirot army until they reached Pyrrhus' camp, where they were turned back by men flinging javelins from the ramparts. Repelled from the camp, the elephants exited the battlefield by ripping through the Epirot army once again. After a forced march over difficult terrain and thereafter being repeatedly charged by their own elephants, the men in Pyrrhus' army were now in ragged shape. The Romans had only to advance and finish them off, which they did with their usual ruthless efficiency.

Accepting defeat, Pyrrhus gathered the remnants of his army and sailed for home in Greece. He never returned to Italy, and in 272 BC he was killed while attempting to capture the city of Argos. His expedition was a failure, but it was a highly significant failure. The Romans had now encountered the Hellenistic armies for the first time. Epirus, as the Romans well knew, was far from the greatest of the Hellenistic powers. The Seleucids and Ptolemies had resources far greater. There was speculation as to what would have happened if Alexander had turned his armies west against Rome instead of east against the Persians (a game of 'what if' which has amused historians ever since). There was also considerable worry that the Hellenistic kingdoms might yet attempt what Alexander had not.

The lesson that the Romans took from the Pyrrhic wars was that Hellenistic armies were so powerful that even a minor state like Epirus could stretch them almost to breaking point. Macedon, the Seleucids and the Ptolemies were ruthless, predatory and unscrupulous. So far only their mutual wars had prevented these kingdoms from turning on the west, singly or collectively. Yet the Romans were now painfully aware that the Hellenistic kingdoms threatened their very existence.

When Pyrrhus left Sicily, he is said to have remarked, 'we are leaving behind a fine arena for the Romans and Carthaginians to fight in', and indeed a decade after his departure the Romans and Carthaginians were at each other's throats. By 250 BC Rome and Carthage had been engaged in mutual slaughter for fourteen years, and even Rome's prodigious reserves of manpower were close to depleted. They had lost army after army, to shipwreck and military defeat. Most recently an attempt to invade Africa had failed, partly because the Carthaginians were ably commanded by a mercenary general from Sparta.

The war was to continue for another nine years. However, even in 250 BC, had any of the Hellenistic kings been interested, either Rome or Carthage was theirs for the taking. However, as we have seen, in 250 BC the Hellenistic kings were preoccupied with internal politics, palace intrigues and wars with each other. Later generations of Hellenes might well have cursed the loss of that opportunity when the eastern kingdoms could have quashed the Roman menace while it was still vulnerable.

Chapter 3

Peak Hellenism

In 255 BC, when Rome's armies were defeated in North Africa, the Roman general Marcus Regulus was captured. By now the Carthaginians were sick of their long unprofitable war with Rome and sent Regulus on parole to Rome to present peace terms. Regulus swore to return to Carthage if those terms were rejected by the senate – as indeed they were, mainly because Regulus himself argued strongly against them.

Regulus returned to Carthage as he had promised, and in 250 BC the Carthaginians executed him. This, the Romans argued, showed how treacherous and cruel the Carthaginians were. Later historians have pointed out that the exasperated Carthaginians might have been upset that Regulus had forced them back into a war they did not want, and anyway, the Romans themselves were not doing much to restrain the wife of Regulus who habitually tortured and killed any Carthaginian prisoners she could get her hands on.

While the Romans and Carthaginians resumed their mutual slaughter in the west, one Erasistratus announced his retirement from the medical school he had founded in Alexandria. The fact that many more people have heard of the heroic Regulus than have heard of Erasistratus tells us something about historiography and about how humans rate personal achievement.

Nor is it only later historians who downplay scientific achievement. Hellenistic writers were fond of deploring the dearth of top-notch literature in their era. This, they declaimed, showed how far Greece had fallen from the golden era of the fifth century. Since Erasistratus wrote about the squidgy bits inside the human body, he was obviously not to be compared to the sublime poetry of say, Bacchylides. Yet a less artistic individual might fairly feel that when Erasistratus published his discovery that the heart acted as a pump, this was as at least as meaningful for humanity as any Bacchylides ode to an Olympic victor.

Most ancient texts and modern histories dealing with this period focus on the war in the western Mediterranean. They pass over the Hellenistic centres of learning which were industriously driving the human race forward, and instead concentrate on the Romans and Carthaginians who were – equally industriously – making humans less numerous.

To their credit, and unlike Livy, Polybius and friends, the Hellenistic kings did see the value of science. It was to be encouraged, both for the practical advantages that research bestowed, but also for the prestige it brought the monarchs who were at the forefront of scientific discovery. Erasistratus was only able to make his discoveries because the Ptolemies allowed the dissection of human corpses – something that was regarded as almost blasphemous by earlier (and most later) ages. If he had worked on living subjects – as horrified Christian writers later claimed he did – it is probable that Erasistratus would have worked out the role of veins and arteries in the circulation of the blood and anticipated that discovery by two millennia. (As it is, he believed that veins carried blood to parts of the body, and arteries carried air – since how else would the air get to where it was needed?)

Erasistratus was but one of a pantheon of great scholars working in the 260s. In Syracuse, Archimedes was taking mathematics to realms well beyond the grasp of most mortals, and indeed about as far as it was to get in the west until the discovery of calculus in the Enlightenment two thousand years later. (The Arabs meanwhile added algebra and the concept of zero to the sum of human knowledge.)

Eratosthenes

Consider also the man who arrived in Alexandria in 245 BC – this was Eratosthenes. Eratosthenes was generally considered a second-rater, because he was merely the second-best mathematician in the world, the second-best astronomer and the second-best poet. Eratosthenes was definitely the best geographer in the world, but he had invented that discipline, so it didn't count.

Eratosthenes was very much a man of his era. His native city of Cyrene (in modern Libya) was dragged into the Ptolemaic orbit when it was captured and administratively attached to Egypt after Alexander's death in 323 BC. Eratosthenes was born a generation later in 276 BC. An outstanding student from an early age, he went to Athens to continue his education as a young man. There he studied under Zeno, the founder of the stoic school, but also spent considerable time at the academy of Plato.

At the time, another Cyrenean, the poet Callimachus, was at the height of his fame. Whether Eratosthenes met Callimachus in Athens or corresponded with him while the latter was in Alexandria, he certainly benefited from the patronage of his famous fellow-countryman. Perhaps due to Callimachus' influence, Eratosthenes first turned to poetry and produced several highly regarded works which led to him being considered the best poet in the world after Callimachus himself.

Yet, even at this time, Eratosthenes' scientific bent was drawing him away from higher things. First, he prepared a chronology detailing major world events since the Trojan War (it is unlikely that he considered the foundation of Rome as worth adding to this list). Then he went on to prepare a chronology of victors in the Olympic games. This latter was no antiquarian fancy, but an important aid to documenting historical events, since the Greeks dated years by each Olympiad – the period between one set of games and the next four years later. Olympic heroes were local heroes, so an event might be described as happening, for example, 'two Olympiads after Callias won the Pankration for Athens'. (That was in 472 BC, as it happens.)

Two events changed the life of Eratosthenes forever. Firstly, in 246 BC Ptolemy II Philadelphos died after a reign of 37 years. The death of a pharaoh and the arrival of a successor inevitably resulted in seismic changes in the royal court, and these changes reverberated through the entire administration. Secondly, Eratosthenes was invited to Egypt to work at the Library of Alexandria as part of the new pharaoh's determination to continue his father's policy of attracting to Egypt the best brains in the Hellenistic world. Within five years Eratosthenes was head of the organization.

Eratosthenes corresponded with Archimedes, and came up with a mathematical tool for finding large prime numbers. This 'Sieve of

Eratosthenes' is still a useful mathematical tool today. Other mathematical discoveries followed, and Archimedes dedicated one of his books on mathematics to Eratosthenes, the man who was widely acknowledged as being the best mathematician in the world after Archimedes himself.

Other achievements followed. In astronomy Eratosthenes prepared a star chart and worked out that the sun was over twenty times the size of the Earth – a good try, but completely wrong, as the figure is nearer a hundred times. Nevertheless, Eratosthenes made a good calculation of the Earth's ecliptic orbit of the sun (or the Sun's orbit of the Earth, as he probably assumed) and realized the need for leap years to keep the calendar in line with reality.

He also worked out that the Sun was 804 million stadia from the Earth. If we assume the stade he used was 185 metres (different states in antiquity had different 'stades' rather as the US and UK today have different sized gallons), then Eratosthenes put the Sun 148.7 million kilometres away. It is actually 149.6 million kilometres. The difference is even less than that, because – as Eratosthenes well knew, the Earth moves 5 million kilometres between aphelion – its furthest distance from the sun – and perihelion, when it is closest. If Eratosthenes had calculated his distance at the spring equinox, he was spot on.

Turning his attention to the Earth, Eratosthenes set about inventing geography. First he correctly worked out the degree that the Earth was tilted on its axis. Then he decided that climate and the seasons depended on how the sun's rays struck the curved surface of the Earth. Using a system analogous to latitude and longitude, he decided that the climate of a region depended on the slope of the Earth relative to the sun in that region. Which is why the word 'climate' comes from the Greek word climein meaning 'slope'.

The flooding of the Nile became more explicable once Eratosthenes accurately traced that river's origins back to the Sudan and decided, again correctly, that heavy rains in the Ethiopian highlands caused the inundation.

The most significant work of Eratosthenes was his now lost treatise The Measurement of the Earth. Like all educated Greeks, Eratosthenes knew that the world was a sphere. He had already calculated that the Sun was far enough away to count as a single fixed point. Therefore, he measured the angle of the sun's rays at a known time in a known location – Eratosthenes chose Syene (modern Aswan) in southern Egypt – and compared this with the angle of the sun at the same time in Alexandria. He got a difference of seven degrees in the angle of the sun's rays over 800km. From there, a quick calculation by the world's second-best mathematician established that 360 degrees for a complete sphere made the Earth 40,000km in circumference.

The Earth is not actually a perfect sphere. Therefore Eratosthenes was out by several dozen kilometres, but he was nevertheless breathtakingly accurate. Much more so than Christopher Columbus whose own calculations reckoned the Earth so much smaller that it should be easy to sail westward from Europe to China. He and his crew would have long perished from thirst and starvation had Columbus not accidentally bumped into America before he got halfway.

Others were also at work. Another researcher at this time, Philo of Byzantium, wrote a book on engines. In this he describes, among other things, the first watermill and an escapement mechanism. Anyone unsure what an escapement mechanism does can probably find the answer by taking the lid off the cistern in their flush toilet. Philo's device was for use in a water basin and did not use an air-filled ball to shut off the water. Instead he used a lump of pumice to do the same job.

Just to prove that the Greeks could also be as blood-thirsty as the Romans and Carthaginians (though more scientific about it), Philo also described the Polybolos, which counts as the world's first machine-gun. By the turning of a handle connected to a windlass, a crossbow fed with bolts loaded from a top-mounted hopper could fire bolts at high speed. (Philo, *Belopoietics* 13)

The only problem was that the machine was actually too accurate and tended to kill the same victim multiple times rather than spreading the pain around. A nineteenth century reconstruction rather proved this when the first bolt hit the target dead on, and the second bolt hit the target in the same place, splitting the first bolt in the process.

The Third Syrian War 246–241 BC

The minds of Alexandrian inventors had turned toward war because, with the death of Ptolemy II in 246 BC, previous treaties that Ptolemy had made with the rest of the world became null and void. This particularly affected Antiochus II, who appears to have been waiting rather impatiently in Seleucia for just this event. It seems that Antiochus had not been getting on very well with Berenice, the wife foisted on him by Ptolemy II as the price for ending the second Syrian war in 253 BC.

It will be remembered that Antiochus had put aside his first wife, Laodice in order to give precedence to this Egyptian bride, Berenice the sister of Ptolemy III. Now that Ptolemy II was dead, Antiochus felt little need to honour the treaty, so he renounced Berenice and set off for Ephesus and a reconciliation with Laodice. It is probable that Laodice had some forewarning of Antiochus' scheme, for she had laid a few plans of her own. Firstly, by way of suggesting that Antiochus' earlier betrayal had not been forgiven or forgotten, she welcomed her husband back by serving him dinner. It is very probable that this meal contained a lethal dose of poison that promptly despatched Antiochus II the God straight to the underworld. Certainly, Antiochus ended up dead on arrival in Ephesus, leaving the throne vacant, and it is hard to believe that the vindictive Laodice did not have a hand in events.

With Antiochus dead, Laodice proclaimed her eldest son as her husband's successor. This lad is known today as Seleucus II – 'Pogon' (the bearded) – though Seleucus himself preferred the considerably less accurate title of *Kallinikos*. The name means 'gloriously victorious', which this Seleucus generally wasn't. There was of course another king of the Seleucid empire also around at the time, namely Antiochus, the five-year-old son of Berenice.

According to treaty, this son was the legitimate heir to the empire and Berenice accordingly proclaimed the boy as such. Berenice also sent urgent messages to her brother Ptolemy III asking for help and support. This was in vain, for Laodice had laid her plans too well. Before Ptolemy could react to recent developments, his nephew was dead also. Seleucus' young rival had been slain by assassins whom Laodice had earlier installed in the royal palace in Antioch. This left Ptolemy infuriated by the unravelling of his father's dynastic plans, anxious for his sister's safety, and in any case, eager for a trial of strength with the Seleucids while their monarchy was in disarray.

Regrettably, before Ptolemy could charge to the rescue in Seleucia, he had business to take care of at home. Egypt's western frontier had long been vulnerable to a sneak attack from Cyrene, a city that had been attached to Egypt by administrative fiat in Alexander's day, and which had been none too happy about it since.

Up to 250 BC Cyrene had been ruled by Magas, a king who had a complicated relationship with Egypt that enabled him to govern with a fair degree of autonomy. Magas died in 250 BC with no sons of his own, but he had a daughter called Berenice. (Not to be confused with the Berenice who was the currently imperilled ex-queen mother in Antioch.) Magas' widow arranged for her daughter to marry into the Macedonian royal line by importing a prince called Demetrios.

Ptolemy II died before he could respond to the threat that Cyrene was about to exit Egyptian control. That task fell to his son and successor, but while Ptolemy III was getting organised, Berenice of Cyrene took matters into her own hands. Apparently, Cyrene's new king Demetrios lived up to his epithet of 'the handsome'. Indeed, so handsome was he that his new mother-in-law became fatally attracted to him. The couple began a short-lived affair – 'short-lived' because a very annoyed Berenice made sure that her husband was also short-lived. Later reports have the king slain *in flagrante delicto* in his mother-in-law's bed while Berenice stood in the doorway directing the assassins and warning them not to harm her mother.

This left Berenice a widow, so Ptolemy took the diplomatic way out of the current crisis and married her. Since Ptolemies usually married their sisters this was rather exogamous of him, although Berenice was still his cousin since their mutual grandmother (a Berenice, naturally) was the mother of the late king Magas. With all that sorted out, Ptolemy was able to leave his new wife Berenice keeping an eye on things in Egypt while he headed off to Seleucia in an attempt to rescue his sister Berenice (and conquer as much of the Seleucid empire as he could while he was about it).

Because he needed to act fast, Ptolemy put forward the disingenuous claim that his intention was merely to visit his sister and ensure her well-being. He set off, with his army gearing up to follow as soon as possible. Berenice the sister had used the Seleucid army around Antioch to gain a degree of local control. Therefore, Ptolemy was unopposed when his ships arrived at Seleucia where his sister was meant to meet him. Sadly, Berenice was unable to make the appointment because she was slain by her Galatian bodyguards – doubtless at the instigation of the scheming Laodice. Indeed, so much responsibility for the subsequent conflict has been laid at Laodice's door that this third Syrian War is also sometimes called the 'Laodician War'.

The odd combination of circumstances that had followed the death of Antiochus II meant that the king, Seleucus II, was stuck in Asia Minor while king Ptolemy III found himself ensconced in the Seleucid heartland of Syria. Ptolemy promptly picked up the reins of government dropped by his murdered sister and took control of Antioch and Seleucia. Because he had naval superiority, there was no chance of the Seleucids invading by sea. Laodice and her royal son would have to wait for the next campaigning season before they could get an army south through the Taurus mountains.

While waiting, Seleucus (or more probably Laodice) was not idle. In a flurry of diplomatic activity, a sister of Seleucus (another Laodice) was married to the king of Pontus, thus ensuring the loyalty of both Pontus and its dependency of Phrygia. At the same time Antigonus Gonatas of Macedon was encouraged to attack Egyptian possessions in the Aegean, which he did willingly enough as retaliation for Egyptian involvement in the currently ongoing revolt of Corinth. It is uncertain whether he also secured his dynasty at this point by getting married also. With a certain degree of inevitability, the wife he chose was a cousin called Laodice, henceforth called Laodice II to avoid confusion with Laodice I (his mother) and Laodice of Pontus (his sister).

Meanwhile, Ptolemy decided to spend the winter going east to Mesopotamia. There is considerable debate whether he got as far as Babylon. It is however certain that despite his propaganda claims Ptolemy did not get as far as Bactria, because that would entail getting through Parthia which had become newly independent under the rebel Andragoras. (p.16)

It seems clear that Ptolemy had no intention of remaining in Mesopotamia. He was too far from home, and already rumours were reaching him of unrest in Egypt. This was apparently inspired by the regency of his headstrong wife, and partly to do with the higher taxes he had imposed to pay for his Syrian adventure. Therefore Ptolemy concentrated on looting from Mesopotamia all the Egyptian treasures the Persians had looted from Egypt while they had ruled the place a century previously. Not only would restoring Egyptian historical artefacts boost Ptolemy's reputation back home, but the bullion extracted from Mesopotamia would put his expedition into profit and so allow his earlier tax rises to be annulled.

The question was whether Ptolemy could hold on to Syria, or if he even wanted to. Ptolemy himself appeared uncertain about that. After all, one reason for the success of the dynasty to date was that the Ptolemies never bit off more than they could chew, and the Seleucid empire was quite a mouthful even without Egypt to govern as well.

Consequently, Ptolemy put up only token resistance when Seleucus marched south in the spring of 245 BC. Seleucus left Anatolia under the control of his brother Antiochus (who bears the distinguishing epithet Hierax – 'the hawk'). As ever with a Seleucid monarch, Seleucus had a choice of crises awaiting his immediate attention. Even with Ptolemy's troops occupying Syria, Seleucus opted to put Mesopotamia at the top of the agenda, which was probably the correct choice. With Parthia already independent, and Bactria gone, it was rather likely that unless Seleucus acted fast, Mesopotamia would be the next domino to topple out of Seleucid control.

Ptolemy observed the eastward departure of his opponent, and nimbly pivoted his attention to the coast of Asia Minor with the intention of making life as difficult as possible for Antiochus Hierax and the depleted garrisons his brother had left there. In time, Ptolemy managed to gain control of several cities on the Anatolian seaboard, including the major centre of Ephesus which Seleucus had recently vacated. Even this was less annoying to Seleucus than the loss of the seaport of Seleucia Piera. Not only was this the port of the major Seleucid city of Antioch, which was further up the Orontes river, but the city also contained the remains of Seleucus I, founder of the royal dynasty. The loss of this shrine to their ancestor was taken very personally by the Seleucids.

Ptolemy did not personally supervise either the new conquests in Anatolia or the slow retreat from Syria. He returned to Egypt, and as was often the case with his dynasty, left the fighting to his generals. He had problems enough at home, where the Nile floods were interrupted for several years resulting in famine and extreme civil unrest. (The lack of rainfall causing the absence of floods was probably due to volcanic activity as shown recently – J. G. Manning et al. 2017. 'Volcanic suppression of Nile summer flooding triggers revolt and constrains interstate conflict in ancient Egypt.' *Nature Communications* 8)

Thus matters stood until the year 241 BC, when peace broke out across the Mediterranean. In the west, an exhausted Roman Republic finally broke the back of a yet more exhausted Carthage. The Romans forced the Carthaginians to abandon Sicily. They also demanded that Carthage pay an indemnity that the bankrupt state could ill afford, thus stoking up resentment which was to erupt into a new war a generation later.

More or less the same thing happened in the east, where Ptolemy and Seleucus brought their war to an end. Ptolemy had a rebellion in Thebes to worry about, and Seleucus had run into more trouble in Anatolia where his brother had decided to set up his own kingdom. It may well be that the root of this rebellion was that Seleucus had started to run his empire himself, and in the process had fallen out with his mother Laodice, who seemed to feel she should be ruling through him. Rebuffed by Seleucus, Laodice had taken up with his younger brother who had obediently set himself up as Seleucus' more amenable replacement.

As the man with the more pressing problems, Seleucus had to give up most. That meant that Ephesus remained Ptolemaic (and was to remain so for another half-century) and Ptolemy kept control of Seleucia Piera. This last rankled as a personal humiliation which almost guaranteed that Egypt and the resentful Seleucids would be back at war as soon as the Seleucids reckoned they had a chance of retaking the city.

Only in Greece were matters still chaotic, mainly because the elderly Antigonus Gonatas seemed content to allow his enemies in the Peloponnese to tear themselves to pieces. This they were doing rather well. Sparta was wracked by civil strife verging on civil war, and just to the north the Achaean League was fighting it out with the Aetolian league. Working on the well-established principle that one should never interrupt an enemy who is making a mistake, Antigonus concentrated on keeping everything north of Corinth secure while he waited for the forces of anarchy to do his work further south.

Attalus I and Pergamon

Although the new ruler of Pergamon took over in 241 BC, the young man was by no means unqualified. He was descended from Seleucus I through the maternal line and had been adopted and trained by his predecessor Eumenes after the death of his parents. He also had the abundant confidence required for the job. Early in his rule, the Galatians demanded the tribute they habitually extracted from neighbouring states as the price for not being attacked. Attalus refused to pay and instead took on the Galatians in battle.

This was quite a gamble, as the Galatians were both warlike and numerous. A migrant tribe of Celts who had settled in central Anatolia, the Galatians were not only a problem for everyone else in Asia Minor, but a regular headache for the Seleucid kings as well. Therefore, relief at the decisive victory won by Attalus over the Galatians was felt far more widely than in just his native Pergamon. While Seleucus may have been delighted to see the Gauls humbled, he was less impressed with Attalus taking the title of 'King' as the result of his victory, thus affirming that his city-state was now a fully independent Hellenistic kingdom.

Nevertheless, Seleucus accepted this, mainly because he had no choice. Since his brother Antiochus Hierax had treacherously declared himself ruler of Asia Minor (with the rest of the empire scheduled to follow in due course), Pergamon's de facto declaration of independence was the immediate problem of the 'king' of Asia Minor. Despite this, Seleucus was determined to eventually settle outstanding business with both Attalus and his family. Therefore, once he had made peace with Egypt and tidied up some minor rebellions elsewhere in the empire, he gathered his army and returned to Asia Minor.

Laodice was an able diplomat and used the time available to prepare alliances. Attalus was a 'rebel' and therefore out of the question, but since the Galatians were enemies of their enemy they could usefully be recruited, and so could her son-in-law Mithridates II of Pontus (for all that he and the Galatians had also fought a recent war). The combined forces put together by Laodice proved sufficient to hold back Seleucus. After two years of indecisive warfare in Anatolia, the armies met in a major battle near Ancyra. Mainly due to the efforts of Mithridates II,

Seleucus was badly defeated – by some accounts losing almost 20,000 men. In fact, Seleucus himself came close to joining the casualty list. After barely escaping with his life, he left Asia Minor to his brother, never to return.

Seleucus headed east in the (unavailing) hope that he might be able to make headway in Parthia, where the rebel Andragoras had run into problems of his own with the leader of the Parni tribe. This was the man who became known as Arsaces I. Arsaces had previously attacked Bactria and been vigorously rebuffed by Diodotus. (In fact it was the credibility gained by that success that allowed Diodotus to appoint himself king of Bactria.) Arsaces had better luck in Parthia, where he defeated and killed Andragoras in battle. Seleucus hoped to exploit the prevailing chaos in Parthia, but his weakened army was unable to make much headway. Arsaces remained in power and is today counted as the first of the Parthian kings.

For the rest of the decade Seleucus focussed on shoring up the rest of his crumbling empire and rebuilding his strength for another crack at his faithless brother. Seleucus was encouraged to prepare for a return partly by the fact that his mother had died some time around 236 BC, and partly because Antiochus Hierax was not having it his own way on Asia Minor. Attalus was proving an unexpectedly hard nut to crack. As was usual with Hellenistic armies, the soldiers captured from Seleucus had seamlessly transferred to the army of the victorious Hierax. With these extra men plus the Galatians, Hierax marched confidently against Pergamon, only to receive a shocking defeat in a battle fought near a temple of Aphrodite near Pergamum. Furious at what they saw as bad generalship, the Galatians briefly seized Hierax.

Though Hierax managed to escape, the Galatian alliance could be definitely considered defunct. Seeing a chance to stir the pot further, the opportunistic Ptolemy lent Hierax troops with which he defeated the Galatians. Despite this success, Hierax was bereft of his Celtic allies and without them he was no match for Attalus. Thereafter the Pergamene army proceeded to beat him up on a regular basis, giving Attalus control of much of Asia Minor in the process. This would have presented an opportunity for Seleucus, were it not for the fact that yet other family affairs were getting in his way, this time as a result of events in Macedonia.

Stratonice of Macedon

Seleucus had an aunt called Stratonice. As usual with Hellenistic royalty, this Stratonice requires an epithet to distinguish her, both from the other royal Stratonices of her time, and also from the half dozen or so Stratonices populating Greek mythology. Seleucus' Stratonice is usually called Stratonice of Macedonia. We shall meet Stratonices of Pergamon, Pontus, and Cappadocia later.

Stratonice of Syria, the wife of Seleucus I, was already dead, having passed away in 268 BC. Her children included Apama of Cyrene, the mother whose relationship with Demetrios the Fair was terminated when her daughter had that son-in-law/lover assassinated, and Antiochus II Theos, recently poisoned by Laodice. Another child of Stratonice of Syria was also called Stratonice, and this is our Stratonice of Macedonia.

Stratonice (of Macedonia) was married to another Demetrios, the son of Antigonus Gonatas. Rather like Attalus of Pergamon, Demetrios had served a lengthy apprenticeship in the art of ruling while under his predecessor. While still crown prince, Demetrios had waged a successful war in Epirus and had fought in Greece and Thrace. It says something for his relationship with his father that not only did this Hellenistic king trust Demetrios with his army, but that trust was repaid. While many another royal son would have taken his inheritance along with command of the army, Demetrios served his father loyally until Antigonus died in 239 BC.

As ever with the death of a Hellenistic king, there were immediate attempts to test the mettle of the successor. In the case of Demetrios, the challenge came from the Achaean League and the Aetolian League. These two inveterate enemies saw the chance of a profitable war in the north, and briefly stopped fighting one another to combine in an attack on Macedonia. Needing to shore up his western flank in a war he was otherwise fighting successfully, Demetrios arranged to marry a princess from Epirus.

Demetrios was already married to Stratonice, but it was normal for a Macedonian king to have multiple wives. Therefore the Macedonian king must have been somewhat baffled by the furious reaction of Stratonice to the new arrival in the imperial bedchamber. In what was quite literally a right royal rage, Stratonice marched out of the palace, out of the country, and into Syria. Once she was there, a somewhat relieved Demetrios II probably reckoned she had become the problem of her nephew Seleucus.

Seleucus had problems enough of his own already. There are different accounts of what Stratonice wanted from her nephew, but these included marriage, a declaration of war against Macedon, and Stratonice's triumphant return to stand over the corpses of her ex-husband and his new wife. Seleucus' preoccupation with securing his eastern frontier and reclaiming Asia Minor struck Stratonice as irrelevant distractions from these objectives. The already enraged queen was further infuriated when Seleucus failed to see things her way.

It is fair to say that Stratonice lacked strategic awareness, for while Seleucus was away raising an army with which to attack Asia Minor, she incited the people of Antioch to rebellion. She apparently failed to realize that since Seleucus was away raising an army he was probably going to come back with one, and that is what he did. Antioch fell quickly to the exasperated Seleucus, and Stratonice fled to Seleucia. From there, she could have sailed away, but she had run out of friendly destinations. Perhaps hoping for a reconciliation with Seleucus, she remained. It was her last misjudgement for, with the recapture of the city, Seleucus had her executed.

An Illusory Stability

Almost a century after the death of Alexander, the Hellenistic world looked as though stability of a sort had been achieved. There were three great powers in the eastern part of the Mediterranean: Egypt, Macedon and Seleucia, with the power of the latter stretching back past the river Tigris to Parthia. Beyond Parthia, Diodotus II had taken over from his father and made peace with Arsaces of Parthia. With his western frontier secured against both the Parthians and Seleucid reconquest, Diodotus concentrated of strengthening his large and prosperous kingdom against nomad tribes from the north and predatory Indian kings to the south-east.

In the western Mediterranean, the minor Hellenistic kingdom of Syracuse was held by the competent and long-lived Hiero II. A former general of Pyrrhus, Hiero took over Syracuse and never gave it back. He remained in power long after the departure and death of his royal master and survived the first Punic War through adroit diplomacy.

After the war, the Romans left Hiero in charge of a tidy little kingdom, which was given scholarly lustre by the presence of Archimedes, one of the few academics of his day who had not succumbed to the siren song of Alexandria. In fact, at this moment Archimedes was in the process of pointing out that the recently deceased Aristarchus of Samos was wrong with his oddball theory of Heliocentrism. Aristarchus had postulated that the Earth revolved around the Sun, as did Mercury and Venus, though more closely, and Mars, Jupiter and Saturn in more distant orbits. (Aristarchus not only put the planets in their correct order but made a fair guess at some of their sizes.)

Archimedes shot down this absurd theory by using parallax. If the position of the Earth changed, he pointed out, then the relative position of the stars would shift also as the Earth moved around the sun. Since that did not happen, then either the Earth was stationary or the stars were millions of millions of stades away. Since it would make the universe vastly larger than the Greeks imagined, Archimedes quite reasonably discarded the second alternative.

His stable world was about to change. Within a decade, Seleucus, Demetrios and Ptolemy would be dead. Their successors would be the most competent kings the Hellenistic world had ever seen. Yet even the skill and sophistication of these men would prove unavailing against the existential threat that the kings of 230 BC had barely considered for a moment – Rome.

Chapter 4

A World at War

The Rise of Rome

While Rome was a democracy (for a given value of that term), the state was in effect ruled by a warrior elite whom the voters regularly returned to power. The legitimacy of the elite rested on three bases. One was the power of the great Roman families who made up the ruling class. The second was the openness of that ruling class to accepting new men with talent and ambition. The third was success in warfare. Rome's was a highly militarized society, and its aristocrats led from the front. Almost every man in public life (the Romans had no word for 'politician') was expected to have some amount of military experience, and unsuccessful generals suffered at the ballot box.

Given the importance of military success to electoral victory, Rome's neighbours might be excused for keeping a low profile lest they become the springboard for someone's next electoral campaign. However, such subtleties appear to have been lost on 'Queen' Teuta of Illyria. ('Queen' is in quotes because, while the Romans treated the lady as such, she was in fact acting as regent for her young son.) Illyria lay across the Adriatic Sea from Italy. In Italy, merchants were getting rich off trade with the Greek settlements in the east. With the peninsula peaceful and increasingly prosperous under Roman rule, there was a growing market for goods from Syria, Persia, Egypt and the oriental lands beyond which populated the trade routes so assiduously cultivated by the Ptolemies.

Italian merchants would be getting even richer were it not for the Illyrians. Pirates infested every bay and island off Illyria's rugged coastline and their speedy fifty-oared warships were the terror of Adriatic shipping. The Romans protested in vain to Illyria's rulers about the predatory habits of their subjects. The Illyrian response was that piracy was a way of life in Illyria, and the government was not going to allow a foreign power to interfere with the rich cultural traditions of the Illyrian people.

There matters might have rested were it not for three things. Firstly, despite the best efforts of Illyria's pirates, Italy's merchants were becoming rich, and rich people tend to also be influential. This was important in Rome where citizenship was generally available for rich influential people, and where elections were held every year. Secondly, Rome was quickly recovering from the rigours of the first Punic War which had ended over a decade ago, and at that point had no significant enemies whose defeat might impress the voters. Thirdly, Queen Teuta of Illyria did not appreciate the value of keeping her head down under such circumstances.

In a series of expansionist attacks, the Illyrians captured a number of coastal cities on the eastern seaboard. Among these captured cities was Dyrrachium, one of the more important harbours for Italian trade with Greece. Since that trade was not substantial (Greece did not have all that much to offer), Rome may have overlooked that. But Teuta went on to capture the island of Corcyra, which put the Illyrian pirate fleet squarely athwart Rome's trade route with the entire eastern Mediterranean.

Doubtless urged on by a panicked merchant class, the senate dispatched ambassadors to Teuta telling her that the Illyrians had to give up either Corcyra or their piratical ways. Teuta loftily replied that she was not in the business of regulating the activities of her seafaring citizens. The ambassadors warmly replied that the Roman state was quite prepared to do this for her. The discussion went downhill from there and ended up with the death of one ambassador and the arrest of the other. No-one was surprised when the Roman senate declared war thereafter.

It is quite possible that the Macedonians regarded the outbreak of this war as a highly positive development. At around this time Demetrios II was fighting the warlike Dardanian tribe, a struggle that was to lead to defeat and his eventual death in 229 BC. Since the son of Demetrios was too young to become king, an older relative called Antigonus Doson stepped into that dangerous role. (This Antigonus was the son of that Demetrios assassinated in Cyrene by his wife Berenice, as described on pp. 30 and 36.)

Antigonus Doson's kingdom was under threat from the victorious Dardanians, the Thessalians were in a state of rebellion, and the Aetolian and Achaean Leagues further south were in an advanced state of truculence. Therefore, the new king was probably relieved to have the Illyrians prevented from joining in the mayhem (as was their wont) by the Romans who invaded Illyria with an army of some 25,000 men. This relief was unclouded by any foreknowledge of the future, for the Illyrian war marked Rome's first venture onto the Greek mainland. In one form or another, the Romans were to remain there for the next 1,600 years.

While the first Illyrian War involved some hard fighting, from the Roman point of view it was a success. Rome took control of several key ports along the Adriatic seaboard, and by 227 BC the Romans had forced Teuta to sue for peace. Renouncing her earlier stance, Teuta promised that she would indeed bring her subjects to heel. No armed ships would in future sail far enough south to threaten Roman shipping.

In any case, Teuta had far fewer subjects than she had started the war with. Rome had detached several tribes from her kingdom along with their territory, and either kept these tribes as independent allies or handed them to Demetrios of Pharus. This Demetrios had been one of Teuta's governors who had opportunistically turned his coat when the Romans arrived at Corcyra and had subsequently been adopted by the Romans as a sort of client king.

With Illyria beaten up to their satisfaction, the Romans turned their attention to the Po valley in northern Italy and its Celtic peoples, and thus briefly drop out of the story of the Hellenistic kingdoms.

Affairs in Anatolia

Another individual who drops out of the picture at this point is Antiochus Hierax, the boy who would be king of Asia Minor (for a start). Hierax had made the mistake of choosing the Galatians as allies, thus almost inevitably pushing Attalus of Pergamon into the opposite camp. Attalus proved a highly successful general. He first defeated the Galatians in a series of battles. (The famous statue of the Dying Gaul, a Roman copy of which is now in the Vatican museum, remains today as a graphic reminder of those victories.)

Then Attalus turned his attention to Hierax and repeatedly defeated him. Eventually the young pretender was reduced to little more than a bandit king in the mountains of Cilicia, but Attalus kept pressing. After a final battle at the Harpasus River saw him defeated once again, Hierax fled Anatolia, probably for Egypt. He was killed *en route*, though it is uncertain which of his many powerful enemies got to the front of the line of those wanting to do the deed.

Seleucus had been working on the principle that while Attalus was the enemy of his enemy Hierax, Attalus was his friend. Now that Hierax was out of the picture, Attalus reverted to being an enemy. Seleucus still had the army which he had used to deal with his militant aunt Stratonice and intended to use this against Attalus. In the end though, the job fell to his son Alexander as Seleucus was killed, apparently after falling from his horse. The caveat 'apparently' is necessary here because it appears that a group of powerful aristocrats were becoming increasingly frustrated by the king's inability to prevent his empire from falling to pieces. The king's horse may have taken the blame for someone else's crime.

While we will probably never know exactly what happened to Seleucus II, the fate of Seleucus III (as the son Alexander chose to call himself on his accession) is another matter. When Seleucus III proved an inept campaigner, his army commanders abandoned subtlety and unambiguously executed their monarch. He was replaced by his younger brother Antiochus, who is known today as Antiochus III the Great.

Dramatis Personae

Thus, by 220 BC, the Mediterranean world had as contemporaries a set of exceptional individuals who have a good claim to be among the greatest leaders in classical history. They were:

Hannibal Barca of Carthage

Hannibal was currently in his late twenties. By now he had been commanding Carthaginian armies for almost a decade, having first served with his father and then his relative Hasdrubal. In 221 BC, after Hasdrubal's assassination (by a disgruntled Celtic mercenary), Hannibal became supreme commander of Carthaginian forces in Spain. This was an important position, because after the defeat of Carthage in the first Punic war, Carthage had been aggressively expanding in Spain as a way of regaining lost wealth and power. Unsurprisingly, the Romans viewed this development with alarm and totally justified suspicion.

Philip V of Macedon

In family affairs, the Antigonid dynasty of Macedon was something of an exception to the unrelieved nastiness of other Hellenistic monarchs. When Antigonus Doson took over the kingdom in 229 BC it was because Philip, the legitimate heir, was only nine years old. Any other Hellenistic king would have made certain that Philip did not live to become ten years old, but Antigonus seems from the start to have decided that his role was to keep the throne warm for his young relative.

Antigonus did a very good job as well. He smacked down the Dardanians, and suppressed the ongoing rebellion in Thessaly. By astute diplomacy, he brought the Achaean League in southern Greece on to his side and used the resulting alliance to destroy the ambitions of the Spartans who were attempting to regain their ancient power. The Spartans were crushed at the battle of Sellasia in 222 BC and their king fled to Egypt.

However, as was usual when the Macedonian army was engaged in the south, opportunistic barbarians attacked in the north. Doson hurried north and successfully defeated the new threat, but at the cost of his own life. He was succeeded by Philip, whom he had groomed for the job for the past eight years. Well trained the newly-crowned Philip V might be, yet what was arguably the most difficult and dangerous role in all the Hellenistic kingdoms was now filled by a lad who today would be too young to drive, drink alcohol or vote.

The Romans

In Rome, two teenagers of very different temperaments and backgrounds were yet to make their mark. The elder of the two was a scion of Rome's great Cornelian family, the Scipiones. Members of this clan were generally called Lucius or Publius – if male. All females were called Cornelia following the Roman convention by which women were given the feminine of the family gentilicium. The father (Publius), grandfather

(Lucius) and great-grandfather (Lucius) of this Scipio (Publius) were all consuls of Rome, and young Publius was expected to follow their example and in his turn lead both the senate and the armies of Rome

The other youngster was a relative nobody from the formerly Samnite town of Arpinum in central Italy. The Samnites were a hill tribe that fought bitterly against Rome, though almost a century after being conquered, the people of Arpinum now were fully-integrated Roman citizens. Many Arpinates retained their Samnite traits of stubbornness, simplicity and strict morality – characteristics which this young man, Marcus Porcius Cato, was later to personify to the Romans. Like the rest of his family, Cato was a farmer, yet the aristocratic Lucius Valerius Flaccus evidently saw something in the young man. He brought him to Rome some time around 220 BC to begin a political career.

Antiochus III (Antiochus the Great)
Antiochus was in his late teens or early twenties when he became ruler of the dysfunctional and disintegrating Seleucid empire. He can be excused of any complicity in his brother's death as he was away in Mesopotamia at the time. Even the most simple-minded of plotters would have arranged to be closer at hand to immediately pick up the reins of power after his victim's demise. As it was, Antiochus had to prise control of the empire from the conniving and vicious subordinates of his assassinated brother.

Taking immediate control of the empire would have been useful for Antiochus. Word of the death of Seleucus III reached Antiochus around the same time as it reached governors just to the east, who promptly rebelled. Another war was developing with Egypt, and Asia Minor was still largely in the hands of Attalus of Pergamon. Antiochus had first to travel west to claim the throne, and then make a brief swerve southward in an (unsuccessful) attempt to control the Egyptian threat. Only thereafter could he focus his energy on successfully suppressing the eastern rebels.

While he was engaged in Persis, Antiochus departed from the tradition whereby the Seleucid king alone personally controlled the Seleucid army in the field. Instead Antiochus sent a separate army under a relative called Archaeus to Asia Minor to deal with Attalus. The strategy of simultaneously fighting on two fronts paid off in that Archaeus made immediate headway against the Pergamene army.

However, the reason why the Seleucid king commanded his own army became apparent soon afterwards when Archaeus followed the example of Antiochus Hierax and declared himself king of Asia Minor. Back in Pergamon, Attalus must have felt he had seen it all before. He had once again become the enemy of the Seleucid king's enemy, and in due course Antiochus would approach Attalus to suggest an alliance. In all, it would be fair to say that the reign of Antiochus III got off to a less than auspicious beginning.

Last (and very much least) Ptolemy IV

In Egypt, Ptolemy III had been keeping a low profile internationally since the end of the third Syrian War. Doubtless this was due to internal issues within Egypt itself, where crop failures had badly damaged the social fabric. By way of demonstrating that the recent problems with the climate were not due to his lack of religious devotion, Ptolemy had worked hard to ingratiate himself with the gods and priestly hierarchy of Egypt. Old temples, such as the temple of Khonsu in Karnak, were embellished and new temples were commissioned, including the famous Serapeum which was to remain for centuries a unifying link between Hellenistic and Egyptian religion. (The closure of the Serapeum in the fourth century AD marked the triumph of Christianity in Egypt.)

Ptolemy III had also enlarged the library at Alexandria, instituting a system whereby customs officers appropriated books from ships calling into the port. If a book was of sufficient value it was confiscated and the owner compensated and given a copy of his original book. Ptolemy also asked the Athenians for the originals of the works of Sophocles and other great Athenian playwrights so that scholars could 'correct' errors in the copies held by the Alexandrian library. Ptolemy paid a huge surety for the safe return of the works, but such was the wealth of Egypt that he happily accepted the loss of that surety in exchange for the priceless original texts.

It was mostly as a result of the hard work of Ptolemy III that his son – inevitably named Ptolemy IV – inherited what was doubtless the richest and best-organized of the Hellenistic kingdoms. Little wonder that Ptolemy IV chose to be described with the epithet Philopater, 'the one who loves his father'. Despite the compliment, Ptolemy III would not have been happy with his son's rule – or lack of it. Right from the start Ptolemy was something of a spineless puppet in the hands of his 'advisors', whose first step when Ptolemy succeeded in 222 BC was to kill off any rivals to themselves. Victims included several members of Ptolemy's own family, including his brother Magas and his strong-willed mother Berenice II.

One notes that the great contemporaries of Ptolemy IV had careers which ended in defeat and failure. Ptolemy avoided this by the drastic step of dying young in 204 BC, possibly through poisoning, but more probably as the consequence of a comprehensively debauched lifestyle. He was fortunate in the timing of his death, for he left a world of problems for his successor – the unfortunate Ptolemy V.

World-shaping wars

The major failure of Ptolemy IV was in the maintenance of peace within the kingdom. Firstly, the series of assassinations which marked Ptolemy's accession to the throne were clearly in the interest of his advisors rather than being the consolidation of power by a new ruler. Thus from the beginning, Ptolemy IV failed to give his subjects even the pretence that the pharaoh himself was running the country.

Making things worse was the single-minded dedication of those advisors to shamelessly grabbing as much wealth and power as they could. This put the palace at odds with the priestly hierarchy. Since peace in Egypt had heretofore been maintained by careful and close co-operation between priests and palace, the breakdown in this rapport was swiftly followed by a breakdown of social order.

The internal turmoil in Egypt was noted by Antiochus III. Unlike the supine Ptolemy IV, Antiochus always intended to rule in person. Soon after suppressing the eastern rebellion he indicated his intention by executing a man called Hermeais. This man was foremost among the advisors who had hoped to rule through the young king, and his execution suitably cowed the others. Then, deciding to leave Attalus of Pergamon to deal with the treacherous Archaeus in Asia Minor, Antiochus headed south.

His intention was to resolve once and for all the question of who owned Coele-Syria – the bone of contention between Egypt and the Seleucids in two of the three preceding Syrian Wars. Though war broke out in 219 BC, active hostilities between Ptolemy IV and Antiochus III began only in 217 BC.

Meanwhile, things were also heating up on the other side of the Mediterranean. In 219 BC, Hannibal attacked the city of Saguntum (modern Sagunto) in Iberia. Hannibal did this in the full knowledge that the city was unofficially allied with Rome. Partly, Hannibal assumed – correctly – that the Romans were currently preoccupied with a rebellion in Illyria which they had recently and partly subdued. Therefore, apart from warning Hannibal to back off from his attack, the Romans did nothing to help the besieged city. Eventually Saguntum fell and Hannibal massacred every male of military age whom he found within.

Despite this outrage, neither the Romans nor the Carthaginian senate particularly wanted to go to war. However, Hannibal had control in Spain and was largely independent of the senate in Carthage, and the other reason why he was happy to attack a city aligned with Rome was because he was looking for an excuse to go to war. While the Romans and Carthaginians attempted negotiations, Hannibal regarded his attack on Saguntum as the unilateral opening of hostilities on his part. Saguntum had been large and prosperous. With the capture and sack of that city, Hannibal had the resources to fund an invasion of Italy. Therefore, without consulting the senate in Carthage, that is what he set about doing.

On both sides of the Mediterranean then, the stage was set for major conflicts which would forever change the destinies of the Hellenistic kingdoms. In Syria, the opening of hostilities was slowed by repeated diplomatic initiatives by the Egyptians. This was not because the Egyptians wanted peace, but rather they wanted time to build up their army. For the first time this army was to include large numbers of native Egyptian recruits trained in the Greek military style, so while these levies were undergoing their training, the Egyptians strung Antiochus along by suggesting that they might be prepared to give him all he wanted without the effort of fighting a war to get it.

In fact, Antiochus had already taken possession of much of what he wanted, because it was given to him by one Theodotus. Theodotus had been commander in Gaza when Antiochus had made his first attempt against Egypt immediately after taking the throne. He had coolly and expertly rebuffed the young king's attacks.

This display of military ability alarmed Ptolemy's advisors who worried that a general of such ability might turn his talents on them. Therefore, they recalled Theodotus to Alexandria, and there the dangerous general would probably have been executed for his competence. Fortunately for him, it became apparent that Antiochus intended to return and make another attempt to take Coele-Syria, and Theodotus was the man best qualified to fight him off. Put back in command in 219 BC, Theodotus did the logical thing and promptly went over to the Seleucid side, taking much of his army and several important fortresses with him. It was partly because he needed to reorganise after this unexpected bonus that Antiochus was prepared to listen to Egyptian overtures which slowed the opening of active warfare.

Hannibal in North Italy, Antiochus in Coele-Syria

Consequently, it was Hannibal who made the early running. The Carthaginian got off to an impressive start. Famously, he had decided to invade Italy by way of the Alps, and this he did by way of an arduous journey through southern Gaul and across mountains already showing the first signs of winter. This initiative threw out the plans of the Romans who had been expecting to fight the war in Spain. The Romans divided their forces into two armies, each commanded by a member of the Scipio family. One army continued to Spain, where it was defeated by Hannibal's relatives, and the other returned to Italy, where it was defeated by Hannibal himself.

In fact, Hannibal won two battles that year. The first was at Ticinus, a largely cavalry action fought not far from modern Pavia. This Carthaginian victory did much to bring over to Hannibal's side most of the Gallic peoples of northern Italy who had only recently been subdued by Rome. Another battle followed later that year at the River Trebbia where Hannibal's superior generalship allowed him to defeat a Roman army of some 40,000 men and defeat it so comprehensively that three out of four on the Roman side were killed or captured.

In the following year, 217 BC, two great battles took place in the same week of June – on the twenty-first and the twenty-fourth. We will first deal with the latter battle of June 24, which was more of an ambush and massacre. The consul Gaius Flamininus had taken over command in north Italy from Scipio and was determined to avenge Rome's repeated defeats in the region. Flamininus was allegedly incensed when Hannibal began devastating the lands of Roman allies and marched to give battle without waiting for the reinforcements which were coming to join his army.

On a foggy morning, the Romans traversed the shores of Lake Trasimene (Trasimeno in modern Perugia). Without warning, the Carthaginians suddenly swept down from the hills overlooking the lake and crushed the unsuspecting army. Almost the entire Roman force of 35,000 men suffered defeat or capture, and Flamininus himself was among the dead.

The result of the battle caused consternation in Rome, but the result was also noted further afield. Philip V of Macedon was busily getting Greece back under control after the rebellions which were a fact of life for any new Hellenistic king. Apart from subduing Greece, the attention of the Macedonians was otherwise naturally focussed on the ongoing war between Egypt and the Seleucids, but in Hannibal's victories Philip scented an opportunity. No matter how the clash of the titans played out, both the Seleucids and the Egyptians were probably going to finish the war with their armies and economies severely debilitated.

This would give Macedon an opportunity, especially if Philip could recruit an ally in the west. Hannibal was a promising Carthaginian general who was spectacularly doing what Pyrrhus had completely failed to do half a century before – effectively beating up the Romans. Perhaps when his Italian war was finished Hannibal might be interested in – for example – liberating from Antiochus Carthage's mother city of Tyre on the Phoenician seaboard? It was certainly something to consider.

If Philip's thoughts were inclined in that direction, then the news from the east would have further encouraged him. In 217 BC Antiochus marched south, and the Egyptians came to meet him. It is an interesting reflection of the relative power of the Hellenistic kingdoms and the Romans that, at Trasimene, Rome had 35,000 men and Hannibal had around 50,000. The army of Antiochus was 70,000 strong and the Egyptian army, boosted by mercenaries and native levies, was slightly larger.

In other words, if the Hellenistic kingdoms could have somehow seen the future and recognized Rome as the existential threat that it was, then their combined force allied with Hannibal's Carthaginians would have massively outnumbered and crushed the Romans. As it was, Hannibal was left to deal with the Romans on his own, while the Egyptians and Seleucids concentrated on tearing each other apart.

The Battle of Raphia

The tearing was currently set to take place near the little town of Raphia in Gaza. Antiochus was naturally in charge of his army, and though the Ptolemies were more comfortable at delegating command, on this occasion Ptolemy had come in person. The personal presence of the pharaoh with his army presented an opportunity to Ptolemy's daring former subordinate Theodotus. With just two others accompanying him, Theodotus slipped into the Ptolemaic camp with the aim of assassinating Ptolemy in his tent.

When a skirmish took place outside the Egyptian camp, Theodotus disengaged and rode into the camp as though he was part of the Egyptian force doing the fighting. It was just before dawn and too dark for faces to be recognized. Rather than sneaking from tent to tent, Theodotus and his fellow assassins boldly walked past the guards and into the command tent. There they wounded two men while searching for Ptolemy and also killed his doctor. They failed to take down their target though, because Ptolemy preferred to sleep in a more private tent erected a short distance away. In the chaos following his failed attack Theodotus slipped away and returned to the Seleucid camp unharmed. Polybius, the historian who reports this incident, was an inveterate opponent of the Aetolians, the people to whom Theodotus belonged. Dark deeds such as assassination were typical of an Aetolian, Polybius remarks, but this particular attempt 'showed no lack of courage'. (Polybius 5.81)

With Ptolemy still alive, the matter was to be settled the more traditional way by armies on the battlefield. The deployment of the two armies was likewise traditional, with each king centring his army around the massive bloc of the phalanx. This would be an interesting challenge for the Egyptians, for as well as some 25,000 Macedonian phalangites, the Ptolemaic phalanx also incorporated almost the same number of the newly-trained Egyptian levies. Lighter-armed contingents of mercenaries and specialist troops were deployed on the side to protect the vulnerable flanks, for while nearly invincible going forward a phalanx quickly fell apart if attacked from the sides or the rear.

The phalanx of Antiochus was smaller, but it included the 10,000 men of the Silver Shields, who were probably the best pike unit in the known world. These were backed up by another 20,000 or so Macedonian phalangites and sundry native levies. Antiochus also had a slight edge in cavalry, having 6,000 horse to his opponent's 5,000 and most of Antiochus' cavalry were of superior quality.

Also of superior number and quality were the Seleucid elephants. The Seleucids had originally obtained their elephants from India and selectively bred them thereafter. Elephants had won the Seleucids a number of victories, especially at Ipsus in 301 BC and against the Galatians thereafter. In the hope that they could do it again, over a hundred of these elephants were now deployed on the flanks, mostly on the right, as the hinge between the infantry and the cavalry on the wings.

Opposing them were seventy-three African elephants of Ptolemy – making this the only battle in which African elephants clashed with Asian elephants. Since we are told explicitly that the Seleucid Asian elephants were bigger, it must be assumed that Ptolemy was not using the African bush elephant (which is much larger but too intractable for military operations anyway), but a smaller now extinct north African breed, rather similar to those which Hannibal had just hauled over the Alps. (Hannibal himself preferred to ride his one Syrian elephant, called Surus.)

The battle opened with the Syrian elephants charging from the Seleucid right and easily routing the Egyptian pachyderms. The Egyptian elephants took the shortest route off the battlefield which entailed going through the left flank of the Egyptian army and Ptolemy's royal guard. In fact, for a moment, it looked as though the king was about to be trampled by his own elephants. On the other flank, the elephants of both sides refused to move at all. Defying every attempt by their handlers to get them to charge, these elephants dug in stubbornly, forcing the rest of the combatants to fight the battle around them.

This worked out rather well for Ptolemy. His Gallic mercenaries were channelled between the elephants and the Egyptian levies so that they fell upon the Arabic troops whom Antiochus had conscripted on his southward march. Most of these troops had not wanted to be there in the first place and now, faced with battle-crazed Galatians, the Arab levies urgently attempted to be elsewhere. This forced the Seleucid cavalry inward to close the gap on the flank of the phalanx. Meanwhile the Egyptian cavalry had been forced to make a wide outward detour around the unmoveable elephant block, so they ended up outflanking their opponents.

Ptolemy had taken himself to the phalanx while the remnants of his left wrapped themselves protectively around the exposed edge of that phalanx. Perhaps roused by his near escape, Ptolemy threw himself with great energy into enthusing his men as the opposing phalanxes came together. Antiochus meanwhile was still charging with his victorious troops on the right, naively believing that the rest of his army had enjoyed similar success and that the battle was all but won. In fact, it was all but lost. On his left, the outflanked Seleucid cavalry had been chased from the field by the Egyptians, and the left of the Seleucid phalanx was now exposed. Also on that side, the Egyptian levies were proving that they could fight every bit as well as the Macedonians. Thus outflanked and outnumbered, with their king away to the races, the Seleucid phalanx eventually buckled.

Some 10,000 Seleucid troops were killed in the battle, mostly phalangites and the unfortunate cavalry caught out of position on the left wing. The survivors sought refuge in the town of Raphia itself while the Egyptians occupied themselves with rounding up (and recruiting) the surviving Seleucid elephants. Eventually the Seleucid survivors were rejoined by their chastened king who sought a truce to bury his dead.

This battle, the greatest for a generation, consolidated Egyptian control of Coele-Syria and thus in effect re-established the status quo. Ptolemy had no ambition for further conquest and was happy to allow Antiochus to take the remnants of his army north to see if he would have better luck in Asia Minor. Ptolemy had domestic problems to deal with

– problems he was to discover that his advisors had made exponentially worse by training those Egyptian levies. Discharged after the Ptolemaic victory, these levies remained under arms as rebels and were to repeatedly prove what they had already proven at Raphia – that they could fight Macedonian troops to a standstill, be those Macedonians commanded by a Seleucid or a Ptolemy.

Cannae

In 216 BC, the year after Raphia, Antiochus was in Asia Minor where he and his former foe Attalus of Pergamon combined to make life miserable for the pretender Archaeus. While the Seleucid king worked to re-establish his authority in his northern domains, the Romans had rather similar plans for their southern possessions.

After winning his three battles in northern Italy, Hannibal had brought his army south, by-passing Rome (and as he did so, narrowly avoiding being trapped by the Romans in a mountain valley). In southern Italy Hannibal received a mixed reception, largely depending on how Romanized the local peoples were and whether they belonged to the inveterately Roman-hating Samnite tribe.

Hannibal was more successful than the Romans would have liked at bringing the locals over to the Carthaginian side, but less successful than he probably expected. Overall, the loyalty of southern Italy to Rome was a testament to the success of Rome's policy of making conquered peoples not subjects, but Romans.

The Romans had pioneered a policy by which a people could simultaneously be citizens of their own city and also citizens of Rome. Heretofore in the ancient world, one was exclusively the citizen of one city (though that city might be part of a greater whole, as were the Greek cities of the Seleucid empire). By giving conquered peoples Roman citizenship – often whether they wanted it or not – the Romans also made these peoples stakeholders in the Roman state. To Hannibal's dismay, many of Rome's former conquests were not resentful subjects of Rome but were now Romans who were prepared to fight hard for their new state.

This enlarged citizen body gave Rome access to reserves of manpower far greater than Hannibal could match. The Roman senate were aware of this and determined to use that advantage to nullify the military skill of their annoyingly competent invader. Basically, they would swamp him with sheer numbers. The Romans also noted that the survivors of the Roman defeat at the Trebbia were those legions which had charged head-on at the Carthaginians and broken through their lines. Therefore, the Romans planned that in their next battle they would do this again, but on a far larger scale. It appears not to have occurred to them that Hannibal might have noted the same phenomenon and made plans for what to do if the Romans tried it again.

Usually the Romans raised two armies each year, and each was assigned to a consul with a particular 'province'. (At this time 'province' still had the meaning preserved in the literal Latin translation of the word – 'for conquering' and it designated the consul's area of operations.) Just for Hannibal's benefit, the Romans decided to combine their army into one unit which would be commanded by each consul on alternate days. Then the Romans literally doubled down on their bet, and, for the 217 BC levy, they called up men not for the usual four legions (two for each consular army) but for eight legions.

This gave the Romans by far the biggest army they had ever fielded – around 40,000 legionaries with about the same number of allied troops. Add light infantry and around 7,000 cavalry and, at best estimates, the Romans had a force of between 80,000 and 100,000 men (though probably at the lower end of this estimate).

Against them Hannibal had an army of about half the size, of which around 10,000 were light infantry incapable of withstanding the shock of a legionary charge. The core of his army was his 8,000 Libyan spearmen – far fewer than the Romans ranged against them, but hardened veterans who would not buckle easily. These were complemented by a larger number of Gallic and Spanish recruits who could be counted on to fight hard but would also break easily. Crucially, Hannibal's cavalry not only outnumbered the Romans almost two-to-one but were of much higher quality. Overall Hannibal had just over 50,000 men at his command.

Hannibal was aware that the Roman army had the population of a large city and needed supplying accordingly. Therefore, he decided to cause his opponents maximum pain by capturing a major supply base at Cannae. Hannibal knew that this would bring the Romans hurrying south to reconnect this vital link in their supply chain, and this would bring them to battle on the wide plain outside Cannae where Hannibal's superior cavalry would have maximum freedom to manoeuvre.

The Romans were prepared to fight Hannibal anywhere he wanted, and consequently the second of August 216 BC saw the two armies squaring off for what both sides probably believed was a decisive confrontation. The Romans were allegedly commanded that day by a consul called Varro. Some modern historians have thrown doubt on this, pointing out that the other consul was the highly aristocratic Aemilius Paullus, and it was his clients and sympathizers who wrote the surviving accounts of the battle. It would be remarkable if these accounts did not do as much as possible to obfuscate Paullus' role in how things turned out, and they might even have demoted him from command after the (disastrous) events of that day.

Insofar as the Romans had a battle-plan, it was the tried and true technique that the Romans were to employ for centuries thereafter. This consisted of basically pointing the legions in the direction of the enemy and once within range allowing them to charge at them like a bull at a gate. The training, tactics and weaponry of individual Roman units were usually all superior to those of any enemy, and these factors, combined with the sheer ferocity of Roman troops, was generally enough to carry the day.

Hannibal's deployments were far more sophisticated. They needed to be if he was to defeat an enemy who outmatched him in everything but cavalry and generalship. His battle-plan required his army to act as an integrated unit with different elements playing their parts in perfect synchronization. This would have been hard enough to pull off with an army from a single nation, yet Hannibal intended to do the trick with a polyglot mixture of at least four different nationalities. That he was able to come up with his plan shows that he was a great general. That he made that plan work despite the imperfect tools with which it was implemented is what makes him one of the greatest commanders in history.

As Hannibal had got to Cannae first with the intention of instigating a battle, he was the one hosting the event. This allowed him to deploy his army to his precise specifications before the Romans had even arrived. Firstly, he had his army facing west, so that the attacking Romans would have the morning sun and the prevailing wind in their faces. This latter was an important consideration, as a large army kicks up a substantial amount of dust and this would get into Roman lungs and into eyes already squinting at the morning sun.

Next Hannibal anchored one flank of his army on the banks of the river Aufidus. With that flank secure, he could deploy most of his cavalry on the other flank. To his great satisfaction, the Romans did not extend their line to overlap his open flank but instead deployed their legions in a deep formation designed to hit the centre of the Carthaginian line like an armoured battering ram.

As the battle lines advanced to contact, the cavalry of both sides clashed in a brutal struggle on the flanks. The more numerous Carthaginians did not have it all their own way, for the Roman horse fought stubbornly before being overwhelmed. Then instead of pursuing the routed Roman cavalry, the Carthaginian commander pulled his men back into formation (something of a feat of discipline in itself) and rode around the back of the Roman army to fall on the Roman horsemen engaged on the other flank. With this accomplished, the Romans were left with just their massive block of infantry. That block brushed Hannibal's skirmishers aside and crashed into the Spanish and Gallic troops whom Hannibal had prepared to take this first shock.

At this point it seemed the Roman plan was succeeding. The Romans were driving the more lightly armed enemy back, though with Hannibal in personal command of this part of his army, the Gauls and Spaniards retreated without breaking. Then, once the Roman army was embedded deep in Hannibal's now crescent-shaped battle line, the Libyan spearmen on the horns of the crescent turned inward and pressed the Romans on each flank – just as the Carthaginian cavalry hit the Roman army in the rear.

The Roman army was completely encircled. Though the Romans still outnumbered the Carthaginians, they were pressed so closely together that most of them could not fight at all. Unable to fight, and with retreat denied, the Romans were cut down in their tens of thousands. In the end, only around 14,000 Romans managed to break out of the trap. The

Carthaginians continued to massacre the others until they were too exhausted to continue, and nightfall brought an end to the slaughter. By then, according to Polybius, 80,000 Romans and allies were killed or captive (mostly killed). Hannibal's losses were less than a tenth of that figure.

Aftermath

And there the Second Punic War should have ended. In the battles before Cannae, the Roman army had been literally decimated – that is one man in every ten Romans of military age had been killed. Then at Cannae, the Romans were decimated again. Meanwhile Polybius, almost in an aside, adds that in Cisalpine Gaul, a Celtic ambush had simultaneously wiped out another Roman army commanded by one Lucius Postumuis. As the historian remarks, Fortune seemed intent on filling the cup of Roman misfortune to overflowing. And worse was to come. The Greek city states of southern Italy, including Syracuse, Cumae and Tarentum, now embraced the Carthaginian cause and most of the southern Italian tribes did the same.

At Cannae, Rome had lost a consul and hundreds of the city's leading men. Many of those left in Rome were making serious travel plans which involved Greece and Egypt. (One such planning session among young aristocrats was broken up by young Scipio who forced the participants at sword-point to swear not to abandon the Republic.)

By the prevailing logic of international relations, the Romans should now sue for peace, abandon Spain and Sardinia, pay Carthage a whopping indemnity and make plans for revenge with the next generation. This is how things generally happened in the ancient world, where few wars were fought to the very last and cities were seldom actually destroyed. In fact, a settlement such as that envisioned above is almost the mirror image of what the Romans had agreed with Carthage after their victory in the previous war.

Hannibal seems to have reckoned that his war was done, and he was thinking along the same lines:

After his resounding success [at Cannae], Hannibal acted more
as though his victory had brought matters to a conclusion rather
than that he still had an ongoing war on his hands...When they
[the Roman prisoners] were brought before him he addressed them
in quite a friendly way. He told them that he was not waging any
kind of vendetta against Rome. He was fighting for Carthage and
that city's honour as a sovereign power. The previous generation of
Carthaginians had yielded to Roman courage, so now he intended
that the Romans should do the same for him.

Livy 22.58

Among those who considered that Hannibal's war with Rome had been
brought to a successful conclusion was Philip V of Macedon, who now
hurried to ally himself with the Carthaginians. To the Romans this alliance
looked like a gross betrayal. The Macedonians were allying with their
would-be conqueror to hammer the final nails in the coffin of Roman
ambitions. It was also the realization of a nightmare which had haunted
the Romans since the time of Pyrrhus – that the Hellenistic kingdoms
would form an alliance and use that to wrest Italy from their control.

In fact, it is very unlikely that Philip V was looking at things that way at
all. As far as Philip could see the Italian war was over apart from the exact
terms of the Roman surrender. Philip had no interest in getting involved
in Italy, but he was very interested in events in Anatolia, where Macedon
had territorial ambitions. Ideally, Philip would like Hannibal engaged in
Phoenicia, distracting Antiochus so that the Macedonians could operate
freely in Asia Minor. Of course, it would be best to wait until the Romans
had ratified a peace deal, but time was short.

In Anatolia, the situation was currently somewhat chaotic, but
Antiochus was already off to a good start in his efforts to restore order
there. Furthermore, at present the Seleucids were still suffering from the
loss of manpower and prestige after their disastrous loss at Raphia, but
the energetic and competent Antiochus was working fast to repair the
damage. Philip wanted his new ally deployed eastwards as fast as possible.

As it turned out, the Romans had every intention of continuing the
war with Hannibal. The surviving consul, Varro, was thanked for his
efforts and because he had returned to Rome was further thanked for

'not despairing of the Republic'. A dictator was appointed to run Rome during the emergency and almost every male capable of growing a beard and standing on two legs was conscripted into the army. As a sign of how desperate Rome was for manpower, even slaves were recruited.

In short, rather as had happened at Raphia, all that the winning side in the battle had done was to confirm the status quo. Ptolemy had not used his victory over Antiochus to do more than consolidate his hold over the southern Levant, and the Romans were determined to demonstrate to Hannibal that his stunning victory had changed nothing.

In fact, perhaps the most significant effect of Cannae was not how it changed things between Rome and Carthage, but in how it affected Rome's relationship with the Hellenic world. After Pyrrhus had been driven from Italy, Rome had hardly interacted at all with the Hellenistic kingdoms either militarily or politically. By inserting Macedon into Rome's war with Carthage, Philip had changed that dynamic. As soon as it was able, Rome would begin taking active measures to contain the Hellenistic 'threat'.

Chapter 5

Kings at Work 217–199 BC

The final decades of the third century BC saw the main powers in the Mediterranean busy with internal preoccupations. Proceeding clockwise around the Mediterranean, we find the Romans grappling with Hannibal who was well established in Southern Italy and eager for another battle.

The Romans had responded to Philip V's alliance with Hannibal by allying with the Aetolian League in central Greece. On Macedon's eastern flank, Philip had fallen out with Attalus of Pergamon. So the Macedonians had plenty to do in Thrace, Anatolia and Greece without getting involved in Hannibal's war.

Antiochus had his chaotic kingdom to knit back together, starting with Asia Minor and then the east. Only thereafter would he be able to turn his attention to foreign affairs. Finally, Ptolemy IV had his own internal issues. Those well-trained and highly competent Egyptian levies which had helped him to defeat the invasion of Antiochus were now highly restive, and Ptolemy (or rather his advisors) were engaged in a long-term and ultimately unsuccessful struggle to keep upper Egypt from breaking away altogether from Ptolemaic control.

Rome v. Carthage (and Syracuse)

The Romans had learned some hard lessons about fighting Hannibal. The cost had been appalling, but they had learned. The major lesson was that one should preferably not fight Hannibal at all. As a result, despite the desperate situation in southern Italy, the Romans worked hard to keep the pressure on Carthage elsewhere. The Romans kept an army in Spain and while this army enjoyed mixed success on the battlefield, it fulfilled its primary purpose – which was to keep the Carthaginians in Spain from sending further reinforcements to Hannibal in Italy. A Carthaginian attempt to recapture Sardinia (which the Romans had annexed after the First Punic War) was rebuffed.

The second lesson was that while Hannibal was the greatest tactician the world had yet seen, he was merely above average as a strategist. (Or as his relative Mago put it – Hannibal knew how to win victories, but not how to use them.) Therefore, the trick in southern Italy was to contain Hannibal without allowing him to bring Rome's armies to battle. In fact, Cannae was to be the last major battle which Hannibal fought on Italian soil, and those battles which he did subsequently win failed to change the overall strategic situation.

In Sicily, Pyrrhus' old lieutenant Hiero had ruled Syracuse for over five decades as an advertisement for the benefits of autocratic rule. He died leaving Syracuse independent and prosperous – and in doing so revealed the fatal flaw of the autocratic system, which is no matter how capable the autocrat, eventually power passes to an incompetent. In this case the incompetent was Hiero's grandson Hieronymous who supplemented his vicious and decadent character with advisors who were both venal and short-sighted. These advisors persuaded the young king to switch his alliance from Rome to Carthage. Hieronymous was assassinated the following year, but by then the damage was done. The Romans landed in Sicily and in 213 BC the last Hellenistic kingdom in the west was under siege.

The Romans were commanded by one Claudius Marcellus. An experienced and competent general, Marcellus assembled a substantial fleet and an array of siege weapons to use against the walls of Syracuse. 'These were worthless in comparison to the engines of Archimedes', remarks Marcellus' biographer Plutarch, who described the siege. Hiero, with his customary foresight had ordered Archimedes to prepare an array of weaponry – though 'these he had never needed to deploy due to spending that part of his life free from war amid the celebration of peace. But now these machines were of great benefit to the Syracusans, as was their inventor.' (Plutarch *Marcellus* 15ff)

Archimedes' defence of Syracuse – 'for the Syracusans were but the body commanded by his mind' remarks Plutarch (*ibid*) – is a testament to the ingenuity of the Hellenistic mind. The abstract ideas of geometry and mechanics dreamed up by the geniuses in Alexandria found terrifying expression in the works of Archimedes.

> 'The engines of Archimedes fired a variety of missiles against the land forces assaulting [the city] along with loads of rock which came whistling down at great speed. Nothing could withstand their weight and men were knocked aside into heaps', Plutarch reports. Nevertheless, those suffering on land probably counted themselves fortunate not to have been on the naval assault.
>
> 'From the walls, huge beams suddenly swung out over the ships. These sank some with huge weights which plummeted through the ships when dropped from a great height. Iron claws and beaks seized others, tipping them stern first into the water. Others were spun around by engines within the city and tossed on to the rocks at the base of the walls, causing huge casualties. The most dreadful spectacle was of whole ships lifted into the air, spun around to throw out the crew, and the empty hulls dropped upon the walls.' (*ibid*)

Eventually the Roman troops would flee in panic merely at the sight of a rope appearing over the city walls. Marcellus resignedly gave up his plans of taking the city by storm and settled down to a long siege. Perhaps the success of Archimedes had made the Syracusans slightly complacent, for they failed to keep a keen eye on the Romans. During a religious festival, the Romans were able to infiltrate the city's defences, and once the Romans were within the walls, the defenders panicked and the city fell.

It is said that when Marcellus saw the wealth and beauty of the city he had captured, he wept at the thought of what his soldiers would do to it, for no commander could deny the Roman army their vengeance. Part of that vengeance was wrought on Archimedes, for all that Marcellus wanted the great inventor taken alive. Legend has it that the soldier sent to capture Archimedes found him immersed in a mathematical problem drawn in sand on the floor of his rooms. When Archimedes refused to be diverted from his calculations, the exasperated soldier cut him down on the spot. 'Don't disturb my circles!' were allegedly Archimedes' last words, though it is uncertain who would have been there to pass that story on.

One major effect of the sack of Syracuse came with the booty which eventually found its way back to Rome. The Romans compared the beauty and sophistication of Hellenistic sculpture with their own crude efforts and observed that many of the slaves they brought back were more educated than the aristocrats who had captured them. From this time forward, there was a growing Hellenistic movement in Rome. Admiration of Greece, its language and culture began to take hold among the Roman aristocracy, and this trend continued to accelerate right into the imperial period. So thoroughly did Greece 'conquer its rough conqueror' (to quote the poet Horace – *ibid*), that modern historians of the first century AD generally refer to the 'Graeco-Roman civilization'.

By 209 BC, Sicily was mostly in Roman hands, and the Romans had gone on to the offensive in Spain, where the young Scipio demonstrated for the first time his military genius in the capture of the major Spanish base of New Carthage. Faced with the choice of holding Spain or conquering Italy, the Carthaginian senate ordered the majority of the army in Spain to cross the Alps to reinforce Hannibal.

Some 30,000 men, under the command of Hannibal's brother Hasdrubal, arrived in north Italy. Lacking the troops to contain the Carthaginian threat in both the north and the south, the Romans managed to withdraw the army facing Hannibal without Hannibal becoming aware that they had gone. In fact, the first time that Hannibal even became aware that the Roman army had withdrawn to fight and defeat his brother on the banks of the river Metaurus was when that army returned victorious to face Hannibal once more. The head of the slain Hasdrubal was tossed over the ramparts of Hannibal's camp as proof that his reinforcements had been defeated.

Ten years after the defeat at Cannae, new Roman reserves of manpower were becoming available as a fresh generation emerged from boyhood to be promptly slapped into armour by Roman recruiters. With much of the Carthaginian army in Spain transferred to Italy and destroyed at the Metaurus, it was left for Scipio to finish the job in Spain in 206 BC. At the Battle of Ilipa, somewhere east of the modern city of Seville, Scipio neatly outmanoeuvred a larger Carthaginian army and comprehensively defeated it. This brought to an end Carthage's domination of Spain and denied Carthage further use of that land's mineral and human resources.

By 204 BC, Scipio was agitating for Rome to take the war to Carthage in Africa.

The Romans were reluctant to launch an African war because, although this would doubtless draw Hannibal from Italy to defend his homeland, it would also probably mean that the Romans would have to fight Hannibal when he got there. To date, fighting Hannibal had produced poor results. Furthermore, there were still Romans living who remembered the fate of an earlier Roman army that had tried to defeat the Carthaginians in Africa in 255 BC. That army had been almost totally wiped out by Carthaginians led by the Spartan mercenary Xanthippus. The Romans were not now keen to repeat that experience with their painstakingly replenished manpower.

Furthermore, Scipio was distrusted by many senators because of his youth. (He had been elected as consul at the age of 31 despite being almost a decade too young for the official qualification.) Many older senators were also made uneasy by Scipio's leadership of the new Philhellenic movement in Rome. Scipio's fondness for Greek literature, dress and gymnastics offended conservative Roman values.

Consequently, Scipio was forced to rely on volunteers and the garrison of Sicily for most of the makeshift army which he raised with little support from the senate. On arriving in Africa, Scipio further 'disgraced' himself by attacking the Carthaginian camp at night, setting fire to the tents and causing lethal chaos. In fact, this night attack had the same effect as a major victory on the battlefield. Tens of thousands of Carthaginians and their allies were killed and the Numidians, who had allied with Carthage now began to wonder if they had picked the right side. Nevertheless, to Roman historians, this night ambush was exactly the sort of dirty trick which Hannibal might have played, whereas upright, honest Romans won their victories on the battlefield.

Masinissa, the new king of Numidia was persuaded by Scipio's success to come over to the Roman side. Now outnumbered and bereft of allies, it was the turn of Carthage to consider accepting peace terms, especially as those Scipio offered were reasonably generous. Then Hannibal returned from Italy with his veteran army. The Carthaginians promptly abandoned peace talks – if they had ever been serious about them in the first place and had not been playing for time.

In the end it came down to a traditional battle at Zama in 202 BC. Scipio had carefully studied Hannibal's previous victories and believed that cavalry was the key. Hence his successful courtship of Masinissa whose Numidians were probably the finest light cavalry in the known world. In addition, as soon as he had begun to raise an army in Sicily, Scipio had worked at training a corps of heavy cavalry.

Hannibal for once had relatively poor-quality horsemen who were mainly citizen levies. He therefore relied on his elephants. These were to charge right into the packed ranks of legionary infantry, which would then be hit by successive waves of Gauls, Spaniards, and finally Hannibal's veteran Libyan spearmen. This plan relied on the elephants causing chaos, since Hannibal's army would struggle against well-formed Roman troops. Scipio had been thinking along the same lines and arranged for the elephants to charge through carefully prepared 'lanes' which his well-drilled troops opened in their formations. Once through the Roman lines, the elephants were picked off by archers and javelinmen prepared for that eventuality.

The Roman horse had driven the Carthaginian cavalry from the field, so the battle now came down to the infantry. Probably to Scipio's alarm, the Carthaginians refused to buckle. The three lines of the Romans – *hastati*, *principes* and *triarii* – were cancelled out by Hannibal's lines of Gauls, Spaniards and Libyans. The infantry might have fought themselves to a standstill had not the Roman cavalry finally rallied from its pursuit of the Carthaginian horse and returned to the battlefield. Once they fell upon the Carthaginian rear, the battle was over.

A decade later, Scipio and Hannibal met at the court of Antiochus III. Scipio, probably fishing for a compliment, asked Hannibal to name the three greatest generals of all time. Hannibal promptly listed Alexander, Pyrrhus and then himself. Somewhat annoyed at being left off the list, Scipio asked where he came in. To which Hannibal replied that if he had beaten Scipio at Zama, he would without hesitation have listed himself as number one. (Livy 35,14)

One thing was certain: while Hannibal's victories generally failed to change the strategic situation, his defeat certainly did. Carthage was forced to terms which amounted to little more than unconditional surrender. With the conquest of Carthage, Rome became a first-rate power, the equal of any of the Hellenistic kingdoms, and considerably better organized. The Romans had a treasury flush with loot and a huge Carthaginian indemnity of hundreds of tonnes of silver. They also had a veteran army ready for redeployment. In short, the time was ripe for the Romans to conclude their unfinished business with Philip of Macedon.

Philip up to 199 BC

Under its young and energetic ruler, Macedon had stamped its authority firmly on Greece. Philip had inherited the Hellenic League from his predecessor, Antigonus Doson and he used the league to break the growing power of the Aetolian confederation which had expanded following the Roman defeat of neighbouring Illyria. Philip was eventually able to make peace with the Aetolians on his own terms in 217 BC.

This peace did not last, because Roman diplomacy had begun seeking allies against Philip after that king declared war against Rome as part of his deal with Hannibal. Although Rome and Macedon had technically been at war since 215 BC, Philip's early efforts had been directed at taking over Rome's client cities in Illyria. After initial setbacks, he was beginning to make progress, which caused some alarm among the Aetolians. Consequently in 211 BC, the Aetolians joined the war against Philip in the misguided belief that the Romans would give them military backing.

Apart from Aetolian enmity, there was always a strong anti-Macedonian sentiment bubbling away elsewhere in Greece. Also, Philip and the Achaean League were working closely together at this point, so Rome had little difficulty aligning the Achaean League's enemies against Philip. Attalus of Pergamon cheerfully joined in the anti-Macedon alliance. He had designs on Macedon's holdings in Thrace, and the Spartans joined the Romans mainly because their enemies the Achaeans were on the other side. Having suitably stirred the pot, thereafter the Romans left their allies to it, confident that Philip now had enough on his plate in Greece to stop him interfering even in Illyria, let alone on the Italian mainland.

Philip rose to the challenge. First he drove Attalus from the Greek mainland. Then he made sure Attalus stayed out by making alliances with other states in Asia Minor, especially Pergamon's rival and neighbour Bithynia. Forced to attend to affairs at home, Attalus largely withdrew from the war. The Spartans had mostly given only moral support to the war against Philip, and with the Romans currently uninterested in Greek affairs, Philip was free to give the Aetolians his full attention. The Aetolians quickly came to realize that attacking the Macedonians had been a misjudgement on their part. Philip had already gained a great deal of experience at fighting the Aetolians in his previous war, and he now enthusiastically re-applied that experience.

This was painful for Aetolia. Philip defeated the Aetolian army and went on to capture a number of the confederation's cities. The loss that hurt most was Philip's capture of Thermium, the confederation's *de facto* capital. Philip comprehensively looted the city, and after he had stripped away enough treasure to pay for his war, he set fire to the major public buildings. After that, he asked the Aetolians if they wanted peace. Though pride kept the Aetolians fighting for another year, their hearts were no longer in the struggle. In 206 BC they agreed to terms.

Without Aetolia, Sparta or Pergamon, the Romans no longer had any proxies with whom to fight their war in Greece. Since the Romans were still fully occupied with Carthage, and from Philip's point of view the Carthaginian alliance had not yielded the benefits he had hoped, it was in the interest of both sides to make peace. This they did in 205 BC, bringing the first Macedonian War of 214–205 BC to an end.

If Hannibal was not going to help Philip fight the Seleucids, perhaps the Seleucids might help Macedon fight the Egyptians? The Ptolemies were inveterate interferers in Greek affairs, and Philip was eager to extend his power into the Aegean where the Egyptians held a number of vulnerable islands. Antiochus III was already actively engaged in hostilities with Egypt and was more than happy for Philip to join in the fight. The pair quickly patched up an unlikely alliance. This quickly brought gains for Philip, both in Asia Minor and in the Aegean. However, before he could realize the full potential of his partnership with Antiochus, Philip's attention was pulled back to the west by the unexpected news that the Romans had declared war on Macedon.

Antiochus III to 199 BC

Antiochus was perhaps the busiest of the Hellenistic kings in the last decades of the third century. He was last reported heading north licking his wounds after the battle of Raphia in 217 BC. That defeat had damaged his standing both with his court and his subjects, and he needed a quick success to repair the damage. His recent experiences meant that Antiochus had become an experienced campaigner in a remarkably short time, and he had a natural talent for diplomacy.

It quickly became clear that the best way to control Anatolia was to follow the earlier example of the Persian kings who had also (with difficulty) ruled the region. The Persians had ruled through satraps who were given the power of minor kings, so Antiochus decided to rule through minor kings whom he attempted – not always successfully – to treat as satraps. Certainly, Attalus of Pergamon was never going to give more than lip service to the Seleucids, and the Bithynians and Galatians were likewise disposed to being awkward.

Nevertheless, such largely autonomous 'subjects' were still vastly preferable to out-and-out rebels such as Achaeus. Achaeus was still claiming overlordship of Asia Minor, and once Antiochus moderated the demands he was making of the region's kings, Achaeus' claim led to his diplomatic isolation. Diminished the army of Antiochus might be, but it was certainly up to the task of defeating one minor rebel, especially with Attalus adding his help and local knowledge. By 214 BC, Achaeus was penned up in his capital of Sardis. He was captured while attempting to escape, and Antiochus had him executed.

Sardis itself held out until sometime in 213 BC under the command of Laodice, the wife of Achaeus. When her soldiers surrendered the citadel against her wishes, she vanishes from history. It is probable though that this Laodice escaped execution, since she was the sister of Antiochus' wife (also called Laodice) and a cousin of Antiochus through her mother (another Laodice).

With Sardis captured, Antiochus struck out eastwards, leaving behind a pacified Anatolia. Since he was headed in the general direction of Armenia with his army, this seemed a good time to demand – and receive – the subservience of the Armenian king. Here again, Antiochus was acting as might a Persian monarch. These monarchs had styled themselves 'King of Kings', not as an empty boast, but because that was how they ruled their sprawling empire. Rather than personally rule every one of the empire's many and varied components, the Persian kings left local rulers in command provided that they recognized the overall suzerainty of the King of Kings.

Antiochus too had more than enough on his hands without having to personally rule Asia Minor, Syria, Armenia and points east. Provided the rulers of these lands offered him fealty (sometimes plus taxes and military levies on demand) he was content to let them do the ruling. This was forcibly impressed upon Arsaces II of Parthia in 212 BC. Arsaces quickly discovered that his army was no match for well-generalled Seleucids. The Parthian king lost his capital to Antiochus and several major cities besides. At Mount Labus, he also lost the battle in which he attempted to get his cities back.

Fortunately, Antiochus knew a competent leader when he fought one, and he was happy to let Arsaces keep his kingdom in exchange for an oath of vassalage. By 209 BC, Antiochus was in Bactria, the first Seleucid monarch to set foot in that kingdom for generations. Euthydemus, the current Bactrian king, was less than welcoming and Antiochus had to get through a brisk battle and siege before Euthydemus acknowledged his sovereignty.

One major issue with the submission of the various rulers subjugated by Antiochus on his eastward drive was that these kings did not offer their fealty to the Seleucid monarchy on behalf of their kingdoms. Instead the submission of (for example) Arsaces II was a personal contract between Antiochus and Arsaces as individuals. Should either king die, then king and successor would have to go through the same process again, with terms re-negotiated depending on the strength of the parties involved. This may have seemed cumbersome, but in an era where assassination was a constant preoccupation for any ruler, anything that made life more difficult for anyone planning a takeover was to be welcomed.

With Bactria, Antiochus went the extra mile, probably because Bactria was very far away and Euthydemus was already well into middle age. Therefore, to keep Bactria loyal, Antiochus was prepared to give the valuable diplomatic asset of one of his daughters (probably called Laodice) in marriage to the son of Euthydemus, a young man called Demetrios. This proved a successful investment, because this Demetrios was to become the most successful of all the Bactrian kings, and as a (nominal) subject of Antiochus he expanded the most easterly of the Hellenistic kingdoms deep into India and lands adjoining the Hindu Kush.

Antiochus took the opportunity to replenish from Bactria's reserves the elephant stocks he had lost at Raphia, and then went personally in search of more. In 206 BC he was in the realm of a monarch called Subhagasena, whom the historian Polybius (11.34) informs us ruled a kingdom on the other side of the Hindu Kush in modern Afghanistan. Since Antiochus had brought along his army for this 'diplomatic visit' he had little trouble strong-arming a further supply of elephants from the Afghan king, bringing his collection for the trip to over 150 pachyderms.

News now reached Antiochus that Ptolemy IV was ill, and very probably on his deathbed. This was the king's cue to come hurrying west, since – as described above – Antiochus' peace deal was with Ptolemy IV personally. Once the pharaoh was dead, all previous peace treaties were void and southern Syria would once again be up for grabs. This time Antiochus and his army were vastly more experienced and Ptolemy's successor, by definition, would not be.

To sweeten the idea further, ambassadors from Philip V of Macedon came to the Seleucid court, suggesting that Philip and Antiochus might profitably gang up on Egypt should Ptolemy IV perish from his illness, which indeed he did in the summer of 204 BC.

Ptolemy IV died just before his fortieth birthday, which was young, even by the standards of his day. This meant that his successor would also be young and rather appropriately Ptolemy V was five at the time of his accession. Since the new Pharaoh could not rule his kingdom personally, there was a short but lethal struggle to determine who would do so in his stead. As with the previous generation, the pharaoh's mother was the immediate casualty. Ptolemy's advisors had reason to fear that this woman – known as Arsinoe III – might seize the regency, for she was as strong-willed as her brother (and husband) had not been. By some reports, she had not only been present at the battle of Raphia but had even commanded a unit of the army.

Two of the advisors of Ptolemy IV now became, in effect, the rulers of Egypt. The rule of these men was far from secure, not least because Arsinoe had been popular with the people and the army. Exactly how popular became clear to one of these advisors when a mob in Alexandria turned upon him and lynched the man. The other vanished without trace, probably the victim of a palace coup. A further power struggle followed with different factions vying to rule in the boy-king's name.

Under such circumstances, no-one was prepared to take an army north to confront Antiochus in Gaza, let alone go much further north to take on Philip who was happily rampaging through Asia Minor, transferring Ptolemaic possessions to the Macedonian throne as he went along. Nevertheless, the Egyptians had a better general than they deserved in the person of an Aetolian commander called Scopas. As soon as word of Antiochus' advance had reached the governor of Coele-Syria, that man defected to the Seleucid side – an advantage of Antiochus' policy of treating defectors well. Scopas took the initiative for Egypt and re-took a large part of the area before Antiochus could get his entire army into place.

Once that army was fully mustered, it was even larger than the force that Antiochus had brought with him on that second excursion into Coele-Syria which had ended with the Battle of Raphia. This time there was to be no impetuous charge to carry a young king off the battlefield. Antiochus was a decade and a half older and a great deal wiser. There was again a cavalry clash to start the battle, and again the cavalry were led by a dashing young man called Antiochus, and again the Seleucid cavalry were victorious. But this young Antiochus was the son of Antiochus III, and he had evidently been warned not to repeat his father's mistakes. Also, as at Raphia, the Seleucid phalanx proved inferior to its Egyptian counterpart. Again, Antiochus had learned from experience and he relieved the pressure on his infantry with judicious attacks by his elephants (this time making certain that they did charge). Then the heavy cavalry commanded by his son fell upon the rear of the Egyptian phalanx, and the battle was effectively over.

Because the Egyptian phalanx was surrounded, the only options for the trapped phalangites was surrender or death. Since surrender involved being painlessly sworn into the ranks of the Seleucid army, it was unsurprising that well over half of the formerly Ptolemaic force took this option. The remainder of the survivors, including Scopas, fled to fortresses in Phoenicia and Judea. There, abandoned by the Ptolemaic government, they were forced to capitulate one by one.

This battle – known as the Battle of Panium after the river at the headwaters of the Jordan where it was fought – was as comprehensive a Seleucid victory as Raphia had been a defeat. Unlike Raphia, this battle did actually resolve something, because it effectively ended Ptolemaic control of Coele-Syria, Phoenicia and Judea. These were to be either independent or Seleucid for the next hundred years.

Antiochus might have considered invading Egypt itself, and certainly he was not deterred by a Roman embassy warning him not to do so. He wisely decided not to do so, even though he stood a good chance of success. But the fact was that the east was getting restless again, Attalus of Pergamon was getting dangerously independent and Antiochus had still to subdue his fresh conquests in the south. The last thing he wanted to add to this list was the steaming pile of problems which currently made up the situation in Egypt.

Egypt to 186 BC – a kingdom in chaos

'Sow the wind, and reap the whirlwind'. So says the book of Hosea in the Old Testament (8.7) and, in training Egyptian levies, Ptolemy IV and his advisors had strewn the seeds of revolt far and wide. 'Ptolemy had an excellent idea for the short time, but he did not take into account the future,' remarks Polybius. 'Puffed with pride by their victory at Raphia, the soldiers were no longer inclined to obey orders. Instead they decided that they could better manage themselves with a figure-head for a leader.' (5.107)

The rest of Ptolemy IV's reign was spent coping with the consequences of his fateful decision. The Egyptian levies might have saved Coele-Syria for fifteen years, but they cost the Ptolemies control of Upper Egypt for twenty.

Polybius attributes the rebellion to the disgust of the Egyptian soldiery for the debauched lifestyle of Ptolemy IV. More realistic modern historians point to the fact that the cost of raising the army which won at Raphia had crippled the Egyptian economy. The coinage of the period is significantly debased, and it appears that taxes were raised at the same time. There was certainly a nationalistic, anti-Greek element to the rebellion also, but because the Greeks tended to be wealthier than the average Egyptian and thus resented for being better insulated from the prevailing economic hard times, these two causes are tightly intertwined.

Since goings-on in upper Egypt were far away both from the physical location and the actual interests of contemporary historians, the course of events in the lead-up to the rebellion are almost totally missing. Even the course of the rebellion itself has only recently been partially reconstructed by modern historians. They have used inscriptions, occasional references and papyri with details of matters such as when tax revenues again became available to the central government and were thus again under Ptolemaic control.

From such sources it is possible to ascertain that the revolt probably began in Edfu, where the hanging of the gates at the reconstructed temple was meant to take place in 207 BC but in fact was only accomplished over a decade later. By 205 BC, most of Upper Egypt was lost to Ptolemy, and a 'Pharaoh' called Haronnophoris ruled in his stead.

The rebel pharaoh did not survive the Ptolemaic counter-attack. The walls of the Temple at Philae on the Nile record that a battle was fought between the Ptolemaic army and the rebels, who were apparently assisted by the powerful African kingdom to the south of Egypt. A 'wicked man' (the inscription grants him no title) was captured and executed. (W.M. Müller, *Egyptological Researches* III.)

If the wicked man was Haronnophoris, then the battle probably took place in 199 BC, for thereafter a new pharaoh called Kannophor was ruling in Thebes. There seems also to have been an element of the ancient rivalry between the royal cities of Thebes and Memphis in play here, with the latter city more inclined to support the government in Alexandria. Surviving inscriptions give reports of temples being robbed or even destroyed. There is no reason to doubt this, because temples were an integral part of the government machinery and as such would have been an obvious target for disaffected rebels.

Thebes was evidently at the epicentre of the struggle for Upper Egypt, for it appears that Kannophor did not remain long in Thebes after his coronation. Inscriptions dated to 199 BC again recognize the young Ptolemy V as Pharaoh, then in 194 BC Kannophor is again the ruler, supplanted by Ptolemy once more in 191 BC.

That the struggle was prolonged and bitter is shown, for example, by a contemporary papyrus where an official writes to his superior asking that, with the population of a particular village all dead, should the official recognize those who had moved on to the land as the new tenants and tax them accordingly?

Step by step the rebels were pushed southward, and Kannophor was finally defeated in 186 BC on the borders of Nubia. An inscription granting a general amnesty is dated to that year and appears to be an attempt by the government to draw a line under the entire business. (W. Clarysse, *The Great Revolt of the Egyptians (205–186 BCE)* Berkeley, April 2004.)

One unexpected benefit for posterity of the rebellion was that Ptolemy V's officials felt the need to keep the priesthood loyal by reducing temple taxes. Accordingly, a decree to that effect was published, and inscribed on a stele in hieroglyphics, a more common Egyptian script called demotic, and finally in Koine Greek. When the stone was found in 1799 near the town of Rosetta (ancient Bolbitinon on the Nile Delta), it proved the key to translating hieroglyphics and so unlocking the door to thousands of years of Egyptian history.

Chapter 6

Philip V Against Rome

The last years of the third century BC were good ones for Philip V. The Ptolemaic kingdom was fully engaged with the secessionist rebellion gathering strength in Upper Egypt and what little energy the government had left for foreign affairs was fully taken up by its unsuccessful efforts to contain the southward advance of Antiochus III into Coele-Syria.

Antiochus actively encouraged Philip's expansionist approach, for this brought Macedon into conflict with a number of states which Antiochus would otherwise probably have to fight for himself. Chief among these was the annoying Attalus I of Pergamon. Attalus had come off second best when he had allied himself with the Athenians and Aetolians against Philip during the First Macedonian war, but he had not yet given up. When Philip made peace with the Romans, this limited Macedonian plans for expansion in the west. Philip therefore turned east and expanded the Macedonian fleet with the intention of gaining control of the straits commanding access to the Euxine (Black Sea).

The Crimea was an important source of grain and the early version of the Silk Road, which channelled trade from the far east at this time, ran through ports on the southern shores of the Euxine. Pergamon would be affected by Macedonian control of trade from the Euxine, so an alarmed Attalus quickly threw together a coalition of other city-states likely to be harmed by this development. These included Cyzicus, which was on the southern coast of the Euxine, Byzantium, which was right on the Hellespont – the strait in question – and Rhodes, the major trading centre in the eastern Mediterranean.

Philip had already taken the islands of Samos and Andros from Egypt and was showing a predatory interest in Crete and Cyprus. His habit of selling into slavery the populations of cities which resisted his encroachments along with his threat to trade combined to turn much of the Greek world against him. Consequently, in 200 BC, Attalus was able to persuade the Athenians to join his coalition and he asked the Romans to join in as well.

The Roman aristocracy were willing for a variety of reasons. Firstly, Rome currently had no major wars on its hands, and any Roman with political ambitions needed a successful military campaign or two on his resumé. (Military operations in Spain were ongoing, but the stubborn Spanish tribesmen were a cause of pain and frustration rather than a source of loot and glory.)

Secondly, Rome was desperately short of manpower after the devastation of the Hannibalic War. By some estimates, the war had killed one man in three of the Italian population. Rome needed workers for the farms and artisans in the cities. A little-noted aspect of Rome's wars against the Hellenistic kingdoms was that, in Greece and Asia Minor, these were also massive slave-taking raids that in time amounted to wholesale population transfers.

Finally, with the disappearance of Carthage as a major threat, Macedon had been promoted to the position of Rome's most dangerous neighbour and, at that, a neighbour with demonstrated unfriendly intentions. To make things worse, Philip had already shown that he and Antiochus were prepared to act in concert when it came to attacking Ptolemaic possessions. What if this *de facto* alliance was turned against Rome? Even without the threat from Antiochus (who, fortunately, had his eastern flank to worry about), given the way that Philip was acting in Thrace, Rome was going to have to deal with Philip sooner or later and since now was a convenient time, why not sooner?

The Roman people could think of one good reason. They had just fought a long, brutal war, and they had no appetite for fighting another. When the senate put the war vote to the Roman popular assembly, the assembly turned it down flat. In democracies both ancient and modern, the governing class tend to keep the people voting until they come up with the desired result. In this case, the Roman senate leaned upon the tribune leading the anti-war party and granted the concession that troops who had served in the African campaign against Hannibal would be exempt from serving in the Macedonian campaign against Philip. Then they put the matter to the vote again. With the tribune muted and the electorate split, the senate got its way and war was declared in 200 BC.

Thereafter, diplomatic and religious niceties required that Philip be informed that he had become an enemy of the Roman state. This proved harder to do than expected because Philip was a busy man. A Roman legate finally tracked him down to where he was besieging the city of Abydos, on the Asian side of the Hellespont. Given Philip's reputation as a merciless conqueror, the citizens of Abydos were determined to fight to the death – after first killing their own children and womenfolk. Philip was more than happy to let them do so.

Under those circumstances, Philip was not prepared to seriously entertain the Roman demand that he give up all his recent gains and retire to within the borders of Macedon, and one suspects that the Romans would have been seriously disappointed if he had. So now, with the formalities completed, Rome and Macedon were now officially at war.

The Macedonian hedgehog

The Romans quickly realized that it was one thing to declare war on Macedon, and a very different thing to fight that war. For a start, for the Romans to 'win' they had to defeat Philip. All Philip required for victory was not to be defeated. The only thing Philip wanted from this war with Rome was for the Romans to go away and let him get on with maximizing his gains in Asia Minor and the Aegean islands before Egypt regained its strength. The Romans were more ambitious. They wanted to restrict Philip and Macedonian imperialism but to do that, they had to attack Macedon and beat the Macedonians in battle. In other words, they had to take the initiative, and this would not be easy.

The usual Roman approach to warfare was direct and effective. The senate levied an army, the army elected a consul in the *comitia centuriata* – which was basically the Roman army in voting mode – and that consul led the army at the enemy. Rome's target would be something that the enemy was desperate to defend (usually the capital city). The enemy would muster their army to defend their capital, the Roman legions would steamroller over that army and the consul would dictate peace terms to the cowed and defeated enemy. It was a tried and trusted formula.

So, the Macedonian capital was the city of Pella, the birthplace of Alexander the Great. The city was not exactly land-locked, for it was accessible by canal from an inlet of the northern Aegean Sea. However, getting a fleet to Pella was practically impossible. For a start, that fleet would have to sail around the inhospitable coast of the southern Peloponnese, which offered not one fleet-killing peninsula but three, the most easterly of which Cape Malea, was a notorious graveyard for ships. Then Rome's fleet (or the survivors thereof) would have to proceed up the east coast of Greece, harassed all the while by Philip's powerful navy. Then supply ships would have to repeatedly make the same journey throughout the campaigning season.

Even in the more friendly waters off Sicily, the Romans had lost tens of thousands of men to shipwreck during the First Punic War with Carthage. Given their precarious shortage of manpower and lack of popular support for the war, the Senate simply could not risk sending yet another army to a watery grave before it had even engaged the enemy.

So this meant taking the army across the Adriatic Sea by the shortest way possible and then fighting into Macedonia by land. The question was how to do this. Pella was on the other side of Greece and supplying an army as it fought all the way there was a logistical nightmare. The north was packed with barbarian tribes such as the Dardanians and Boii and subduing these just to get to Macedon would be at least as difficult as fighting the Macedonians themselves.

The south would at least put the Romans into relatively friendly territory in Greece but if the people would be on the Roman side, geography would not. The Olympus range lay between Greece and Macedon like the ultimate border wall, with peaks up to three kilometres above sea level. Passes through the range were few and those were easily defended.

This left the west. Philip had abandoned his attempts to expand westward through Illyria due to the roughness of the terrain and the hostility of the natives. The Romans could try going the other way, but, after their recent war, the Illyrians were none too fond of the Romans either. Getting through their mountainous land would be difficult. Getting regular supply trains through the lands of a hostile people who had a history of enthusiastic brigandage would be more difficult still.

Further south, the Aetolians looked like a good prospect. After all, they had been allies with Rome before and Aetolia offered access to Macedonia at least as far as Epirus, which would be a good start. The problem was that the Aetolians were currently at least as anti-Roman as the Illyrians. They felt – with considerable justification – that they had been very badly treated by the Romans in the previous war with Macedon. The Romans had allied with the Aetolians then left the Aetolians to do all the fighting. Then, after Philip's armies had ravaged Aetolian farms and pillaged their cities, Rome had made peace at its own convenience and with nothing in the peace terms that compensated the Aetolians for their suffering.

So, when Roman ambassadors turned up in Aetolia hopefully offering a renewal of the earlier alliance, the response was somewhere between derision and outrage. When blandishments failed, the Romans tried unsubtle threats (as a nation, the Romans prided themselves on their lack of subtlety, a characteristic they associated with weakness). All that threatening the Aetolians achieved was to cow them into a grudging neutrality as they awaited developments.

Since all that remained for the Romans were bad options or worse, an attack was proposed via Illyria on the basis that, having been recently beaten up by the Romans, the Illyrians might at least be passive while Rome's armies moved through their territory. With this decided, a Roman army landed in Apollonia under the command of the consul Sulpicius Galba. Philip accordingly put his campaign in the east on hold and moved west to face the Roman threat.

The opening round

It was almost traditional that, whenever the Macedonian army had to move from the Macedonian heartland, the barbarians to the north would launch a plundering expedition to take what they could before the army returned. Galba was well aware of this and had accordingly taken care to inform the Dardanians that he would be attacking Macedon from the south, should they care to join in by attacking from the north. Galba had also carefully sacrificed to Neptune in the hope of getting a Roman fleet around Cape Malea so that Philip would also have to deal with naval operations on his eastern flank.

This fleet successfully rounded the Peloponnese, rendezvoused with the fleets of Pergamon and Rhodes and commenced operations. The combined allied force enjoyed mixed success – the island of Andros was taken before the Macedonians were properly aware that there was even a threat and, since the Romans had no interest in acquiring Aegean islands, Andros passed into the possession of Attalus. On the other hand, an assault on the Chalcidice peninsula on the Greek mainland resulted in a humiliating defeat. The allies withdrew to Euboea where they captured another Macedonian naval base and thereafter wrapped up operations for the year. Though the fleet had overall more gains than losses, the effort-to-reward ratio was low, particularly considering the expense of equipping a fleet in the first place.

On land, Sulpicius advanced through the mountains as far as the Macedonian border town of Ottolobus. There, partly because Philip had to divide his army to also cope with the Dardanians, the Romans won a minor and pointless victory. Pointless, because it was too late in the year for Galba to follow up and risk being trapped in Macedonia when winter closed the mountain passes.

Thus, the battle had only two effects. The first was to formally introduce Macedonian pikemen and Roman legionaries to one another on the battlefield. The Romans were somewhat confounded by the bristling wall of spears presented by a well-formed phalanx and, in their turn, the Macedonians were horrified by the *gladius Hispaniensis* which the Romans had recently adopted from Spain. This sword was considerably more brutal than the *kopis*, its Greek counterpart. The gaping wounds and severed limbs inflicted by legionaries when they got to close quarters were thereafter a hidden drain of Macedonian morale.

The other effect of the Roman success at Ottolobus was that it persuaded the Aetolians to enter the war. After all, if the Dardanians were coming in looting from the north and the Romans were keeping Philip busy in the west, they might as well charge through Thessaly in the south and grab what they could. This proved something of a misjudgement, as Philip had correctly divined that the Romans would have to pull back to the Illyrian coast for the winter. He therefore took his own army back to Macedonia and from there southward and spent the remainder of the year giving the invading Aetolians yet another beating. The Romans did little to help because the Aetolians had forcibly rejected their offer of alliance. Therefore, the Aetolians were merely *hostes hostis* – the enemies of their enemy. The Romans would encourage them but when it came to actual support, the Aetolians were on their own.

As 199 BC came to an end, Philip could reflect that the war was so far going his way. He had taken some minor losses which in no way repaid the alliance against him for the manpower and treasure they had paid to inflict them. If the war continued as it had begun, Rome and Pergamon would be bankrupt a century or two before Macedon was defeated. The truly annoying thing about the war as far as he was concerned was that he was forced to abandon his expansionist plans in Asia Minor in order to fight it.

There was also the worrying fact that he was fighting Rome. The Romans did not mind long wars. It had taken them 23 years to defeat the Carthaginians in the First Punic War, and seventeen to defeat Hannibal. This was radically different to most Hellenistic wars which generally lasted for two or three years before the kings found something better to do and patched up a peace between them.

Still, Philip would have taken heart from the consulship of Villius Tappulus. Villius was the successor to Galba, for the Romans changed consuls and therefore army commanders every year. Yet, commanding armies was not all that a Roman consul had to do as head of the Roman state. Politics and administrative matters kept Villius in Rome for most of his consulship, and the consul was only able to get out to the army in Illyria in time to hand it over to the consul for the next year.

It is quite possible that Villius had observed Galba's struggles to get anywhere with the war and had simply decided that he wanted no part of it. Apart from anything else, the veterans in his army had also had enough and were riotously advocating to be discharged, and Philip, learning from his experience with Galba, had taken up a position in a narrow gorge along the river Aous. Now anyone wanting to attack along Galba's route would first have to dislodge Philip from his fortifications. Not only would that prove painful, but all that Philip needed to do upon being dislodged was to fall back to the next narrow gorge and there invite the Romans to repeat their experience. Villius was not enthusiastic.

Nor were things going any better in the Aegean. The Macedonians had a strong fleet which could overpower the allies without the support of Pergamon. Yet Attalus had problems of his own, for Antiochus III had observed that Pergamon had committed significant reserves to the Macedonian war, which gave Antiochus the chance to regain lost Seleucid territory in Asia Minor.

Also of course, Philip was preoccupied with fending off the Romans and was no longer able to mop up Ptolemaic possessions along the Anatolian seaboard. The Egyptians were unable to defend their overseas territory as all their energies were engaged in their civil war, and since Antiochus had already taken all he wanted in Coele-Syria, this left him free to take what he wanted. Attalus alone was hardly a match for the power of the Seleucid empire, and certainly could not defend all of Anatolia. Therefore, he pretty much abandoned the attack on Macedon and focussed on fending off Antiochus from Pergamon's heartlands.

In all, 199 BC was another good year for Philip. He had merely to hold off the Romans to get what he wanted from the war, and he had done that with minimal effort. At current rates, Macedonia could hold out for a few centuries yet. All this was about to change with the arrival of the Roman commander for the following year – Titus Quinctius Flamininus.

Flamininus and the 'freedom of Greece'

In Flamininus the Romans found the perfect commander for the war against Macedon. Flamininus was a good general. This was almost self-evident for he, as a young man, had campaigned in southern Italy against Hannibal and survived. His commander in the theatre, Claudius Marcellus – the conqueror of Syracuse – had not. After the death of Marcellus, it fell to Flamininus to hold things together in southern Italy until a replacement arrived.

Yet Flamininus was more than a grim general of the type of Galba. He was a Philhellene, fluent in Greek and of an aristocratic family cultured enough to reassure diplomats that they were not dealing with some western barbarian which is how Greeks generally considered contemporary Romans. Not only a general and a diplomat, Flamininus was also a strategist. He realized that Macedonian strength was largely derived from its occupation of Greece, and that there would be no defeating Macedon unless the Greeks no longer supported Philip, whether they did so willingly – as did the Thessalians and Achaeans – or unwillingly, as did almost everybody else. Flamininus was already working on the Achaeans and was soon to bring them over to his side.

It helped that Philip himself was a far less sympathetic character. His sense of humour was darkly sardonic and he was only prepared to negotiate when the merciless use of force was not available as an option. Merciless force was certainly not an option in the case of Rome, where the senate was demonstrating its usual tenacity in grinding on with a war whatever the initial setbacks. When Flamininus arrived in Illyria, he did so with substantial reinforcements for the army he was joining. Philip realized that the Romans were in this for the long term and, reluctantly, he announced his readiness to negotiate.

Flamininus, on the other hand, wanted a war. He was a young man who had skipped numerous rungs on the usual ladder of Roman offices and vaulted straight to the consulship. Not unexpectedly, this speedy ascent to the top had earned Flamininus a host of enemies who felt they had been ahead in line for his current job. If these enemies were not to be given their opportunity to take him down, Flamininus had to bring news of a highly successful war home to the voters. A tamely negotiated peace would not do that.

Therefore, when Flamininus and Philip met outside Philip's fortified blockage of the Aous River gorge, Flamininus' position was basically that they should skip the war, pretend that the Romans had already won, and discuss surrender terms. Naturally enough, Philip refused indignantly. Yet the meeting was by no means a failure from the Roman point of view. It got Flamininus close enough to the gorge for his agents to recruit a local who knew another way around it.

This walk-around was not enough for the entire army, but it made all the difference when the Romans threw themselves at Philip's fortifications. His insider knowledge allowed Flamininus to send a force large enough to create total confusion when it turned up on the Macedonian flank at a crucial moment in the battle. Philip's plans to make a fighting retreat to his next strong point had been predicated upon pulling back his army on good order. As it was, he was caught up in a chaotic retreat in which the

Romans did not stop pressing until they were through the Vale of Tempe and into Thessaly.

Flamininus grandly declared the 'freedom of Thessaly', thus loosing the region from the vassalage to Macedon which the region had endured since the time of Philip II in 353 BC. It quickly became apparent that Thessaly did not want to be free, and the cities would fight ferociously not to be liberated. This was in part due to loyalty to Philip, but also because much of the actual liberating was being done by the ravenous Aetolians, whose struggles to prise Thessaly from Macedonian tyranny were, in reality, little different from the pillaging expeditions they had launched in the past.

With a large Roman army on its doorstep, Epirus had little choice but to surrender to Flamininus, or as Flamininus would have it, voluntarily join the campaign to free Greece. Elsewhere, however, the Thessalian city of Atrax resisted stubbornly, and it was but one of a series of strong points between Epirus and Macedonia. Reluctantly, Flamininus was forced to concede that, against that sort of resistance, he was not going to get into Macedonia that year. Accordingly, he led his army south to the Gulf of Corinth where it could be supplied over the winter.

Peace and war

Flamininus' consulship was only for a year, but he had hopes of his command being extended. The Roman constitution allowed this when a commander was deemed indispensable or if he could not be replaced because the the new consuls were too busy elsewhere. Whether his command was renewed or not, Flamininus was determined to claim the glory of finishing the war.

Accordingly, he sent word to his extensive network of political contacts in Rome that he was going to try to negotiate peace terms with Philip. If his command in Greece was not renewed for another year, then those friends should lobby for the peace to be accepted and Flamininus would get the credit for finishing the war. If Flamininus retained his command, the peace should be rejected and Flamininus would have another chance for glory in defeating Philip. In short, thousands of lives and the geopolitical situation in the north-eastern Mediterranean depended on how far one man's political ambitions could be satisfied. No wonder Philip was deeply cynical about dealing with Rome.

That cynicism was immediately apparent when the Macedonian king turned up for talks at the port city of Nicaea. Philip was happy to talk, but not prepared to leave his ship to come to the negotiating table. When Flamininus asked what he was afraid of, Philip replied that he feared only the gods. However, he certainly did not trust either the Romans or Aetolians. After the first day of negotiations, Philip sailed away. He returned late in the day on the morrow, saying that a late start was the only way to get any negotiating done. Flamininus' windbag Greek allies would only keep their speeches short if talking too long cut into the dinner hour.

Eventually peace terms were roughed out, and it was decided that those points upon which Philip and Flamininus could not agree would be presented to the Roman senate. The senate could either take Philip's side, or agree with Flamininus that the Macedonians were being intractable and resume the war. As it happened, by the time the ambassadors from the peace talks had arrived in Rome, the consular dispositions for the coming year had already been decided. Both consuls would campaign in Gaul and Flamininus would keep his Greek command.

With the consular commands already decided, so was the fate of the peace talks. The senate listened sympathetically to ambassadors from the Greek leagues and Pergamon who spoke at length about the advantages of continuing the war. As the historian Polybius reports, 'Philip's envoys had prepared a detailed rebuttal, but when they rose to speak they were silenced, and their arguments cut short.' (*History* 18.11.11) The war would continue.

The campaigning season of 197 BC opened with Philip in dire straits. While Flamininus had kept his promise not to engage in military operations while the Macedonian ambassadors were in Rome, this had not prevented a winter of furious diplomacy. One by one Philip's allies were peeled away, with the last defectors hurrying to leap on the Roman bandwagon before they alone in Greece were left to face Rome's power.

Even Philip recognized that he had lost his control of the cities of Greece. He handed Argos in the Peloponnese to his last ally, Nabis of Sparta, in recognition of the fact that he would be powerless to stop the city from falling into the hands of his multitude of enemies. Then he mustered his army and prepared for a last gamble. If he had been unable to prevent the Romans from defeating him diplomatically, there was still the chance that they could be defeated in the field. It was a hotly-debated topic among military men of the day whether the Roman legion was superior to the Macedonian pike phalanx. In his last throw of the dice, Philip was going to give them the chance to find out.

The battle of Cynoscephalae 197 BC

At Pherae in Thessaly, Philip's army and that of Flamininus prepared for a showdown. The Macedonian phalanx was certainly inferior to the Roman legions in one way – it required a stretch of open ground, preferably flat, on which to operate. His experience at fighting the Romans in the broken canyons of Illyria had given Philip the patience to wait until he could find a suitable battleground, so the two armies moved parallel to one another on either of a long ridge of hills shaped like dogs' heads (Cynoscephalae).

The two armies were well-matched in numbers. Overall Philip had some 25,000 men, of whom two thousand were cavalry. Flamininus had about the same number of cavalry, and his legionaries were equal in number to the Macedonian phalangites, being around 16,000 apiece. The remainder of Flamininus' army consisted of lighter-armed Greek troops, against which Philip had a similar number of mercenaries. Unlike the other Hellenistic kingdoms, the Macedonians had no elephants, while the Romans had procured over a dozen – presumably from their Pergamene allies.

For all the careful planning and strategizing of the two generals, the decisive battle happened more or less by accident. The night before the battle, there was a heavy rainstorm and when the armies awoke to a chilly June morning, they found they were surrounded by fog.

Aware that his army was blind and losing its direction, Philip dispatched a force to take and hold the Dogs' Heads lest the Romans take command of the heights and come down on him out of the mist as Hannibal's troops had done to the Romans at Lake Trasimene. (p.49) Meanwhile, Flamininus was trying to work out the current location of the Macedonian army and he sent a force of light infantry to the Dogs'

Heads presumably because, once the fog cleared, they would have a good view of the enemy's location and disposition.

While engaged on different missions to the same location, Romans and Macedonians bumped into one another and a heated little battle broke out. Both sides pumped reinforcements into the fight, and eventually the Macedonians prevailed. It was only a temporary victory, however, because Flamininus was already pulling his army into full battle order.

This left Philip with a tricky decision. On the one hand, his side was currently winning and secondly, the slope was in his favour. A Macedonian phalanx was hard to beat even on level ground. Coming downhill with pikes levelled, it was literally the stuff of opposing general's nightmares. (The later Roman general Aemilius Paullus was to confess that the memory of a phalanx rolling down on him used to wake him up at nights in a cold sweat.)

On the other hand, the ground was rocky and uneven. Thousands of men, pushed into close formation, had little ability to manoeuvre around obstacles because the phalanx was designed simply to go forward without changing formation. It was something of a gamble therefore – would the benefit of the slope be worth the drawback of rough terrain? In the end Philip decided to take the chance and ordered his army into battle.

Flamininus was in command of the Roman left wing which took the first shock of the Macedonian advance. Observing that his men were being driven back, Flamininus transferred his command to the right. Here the legions were having more success, mainly because the Macedonians hurrying into formation had not been given time to form their lines properly, and much of a phalanx's success depended on everyone being in the right place.

At this point, the battle was in the balance though hardly deadlocked. The Roman right was advancing and the Roman left was retreating. Flamininus now committed his reserves, including the elephants on to the right and this forced the Macedonians back even further. The battle was now a story of two halves – on one, a Roman army was literally going downhill towards defeat and, on the other, the Romans were slogging uphill against a wavering enemy.

At some point, as they went in different directions, the two halves passed one another. This was when an observant Roman military tribune, on the advancing wing of the Roman army, noted that the Macedonians pressing downhill were presenting their backs and flanks to his men. Acting on his own initiative, the tribune stripped every man he could muster from the back of the advancing Roman force and led them in a wild downhill charge at the rear of the Macedonians.

The phalanx was not designed to take an attack from the back. With their pikes pointing forward through two ranks of their fellow phalangites, the Macedonians could not even turn to face their attackers without dropping their weapons. Chaos in the rear led to confusion at the front and, within minutes, the Macedonian battle machine had dissolved into a mass of disorientated, frightened men.

The phalanx was beaten and the men within knew it. Accordingly, they did what Hellenistic armies had done for generations. To show they had stopped fighting, they grounded their pikes. That is, they lowered the pikes so that the butts were on the ground and the points in the air. It was a clear indication of surrender. Unfortunately, their enemy was unused to the more genteel rules of Hellenistic warfare. Most were Roman veterans of the war against Hannibal, and the only fight they understood was to the finish. They cut down the defenceless phalangites in their thousands.

Overall, the Romans killed far more Macedonians after the battle was over than while their enemy was still fighting. Eight thousand men – almost half the phalanx – was slaughtered before the Romans started taking prisoners, and they took five thousand of these. In short, Philip had lost his army while the Romans had lost 700 men. The gamble had failed, and Philip had lost the war.

The Peace

Having adroitly transferred from the losing to the winning flank, Flamininus was literally on the winning side in the battle. We also note that somehow the name of the junior officer whose initiative won the battle for Flamininus never made it into the historical record. Therefore, credit for the victory goes to Flamininus alone. The question now was how he would use this success, for Philip would now have to accept whatever terms were dictated to him.

The terms proposed by Flamininus were intended to break Macedon as a Mediterranean power but leave it intact as a Hellenistic kingdom. At this time, the Romans were not interested in eastern expansion. They had fought their war with Philip to prevent any risk of his westward expansion and the terms of the peace were designed to reflect this.

Philip was stripped of his fleet largely on the basis that, if he was to be confined to Macedonia, then a fleet was completely unnecessary. Also, as Flamininus had observed, Macedon's power was drawn from the kingdom's occupation of Greece. Therefore, Philip was ordered out of Greece. The Romans had no interest in taking over Greece in Philip's place, but they also did not want anyone else there. Accordingly, they made good Flamininus' promise to 'free' Greece. Flamininus himself made the declaration to rapturous applause in a speech given in Corinth.

As rhetoric, the speech was superb. As a legal statement it was defective. As it turned out, Romans and Greeks had different interpretations of 'freedom', quite possibly due to an imperfect understanding of each other's culture. To the Greeks freedom meant much as it would today. It meant that the Greeks were fully independent and free to return to life as it was two centuries earlier when they barely needed to even acknowledge that Rome or Macedon existed.

For the Romans, Greek 'freedom' had a different sense, which was more that of the status of a freed slave who remained under the tutelage of his former master. This meant that though free, the freed people had an obligation to their liberator to do as he required of them and to give their support when and as demanded. In return the Romans would give the Greeks their protection but would expect to be consulted before the Greeks undertook any initiatives of their own. From the Roman point of view, the Greeks signally failed to live up to their obligations and this led to the eventual breakdown of the relationship.

Philip might have been able to bridge this cultural divide but, after hurriedly accepting the Roman terms, he left the peace talks at speed. The northern barbarians had again gotten word that the Macedonian army was fully engaged in the south so they had yet again embarked on a plundering raid into Macedonia's heartlands. Philip took with him the remnants of his army, some 5,000 men. The terms of the peace said that Philip was not to increase his army beyond that and nor was he to add any elephants, though where the elephants would have come from anyway is an open question.

Finally, the Romans – as was their wont – insisted that the defeated party pay for the war which Rome had just fought. Philip agreed to pay 500 talents of silver to cover Rome's immediate expenses, and further instalments of 50 talents for the next decade. (Given that Philip had just eliminated his fleet and cut his army by seventy-five per cent, the savings in manpower and operating expenses paying the indemnity probably left him with an annual profit.)

Overall, once he had repelled the barbarian invaders, Philip could reckon that he had come off relatively lightly from his catastrophic defeat. His kingdom remained intact, albeit stripped of its overseas possessions. Greece was no longer under his control, but there was a certain satisfaction in knowing that the peninsula was now Rome's problem. Since the main strategic reason for Macedon wanting to control Greece was to ensure that the kingdom's southern flank was protected, Philip could take comfort in knowing that security on that side was now underwritten by the formidable Roman army.

Like any Hellenistic king, Philip probably reckoned that the terms of the peace would endure for his lifetime. Thus he would now quietly build the kingdom's resources, keep a low profile in international affairs, and let his successor make of the situation what he could.

Meanwhile Rome's problems with Greece had already begun. The Aetolians felt that, since they had fought alongside the Romans, they were entitled to a share of the booty and some of the land which they and the Romans had jointly conquered – not least because some of that land had formerly been part of the Aetolian League. Flamininus was of a contrary opinion and held that the Aetolians had been fighting on their own behalf and Rome owed them nothing. However, he had settled affairs in Greece and Macedon to his satisfaction and the Aetolians interfered with these arrangements at their peril.

Philip cheerfully surrendered possession of his Greek fortresses to the Romans, knowing well that the Aetolians were itching to get hold of those nearest to their territory. Roman legionaries in those fortresses cramped Aetolia's ability to make war almost as severely as Macedonian occupation of the strong points had done. In the end all the Aetolians got from their war was blood, sweat, toil and tears. Even their most basic request was not met. When they demanded that at the very least their enemy, Philip, should be deposed and a replacement put on the Macedonian throne, Flamininus simply told them not to be ridiculous.

In short, the Peace of Tempe (also called the Peace of Flamininus) was far more satisfactory to the conquered Macedonians than to the Aetolian allies of the conqueror. As peace settlements go, it was doomed to fail because the Aetolians were determined to rewrite several major clauses at the first chance they got. One part of the peace terms that the Aetolians did like was that Philip could not move his army out of Macedonia without the express permission of the Roman senate. From their point of view, since the Romans had promised the Greeks their freedom, all they had to do was wait until the Romans withdrew their army from Greece, and then their intention was to use that freedom in ways that the Macedonians and their neighbours certainly would not appreciate.

For a start, miscalculated the Aetolians, if the Romans really did intend to leave the Greeks to decide their own fate, then the Aetolians were free to make their own arrangements with other powers. Chief among those powers which assumed that Greece was now a tasty morsel abandoned to the predators was the very predatory Antiochus III.

Chapter 7

Rome and Antiochus III

The decade 202–192 BC was a good one for Antiochus III. With Philip of Macedon completely engaged in his ever-more dangerous struggle with the Romans, and the Egyptians preoccupied with palace intrigues and the rebellion in the south, Antiochus had as near to a free hand as he was ever likely to get. Furthermore, dissent within the borders of his empire was at a low point. The Seleucid empire was ruled by the Seleucid king as overlord of other monarchs. So, provided he did not push those kings too far, Antiochus could currently count himself as supreme ruler of Armenia, Parthia and Bactria as well as the lands he ruled directly. All these nations were currently submissive.

The only fly in the ointment was that Antiochus still felt unable to take complete control of Asia Minor. Just before the start of Philip's war with Rome, the Macedonians had attempted an invasion of Pergamon. The attack was observed with intense interest by the Seleucids, who had frequently yearned to do the same thing. It failed, because the cautious Attalus had spent a lot of time and money fortifying his city against just such an eventuality. Antiochus took note, and he left Pergamon alone, even while Attalus was away waging diplomatic warfare in Greece on behalf of his Roman ally Flamininus.

Instead, Antiochus took over where Philip had left off in Asia Minor and the Aegean. His army and fleet steadily picked off Ptolemaic possessions in the northern Aegean and along the seaboard of Asia Minor until there was nothing worthwhile left to acquire. Then Antiochus made his peace with Egypt by marrying his daughter Cleopatra to Ptolemy V. (This daughter was to be the first of a long line of Egyptian Cleopatras, culminating in Cleopatra VII who, 150 years later, was to be the last Ptolemaic ruler of Egypt.) At the time of her marriage Cleopatra I was around ten years old and Ptolemy was fifteen or sixteen. The Egyptians were later to claim that Cleopatra brought with her Coele-Syria as her dowry, but while the canny Antiochus may have hinted that he might do so, he never put that particular offer in writing, and Coele-Syria remained a Seleucid possession.

Thus in 195 BC, with the betrothal of his daughter to the Pharaoh, Antiochus had inserted his family into the Ptolemaic royal line. Furthermore, two years previously, he had received the news that the annoying Attalus I would no longer trouble him in Asia Minor. While travelling on a diplomatic mission to Boeotia, Attalus had suffered what appears to have been a severe stroke. Partly paralysed, Attalus was taken back to Pergamon where he may have lived just long enough to hear of Philip's final defeat in the Macedonian war.

The bad news was that the successor to Attalus was his eldest son, Eumenes II, who was to prove every bit as competent and annoying as his father. But in the late 190s BC, Eumenes was still feeling his way into his new job and as yet he had not demonstrated that he too was going to menace Seleucid ambitions in Asia Minor.

Furthermore, Rome had finally demonstrated that it was getting interested in affairs east of the Hellespont. The senate designated a number of cities in Anatolia as 'free', much as they had declared all of Greece as free. The intention was clearly to put a buffer zone of cities between the Seleucids and the Romans' Pergamene allies. Therefore, getting too involved in Asia Minor would bring Antiochus into conflict with Rome. And if Antiochus was going to clash with the Romans, he might as well do so in Greece, where things had been getting interesting.

Events in Free Greece

After he had dealt with Macedon, Flamininus had a few details in Greece to tidy up before he returned to celebrate his triumph in Rome. Chief among these was the issue of Nabis of Sparta. For over a century, Sparta had been failing as a state. Soon after Sparta's great victory over Athens in the Peloponnesian War, the Spartans had fallen out with Thebes. A major flaw of Spartan society was that the ossified system made it very easy for poorer Spartiates to drop out of the top rank of Spartan society which provided the nation's hoplites, the feared Spartan warriors. At the same time, almost the only way to become a Spartiate was to be born one.

Lacking warriors, the Spartans were unable to prevent the Thebans and their allies from defeating them and taking Messenia from their control. Just as Macedon had drawn its strength from its domination of Greece, Sparta had been a great power because of its domination of Messenia. Without Messenia, Sparta was reduced to a third-rate Peloponnesian city with over-sized dreams of glory and a dysfunctional government paralysed by coups and intense social strife.

The last king of Sparta was the usurper Nabis the First (and only). He took power in 207 BC and ruthlessly executed a reform programme while also executing or exiling anyone who opposed him. The only historians who have described his reign are the implacably hostile Polybius, and Livy, the faithful echo of Polybius in contemporary matters Greek. These two historians describe Nabis as almost a picture-book villain, though modern historians believe that – while doubtless brutal – Nabis was no-where near as bad as he was painted.

Nabis had sided with Philip in the war, and as Philip prepared for his final confrontation with Rome, he gave Argos to Nabis for safekeeping. Nabis took control of the city and then abandoned Philip by joining the Roman side. After the defeat of Macedon, Flamininus politely asked Nabis to leave Argos. When Nabis refused, the Romans took it from him in a short but nasty war. With Nabis down (but not out), the Romans had little reason to remain in the Greece they had allegedly freed from foreign domination so the legions returned to Italy.

With Rome gone, the enemies of Nabis prepared to finish the job that Rome had started. Meanwhile, the Aetolians were furiously plotting to gain the spoils they felt that Flamininus had denied them. Nabis allied himself with Aetolia and the Aetolians opened negotiations with Philip and Antiochus with an eye to radically re-arranging the power structure of Greece. Philip had given his son as a hostage to the Romans and, despite his recent defeat, he and the Romans were getting along rather well. Consequently, Philip not only declined to join the proposed alliance, but very probably warned the Romans about what was going on.

Deciding that Nabis was an unreliable ally, the Aetolians assassinated him and attempted to rule Sparta as a subject state. This failed because the indignant Spartans and neighbouring Achaeans turned viciously on the Aetolian garrison. By 191 BC, Sparta had ceased to exist as an independent state, having been captured by the Achaeans and forcibly incorporated into the Achaean League.

Meanwhile, Antiochus had acquired a new advisor. This was no other than Hannibal of Carthage. After the defeat of Carthage in the Second Punic War, Hannibal had stayed on in his native city as a senior politician working with considerable success to rebuild his city's fortunes. Like any successful politician, Hannibal quickly acquired enemies. Those enemies were quick to take advantage of the deep suspicion that Rome still harboured for their former foe, and eventually Hannibal was forced to flee from Carthage before he was arrested for conspiring against the Romans.

The only great power presumed capable of withstanding Rome was the Seleucid empire and, though Hannibal had his doubts about Antiochus' military capability, he fled to him for protection. (There is a story that Antiochus, aware that his planned move to join the Aetolians in Greece would bring him into conflict with Rome, paraded his army for Hannibal to inspect. Then Antiochus asked the great Carthaginian general, 'Well, do you think these will be enough for the Romans?' Hannibal regarded the richly-decorated armour of the soldiery and replied, 'I am not sure. The Romans are very greedy.')

Despite Hannibal's reservations, Antiochus began to expand his power across the Hellespont. His first stop was not in Greece but in Thrace. Philip had been ordered to withdraw to within the boundaries of Macedon and, while he interpreted these boundaries as inventively as possible, he could not extend them to include all of Thrace. This left the Greek town of Lysimachea unprotected and the native Thracians, always resentful of this foreign imposition upon their soil, took advantage of Philip's withdrawal to attack and pillage the town.

The Thracians may well have intended to destroy the place completely, but they were thwarted by Antiochus who turned up in time to save and occupy what remained of the town. Antiochus disingenuously informed the Romans and Macedonians that as a Seleucid king he had a valid claim on the town which, as its name indicated, had been founded by Lysimachus, a former general of Seleucus I. The town was not on the list of places which the Romans had declared off-limits (probably because it had not occurred to them to do so) so there was no reason why Antiochus should refrain from (re)including the place in his empire, nor any reason why anyone should be alarmed because he had done so.

These reassurances would have been considerably more effective if Antiochus had not turned up with remarkable promptitude together with an army which he coincidentally had handy. Indeed, a suspicious mind – such as Philip's – would have thought that Antiochus was planning to move into Thrace anyway, and Lysimachea had provided a convenient pretext. Furthermore, even a cursory check would reveal that Antiochus was busily preparing his new possession as a staging post for further attacks upon Greece and Macedon. We can safely assume that Philip made more than a cursory check.

Philip took his suspicions to the Romans. Following their usual custom, the Romans had dispatched a senatorial commission to settle affairs in the lands they had just conquered. In this case, even though Greece was technically 'free', there were still a number of issues for the commission to sort out. For example, Thessaly was declared an independent entity, which caused anger among the Aetolians who felt that they had earned suzerainty there.

The same happened in Arcania, neighbours to the Aetolians, and therefore targets for Aetolian expansion until the Romans placed them off limits. Thereafter, control of a number of important fortresses was arranged in such a way that – not coincidentally – those fortresses remained a check upon Aetolian ambitions. This caused further anger in Aetolia and this anger became incandescent fury when Philip's reported evidence of Antiochus' plans to the Roman chief commissioner resulted in the Macedonians and Romans declaring an official alliance.

Rome's reconciliation with Macedonia was greatly helped by the death of Rome's ally Attalus, which somewhat weakened the bond between Rome and Pergamon, and by the presence of Philip's son Demetrios in Rome. Demetrios was officially a hostage for his father's good behaviour, but Philip had no intention of misbehaving anyway. Therefore, Demetrios was more an ambassador-in-place, an eagerly sought guest at aristocratic dinner parties and a persuasive voice in the ears of influential Romans.

Finally, the Dardanian invasion of Macedon after the battle of Cynoscephalae had demonstrated to the Romans the importance of maintaining a solid bulwark against barbarian invasions of Greece from the north. Philip's expert quashing of that Dardanian invasion persuaded the Romans that he was the man for the job. Overall, given the new rapport between Macedon and Rome, the chances of success for the plans of the unofficial Aetolian-Seleucid alliance had dimmed considerably. Nevertheless, they doggedly went ahead.

Antiochus now sent an official ambassador to the Aetolians. This ambassador declared that the Seleucid empire intended to stand shoulder-to-shoulder with the Romans in defending the 'freedom of Greece'. This declaration was intended less as a gesture of solidarity with the Romans than to put them in a tight spot diplomatically. The Romans could hardly object to someone enthusiastically endorsing the very objectives for which they had ostensibly gone to war with Philip in the first place. Yet at the same time, everyone was well aware that, at present, the only people forcibly meddling in the affairs of the Greeks were, in fact, the Romans.

In response, the Romans issued a degree of their own demanding that Antiochus respect the liberty of all autonomous cities within his empire. Since, in practical terms, this decree would have led to the dissolution of the Seleucid empire in the west, Antiochus ignored it.

It is probable that Antiochus planned his invasion to 'protect' the Greeks from Roman intervention in the spring of 191 BC. He would spend the winter mopping up the last of the Thracians still indignant over his reconquest of Lysimachea, and thereafter, the army he had been collecting from across his extensive domains would be ready to cross the Hellespont as soon as the winter weather relented. The invasion of Greece would go ahead, with the Greeks prepared for the event over the winter by diplomacy, bribery and threats.

This tidy plan was disrupted by the Aetolians. The Aetolians were eager to get control of three fortresses so vital that they were collectively known as the 'fetters of Greece'. These were the Acropolis of Corinth, Chalcis on the island of Euboea, and Demetrias in Thessaly. The Aetolians had expected that any peace after the war against Philip would give them at least Demetrias, and ever since the Romans had denied them, the Aetolians had been scheming furiously to take these strong-points anyway.

In the late summer of 192 BC, matters were finely poised. The Aetolians reckoned that, while Corinth was firmly in the hands of the hostile

Achaeans, they had a good chance of taking Chalcis and Demetrias, where key members of the garrisons had been suborned. The problem was that, if they waited until the late spring of 191 BC, as Antiochus wanted, then the chances were high that someone would reveal the Aetolian plans and betray their sympathizers. The Aetolians had to act now.

Act they did. They made lightning attacks upon Demetrias and Chalcis, combining attacks from without with treachery within. Something went badly wrong at Chalcis, where the Aetolians were rebuffed, but all went well at the prize of Demetrias, which fell into Aetolian hands. The Aetolians now sent urgent representations to Antiochus. They pointed out that they now had a key fortress in Thessaly, the perfect gateway into Greece for an invading force from Thrace. The Greeks were restless under Rome's increasingly heavy hand and Philip was likely to join with the Seleucids if it seemed that they were going to take control of Greece without him. What was Antiochus waiting for?

The short answer was that Antiochus was waiting for spring and the rest of his army but, as the Aetolians pointed out, they could not hope to hold on to Demetrias for that long now that they had practically declared war on Rome. It was now or never. At present, Antiochus could muster an army of 10,000 men, a few elephants and some 500 cavalry. That was all he needed, the Aetolians assured him. They themselves could supply more infantry, and the Thessalians whom Antiochus was liberating would supply the cavalry. Indeed, now that the great enterprise was underway, perhaps Philip might also contribute a few thousand phalangites.

Thus, on a wave of wild optimism, half-baked plans and deeply misplaced assumptions, Antiochus launched his invasion to re-liberate Greece in the late summer of 192 BC.

Antiochus in Greece

For Antiochus, the only good thing about having his plans hurried was that the Romans were even more unprepared for the invasion than he was himself. It would be 191 BC before the Romans could get a decent army into Greece, so Antiochus had until then to get the entire peninsula united solidly behind him. This was to prove no easy task.

It quickly became apparent to Antiochus that the Aetolians had – to put it charitably – erred in their assessment of sentiment in Greece. Rather than a rapturous welcome from Greeks overwhelmed with gratitude at being freed from the heavy hand of Rome, Antiochus found himself greeted with deep scepticism which bordered upon hurtful cynicism about his motives.

The fortress town of Chalcis, for example, coolly informed Antiochus that its people were currently enjoying all the freedom they wanted. That freedom included the right to stay out of the current fight, and if Antiochus wanted to make the place any more free, he would have to come with his army and make them so. (In fact, because Chalcis was vital to naval operations on the east coast, Antiochus was forced to take up the people of Chalcis on their challenge and he eventually took the place by armed force.)

Elsewhere, the Seleucid diplomats faced more challenges to their negotiations. Even the people of Thessaly, upon whose soil the army of Antiochus was currently standing, were notably unenthusiastic about developments. Rather than believing that Antiochus had freed them once and for all from the threat of Macedonian domination, the Thessalians were clearly anxious about Antiochus' Aetolian allies, and deeply suspicious of their intentions.

After some dithering, the Athenians declared themselves on the Roman side (as they had been on the previous war). The Boeotians declared for Antiochus, but less out of enthusiasm for his cause, than because the Boeotians tended to take the opposite side to the Athenians almost as a reflex action. Even in this case though, it required the personal presence of Antiochus plus army to tip the scales in his favour.

There was little doubt which side Philip was going to choose. The idea of the Seleucids making themselves at home in Thessaly – a region that the Macedonians considered almost an adjunct of their kingdom – was anathema. Philip had already offered his kingdom to the Romans as a launch pad for the reconquest of Greece and had given hospitality to those Romans in Greece fleeing from Antiochus. Once Antiochus started military operations to subdue the Thessalians, Philip and Rome came to an agreement that any Thessalian cities which Philip re-took from the Seleucids, he could keep.

The year 192 BC ended on that note, with both sides working hard on the logistics of bringing in much larger armies as soon as the winter relented enough for them to do so.

Spring that year came first on the Adriatic side of Greece, and 20,000 Romans arrived to support the Macedonians and the small army Rome already had campaigning in Thessaly. Antiochus, meanwhile, was frustrated by late spring storms in the Aegean. As the Romans swept through Thessaly, the army that could have stopped them remained frustratingly penned up in the ports of Asia Minor. In the end, Antiochus had to ask the Aetolians to deliver on their promise to supply him with the manpower he was lacking.

The answer was a somewhat embarrassed silence. There were two reasons for this. One was that the Aetolians had already seen at close quarters what 20,000 legionaries had done to Philip's army and had no wish to be at the receiving end of that experience. More importantly, Philip had left the Romans to deal with Antiochus and was moving east towards Aetolia with the very clear intention of paying off some long-standing grudges. The Aetolians needed everyone back to defend their homeland. Nevertheless, they grudgingly sent Antiochus several thousand men.

While Antiochus had no way to stop the Romans from re-taking Thessaly, there was a time-tried formula for keeping invaders from the north out of the rest of Greece. The best way to get an army south was to lead them through the pass of Thermopylae. At Thermopylae, as had the Spartan king Leonidas 350 years before him, Antiochus decided to make a stand. Not trusting his Aetolian allies to hold the line, he assigned them garrison duty guarding the paths that led around the back of the pass.

Of course, it would have helped greatly if the Romans did not have a steadily developing interest in Greece and its history. They knew the story of Leonidas and his heroic 300 as well as did Antiochus, and they knew that the Persians had turned the pass with a night march around Mount Kallidromon. Following the Persians' footsteps, the Romans set out with two columns. This was presumably on the basis that one column could get around the Aetolian garrison guarding the route while the other engaged it. Ironically, the man charged with the job of repeating the Persian feat of getting around the pass was a politician renowned for his anti-Hellenistic views. This was Marcus Cato, known to posterity as Cato the Elder or Cato the Censor.

Cato had a miserable time of it on his march, and he and his troops came close to getting lost, even though at one point an exasperated Cato attempted to scout the way personally. In the end, his men were drawn in the right direction when the Roman commander, Marcus Glabrio, decided he could wait no longer and attacked the Seleucids at the pass head-on. The sound of battle guided Cato's force, which turned up at the Seleucid rear at about the same time as Antiochus was hit in the face by a Roman missile that cost him most of his teeth.

With their king understandably distracted, and Romans suddenly attacking on all sides, the Seleucid army broke in a wild dash for the rear. It did not help that, while in Thessaly, Antiochus had cleaned up the battlefield at Cynoscephalae and given the Macedonian dead a long-delayed funeral. This had partly been intended to illustrate that Antiochus was doing what Philip could not, since at that time the Romans had barred him from Thessaly. Yet it had also graphically shown to the Seleucid army what the Romans were capable of doing to a defeated force.

In consequence, even had the Romans stood back (and they emphatically did not), it is estimated that around a quarter of the Seleucid army would have trampled itself to death in the panic to get out of the narrow pass that had turned into a death-trap. It did not help that the elephants which Antiochus had brought along turned out to be worse than useless. Infected by the general panic, they blocked one narrow stretch and refused to move even as the Romans at the other end of the trapped mass of Seleucid soldiery hewed down their defenceless enemies.

The Second Battle of Thermopylae ended as had the first, with the defenders defeated and almost wiped out. The Romans later claimed that they had lost only 200 men, while the Seleucid army in Greece had basically ceased to exist. Antiochus realized immediately that his attempted occupation had failed completely. Pausing only to pick up the garrison at Chalcis, he left Greece – never to return.

It may have consoled the Seleucid king that, while at Chalcis, in Euboea he had found and married a beautiful Greek bride. And while he had lost an army of 10,000 men, there were ten times that number still waiting for him on the Asian side of the Aegean. Overall, his foray into

Greece had been an expensive adventure, but with Macedon subdued by Rome and Ptolemaic Egypt still preoccupied with internal divisions, Antiochus might have consoled himself that it was a defeat without serious consequences.

That the Romans might follow him into his Asian heartlands seemed at that time to be a very remote possibility indeed – despite the heartfelt assurances of Antiochus' advisor Hannibal that the Romans would very much intend to do this. Antiochus reckoned that he had gone to war with the Romans over who would control Greece, and that question had been decisively settled in Rome's favour. The matter was settled, and there was no remaining *causus belli*. Antiochus might have confidently expected the imminent arrival of Roman envoys bearing peace terms.

In fact, the Romans were already making preparations to cross into Asia. Glabrio in Greece informed Philip that he would take over the task of dealing with the hapless Aetolians, and this left the Asian theatre of war free to be assigned to one of the consuls of the following year. From the Roman point of view, they were at war with Antiochus, they had no other pressing concerns at the moment (apart from the perennial headache of Spain's recalcitrant tribesmen) and so there was no reason why the war should not continue.

Chapter 8

The Romans Go East

The first indication to Antiochus that the Romans intended to keep fighting came from Aetolia. Guided by Philip, whose Macedonians had considerable experience at invading the place, Glabrio marched west, receiving en route delegations from various Greek states which vehemently protested that they had only taken the Seleucid side through coercion, and secretly they had been pro-Roman all along, really. Clearly, Glabrio intended to deal with the Aetolians before Rome moved east to take on the Seleucids.

The Aetolians could not convincingly offer the excuse of other Greeks that Antiochus had forced them to fight against Rome. Especially as their general Democritus had boasted that, after defeating the Romans, his army would make camp on the banks of the Tiber. In fact, rather than defeating the invading Romans, the Aetolians basically refused to fight at all. Democritus himself was captured in hiding and hauled out to explain himself to an unamused Roman general.

What preserved the Aetolians from total defeat was not the embassy which they had sent to Rome seeking peace on whatever terms might be offered. Instead, the Aetolians were saved by the Roman consul Lucius Scipio, the brother of the Publius Scipio who had defeated Hannibal. L. Scipio was the consul charged with taking the war to Antiochus. (Publius himself was along as an advisor to his brother.) The Scipios could not really have cared less what happened to the Aetolians, but they were deeply interested in the army with which Glabrio was beating the Aetolians up. L. Scipio wanted that army, which he intended to merge with his own and take the combined force to Asia Minor.

Glabrio was persuaded to offer the Aetolians a six-month truce while peace terms were worked out and the grateful Aetolians accepted almost before the Roman ambassador had finished speaking. This gave the Scipios a total army of some 40,000 men – less than half of what

Antiochus could muster against them but by now Rome's legionaries were confident that they could beat any army in the known world, no matter what the odds.

The first step towards defeating Antiochus in the east was to actually get there. This would, at some point, involve a sea crossing and the Roman experience of attacking the Carthaginians in Africa had made them very wary of doing this. In the first Punic war, they had lost at least as many men at sea as they had to enemy swords on land and they were not keen to repeat the experience. So even before L. Scipio advanced into Greece, the Romans were taking steps to make the eastern seas as safe as possible.

An admiral called Livius was charged with securing the Aegean sea lanes. He had help from allies, such as the ships of Rhodes, the island trading nation, and the fleet of Eumenes of Pergamon. The Roman ships were heavier and slower than those of Antiochus. If the Romans did actually get close enough to secure a Seleucid ship to theirs with grappling hooks then the ferocity of the legionaries storming over the gunwales practically guaranteed a Roman victory, but the faster and more nimble Seleucids were generally successful in evading their lumbering opponents.

Technically then, in 191 BC, the first sea battle fought between the two sides at Corycus (on the south coast of Asia Minor) was a Roman win but the Seleucids were able to get away with only light casualties and retreated to Ephesus to regroup. The fact that the Seleucids still had a fleet on the water was enough to cause the Roman commanders some worry and this disquiet was reinforced by the news that Antiochus had now put Hannibal in charge of another fleet, further to the south in the Levant.

Since a Roman army was happiest with its feet on the ground, the Scipios opted for the somewhat slower but much safer route to the Hellespont via Macedonia and Thrace. At the start of the journey, there was certainly a great difference between the difficulties that Flamininus had encountered trying to get into a hostile Macedonia and the ease with which Scipio was ushered into a friendly one.

Philip had decided that the best future for Macedon was as an ally of Rome, and he threw himself into the role unstintingly. Warned that the Romans were on their way, Philip worked out the optimum route and repaired the roads along the way. He bridged any streams that might slow down the Roman army and laid on provisions for the troops and entertainment for their officers.

So impressed were the Romans with Philip's enthusiastic co-operation that they relieved him of the outstanding debt on the indemnity which he owed Rome under the terms of the earlier peace treaty. All this amity had a knock-on effect elsewhere. Prusias, king of Bithynia in Asia Minor, had aligned himself with the Seleucids primarily on the basis that his neighbours and enemies, the Pergamese were Roman allies. However, following the mutual generosity and growing friendship between the Romans and their former enemy Philip, Prusias was persuaded that he would receive the same liberal treatment if he switched sides, and he promptly did so.

This was enough for Antiochus who anyway was not planning to wait passively for the Romans to arrive. Now he sent a strong force into Asia Minor, commanded by his son Seleucus. Seleucus had orders to try to take Pergamon out of the war before the Romans arrived, preferably by capturing the city of Pergamum itself. Following paternal instructions, Seleucus duly invaded Pergamene territory and fought his way to the walls of the city. There, like other invaders before him, he found that he could make no impression upon Pergamum's formidable walls. Eventually, low on supplies and with his foragers constantly harassed by native troops, the Seleucid heir was forced out of Pergamene territory altogether.

With Pergamon still in play, the war at sea became critical to the Seleucid plans. At present, Antiochus was aiming to make a stand at Lysimachea, the base in Thrace which he had occupied at the start of the conflict with Rome. The problem for Antiochus was that if he fought and was defeated there, he needed a line of retreat into his Asian heartlands. If Pergamon had been subdued then his army could have made the short hop over the Hellespont into Asia Minor. Now with Pergamon undefeated, Eumenes army and fleet would be waiting to meet him on the Asian shore with the Romans closing in from the west. Another line of retreat was needed. So now Antiochus needed command of the sea in case he had to evacuate his army from Thrace. With the sea lanes clear, he could take his men somewhere safe further south, such as Ephesus, and regroup there.

The problem with securing the sea for his troopships was Rhodes. The Rhodians were the most capable sailors on the Roman side. Just as importantly, the home island of that competent Rhodian fleet was inconveniently located between the main Seleucid fleet in the Levant and the shores of the Hellespont where it needed to be. Hannibal was in command of the fleet in the south, trying with all his considerable ingenuity to get past Rhodes to Asia Minor. Meanwhile a Seleucid admiral called Polyxenidas struggled to keep a fleet together in the north while he waited for Hannibal to reach him.

The fate of the Seleucid presence in Thrace was effectively decided by two naval battles. The first was fought by Hannibal at Side, not far from the Eurymedon where the Greeks had once crushed the Persian fleet that had invaded their shores. The battle of 191 BC was indecisive, but that in itself counted as a Roman victory because Hannibal remained unable to get past Rhodes to relieve Antiochus. Then, at Myonessus (near Teos halfway up the coast of Anatolia), the Roman fleet was finally able to get hold of the slippery Polyxenidas and decisively defeat him.

Antiochus now had no choice. He had to evacuate his army – and quickly – before his enemies got their act together enough to deny him a safe crossing. Antiochus was helped by the fact that, once beyond the borders of Macedonia, the Roman advance had slowed dramatically. Unlike the Macedonians, the Thracians were decidedly unwelcoming, and the Romans needed to now gather supplies for what was looking like an extended stay in hostile territory.

Nevertheless, Antiochus could not afford to be caught in hostile Thrace with no way back to his kingdom. He had to act before the allied fleet blocked the Thracian shore. Accordingly, he abandoned Lysimachea so hurriedly that he left behind a considerable stockpile of provisions which were gratefully seized by the Scipios when they eventually got there. The historian Appian claims that, in abandoning Lysimachea with such haste, Antiochus showed his febrile and indecisive nature.

The reality is that Antiochus had burned through his plan A (securing his line of retreat by taking Pergamon out of the war) and his plan B (making sure he could get away by sea whenever he wanted or needed to) and this left only plan C (leaving Thrace immediately). The final option (D) would have involved actually fighting the Romans in a pitched battle in Thrace. Future events were to show that Antiochus was very wise to avoid this, even at the cost of sacrificing all the material which he had stored at Lysimachea. The Seleucids therefore abandoned Europe, and Antiochus noted gloomily that Hannibal had been right – the Romans promptly crossed the Hellespont in pursuit.

Antiochus now sent envoys seeking peace. After all, the reason Antiochus was at war with Rome was because the senate had reacted violently to the Seleucid presence in Europe. With Greece abandoned and Thrace evacuated, there was not now a single Seleucid soldier on the European side of the Hellespont. Antiochus might have hoped that the Roman army's slow advance through Thrace had been deliberate, aimed at pushing him out of Europe without unnecessary bloodshed. It may have been that the Roman presence in Asia Minor was a tactic designed to force him to the negotiating table.

There was another reason to hope for the best. Publius Scipio's son had been captured by the Seleucids, under uncertain circumstances. The historian Livy gives two different accounts. By one, the young Scipio had been captured by Seleucid ships early in the war while he was en route by sea to join the army of his father and uncle. By another account, young Scipio had made it safely to the Roman army but fell from his horse during a cavalry skirmish while the Romans were establishing a beachhead on the Asian shore.

Either way, Antiochus treated his aristocratic captive with great kindness and hospitality and, in freeing the son without conditions, Antiochus hoped that he had laid the foundations for an amicable peace settlement. He was to be disappointed. The Scipios knew that the Roman people would not be satisfied with anything less than a resounding victory and for their own political advancement they were determined to supply one. Therefore, Publius Scipio bluntly informed the Seleucid envoy that the only way that Antiochus would make peace was to skip the preliminary stages of fighting, getting defeated and surrendering and proceed straight to having the Romans dictate peace terms.

Livy remarks, 'Antiochus was not in the least impressed by this. He felt that he had little to lose from fighting if the only terms proposed to him were those he would have to accept anyway if he were defeated.

Therefore he abandoned attempts to make peace and dedicated himself to preparing for war.' (Livy 37.36)

At this point the Egyptians complicated everyone's plans by raiding and sacking a Seleucid coastal city. This was a blatant violation of the earlier peace treaty which Antiochus had made with Ptolemy V so, to avoid charges of bad faith, the Ptolemaic government tried to pretend the raid was an unauthorized private initiative by one of their own high officials. The intent was clear – the Egyptians wanted Antiochus to declare war on them at a time when he could do no active fighting on that front because he had his hands full with the Romans.

Then, when the time came to make peace, the Egyptians could claim that, as Roman allies, they were entitled to a share of the spoils. Coele-Syria, for example would do nicely. The gambit failed because both Romans and Seleucids pretended to take the Egyptian excuse at face value insofar as they acknowledged that the attack had taken place at all. Nevertheless, Antiochus had now been warned that the Egyptians were untrustworthy and he was consequently forced to strengthen the garrison in Coele-Syria with troops he would much rather use to fight the Romans.

The Battle of Magnesia – 190 BC

The Romans spent a while in friendly Pergamon, which again suggests that recovery time was needed because their passage through Thrace had been harder than the historical record tells us. At this point, Publius Scipio fell ill so sole command of the army fell to the man who was anyway its nominal leader, Lucius Scipio.

Perhaps Antiochus was informed of this, for when the Romans did move from Pergamon, Antiochus remained exactly where he was. This was at a secure position that blocked the Romans from advancing either to the old Persian provincial capital at Sardis or south to where the remnants of the Seleucid fleet were anchored at Ephesus. In short, Antiochus was inviting a decisive battle. Even without the military genius of his brother to guide him, L. Scipio was more than ready to meet the challenge. His consulship was coming to an end and he wanted his legacy to be more than that of the man who brought a Roman army into Asia Minor so that his successor could finish the job of defeating Antiochus.

The Romans duly advanced to where the Seleucids had made camp alongside the banks of the river Phrygius, not far from Magnesia, the town after which the battle was to take its name. Once the Romans got there, something of a stalemate ensued after the preliminary skirmishes. Antiochus wanted to fight on ground highly favourable to himself, a prospective battleground about a mile from his camp. The Romans preferred to fight on more open ground somewhat further out. Consequently, for the next four days, both sides either marched out to their chosen battlefield or waited in their camp, ignoring the enemy as they marched out to theirs.

In the end Antiochus caved. This may have been because he had by far the larger army and this army was getting demoralized by their general's refusal to take on a smaller enemy force. At least our ancient sources tell us that this is the case. According to both Appian and Livy, Antiochus had some 70,000 men to the Roman 30,000. If true, this suggests that Antiochus had been forced to send some 30 000 men to reinforce Coele-Syria, and that the Romans had indeed a very tough time of it crossing Thrace (it will be recalled that they started with 40,000 men).

Modern historians are somewhat sceptical of the ancient figures which they feel are flattering to the Romans. (It must be remembered that both Livy and Appian probably draw upon figures supplied by Polybius, a historian who was also a client of the Scipios.) For example, it is rather probable that the pro-Roman historians conveniently under-counted the force provided by Eumenes of Pergamon which occupied the left wing on the battlefield – a force which was to prove crucial in the events which followed. Generally, most military historians are more comfortable with a more even balance of power, giving Antiochus approximately 65,000 men and the Roman side 55,000.

It helped them considerably that the Romans credibly claimed that they had no interest in conquering and holding territory in Asia Minor. After all, they had even withdrawn to Italy after their first successful campaign in Greece. Antiochus, on the other hand, made no secret of the fact that once he had seen the Romans out of Asia Minor he would use his army to firmly stamp his authority upon the region. This meant that those cities and minor states that were inclined towards autonomy were also inclined towards the Roman side. Consequently, Antiochus received less local support than he might have been expecting. He did, of course, get the support of the Galatians because the Pergamenes were fighting on the Roman side and the Galatians automatically sided with whomever was fighting their inveterate enemies.

The core of the Roman army was the two consular legions which the Scipios had brought with them from Italy. To this we should probably add another legion, that being the one which Glabrio had been using to terrorize the Aetolians and which was added to the Scipionic force after a truce was patched up in Greece. With the legions came the usual accompaniment of auxiliary forces from Rome's Italian allies, giving the Romans around 36,000 heavy infantry. There were also a collection of Macedonians and Thracian peltasts who had signed up for the campaign, presumably in the hope of booty. (These a distrustful Scipio assigned to guard the camp, rather than placing them in the line of battle.) There were also a number of soldiers contributed by the Achaean League of Greece, and the entire Pergamene army, the size of which can be estimated at around 6,000 men, of whom 800 were cavalry. Among the other bits and pieces bolted on to the Roman force were sixteen elephants, but these were the smaller north African breed, and Scipio kept them in reserve fearing that they would be easily defeated by the larger Seleucid elephants.

Scipio formed his army in classical battle array. His legions occupied the centre, with a triple battle line. The *hastati*, the younger soldiers, were at the front. In the next line were the more experienced *principes*, while the veterans of the *triarii* formed the final line. While the first two lines were armed with the heavy throwing pilum, the *triarii* were primarily defensive in nature – should the first two lines be broken, the *triarii* would hold back the enemy with their long spears until the first two lines could rally again. ('It's come to the triarii' remained a common Roman expression for a desperate situation long after the *triarii* had been retired from the Roman legions.)

The cavalry on the right wing had the task of holding the space between the legions and the river Phrygius which secured the Roman flank, while most of the cavalry – some 3,000 strong – were on the open wing alongside the Pergamene army.

This marble head probably depicts a Ptolemaic queen of the period 270–250 BC. 'Portrait' heads such as this were often slotted into statue bodies made by less sophisticated sculptors. (*Picture from the Metropolitan Museum, NY*)

The god Osiris is here depicted in classical Egyptian style, though is from the Ptolemaic era. Apart from inserting themselves into the Egyptian pantheon, the Ptolemies interfered little with Egyptian religion. (*Picture from the Metropolitan Museum, NY*)

War elephants as depicted in a nineteenth century woodcut. African war elephants were from a now extinct species which, unlike the sub-Saharan bush elephant, were actually smaller than the Syrian elephants. (*Public domain picture*)

Antiochus III the Great.
(*From a bust in the Louvre, Paris*)

Parthian coin of the Hellenistic era. These coins were often used by Greek merchants within Parthia, hence the Greek lettering on the obverse. (*Public domain picture*)

Apamea on the Orontes. Named after the wife of Seleucus I, this became a major city under later Seleucid kings. (*Creative commons license 1.2 Bernard Gagnon*)

Head of an 'Ethiopian' showing how both the Egyptian and Greek elements of the upper classes in Egypt subscribed to Hellenistic conventions of sculpture.

Ptolemy IV Philopater 221–204 BC. His coinage was perhaps the best thing about a reign that saw the dynasty go into steep decline amid war and revolution. (*Contemporary coin*)

Timeless art. This Bronze statuette of a veiled yet nearly nude dancer is from the Hellenistic era. The style was widely copied by the Romans and would not look out of place in a modern gallery. (*Picture from the Metropolitan Museum NY*)

Hellenistic portrayal of a Bactrian camel. The ability of these camels to transport goods along the Silk Road was one of the reasons for the durability of the Bactrian kingdom. (*Picture from the Metropolitan Museum, NY*)

Part of the Rosetta Stone, with hieroglyphics at the top. Because the stone had the same message in three languages, scholars were finally able to understand Egyptian hieroglyphics. (*Public domain photograph*)

Nabis, last king of Sparta 207–192 BC. By the time of his reign, Sparta had lost all importance in world affairs and was a minor Peloponnesian city. (*From a coin of c.200 BC*)

The tomb of Archimedes in Syracuse as imagined by the German artist Carl Rottmann (1797–1850).

The goddess Cybele on her chariot. Originally an obscure deity from Phrygia in Asia Minor, worship of Cybele was adopted by the Greeks and later by the Romans. (*P. Matyszak*)

The theatre in Syracuse. The design of the Greek theatre, like the culture the theatres spread, was almost the same from Spain, through Egypt and Mesopotamia to Bactria, thousands of miles away. (*Jeremy Day*)

Merchant ship of the classical era. The design of these ships was almost unchanged through antiquity, and were essential to trade in the Hellenistic era. (*P. Matyszak*)

Cornelius Sulla, 138–78 BC, the Roman general, who broke the power of the Pontic king Mithridates VI and recaptured Greece for Rome's growing empire. (*P. Matyszak*)

Gnaeus Pompeius Magnus 'Pompey the Great' – the man who finally laid the crumbling Seleucid empire to rest and instituted a new era in the Middle East. (*P. Matyszak*)

Officer of the Roman army contemporary with the eastern conquests of Caesar and Pompey in the East. (*From a bas-relief in the Louvre, Paris*)

Portrayed sitting pensively with his head on his knees, the man in this Hellenistic statuette seems to be contemplating the folly of the dynastic struggles which, every bit as much as the Roman legions, destroyed the Hellenistic kingdoms. (*Metropolitan Museum, NY*)

The death of Cleopatra painted following the description by the biographer Plutarch. (*Jean-Baptiste Regnault, c. 1783–1829*)

Facing the legions was the Macedonian-style phalanx some 16,000 strong and composed of veteran soldiers. There were lanes between each block of 1,600 men kept clear for elephants, the plan being for the elephants to charge down the lanes into the legions just as the phalanx hit at the same time. The combined impact was intended to break the Roman centre. Meanwhile, the strong force on the open flank would work its way around and through the Pergamene army. The troops allocated for this job were formidable in themselves, consisting of scythe chariots, heavily armoured cataphract cavalry, Galatian warriors and a mass of peltasts and archers from the Anatolian interior.

Antiochus took the river flank, his son Seleucus took the centre along with another commander called Philip, and another Antiochus (the king's nephew) commanded the far flank. With their dispositions made, both sides prepared to fight.

As the Romans moved forward, a gap opened on the river flank, and the experienced Antiochus immediately charged his cavalry into it. The numerically inferior Roman cavalry were pushed back and Antiochus drove forward all the way to the Roman camp. The sudden success of the Seleucid king seems to have caught the Antiochus commanding the other flank off balance. His scythe chariots were still getting into position for their charge when Eumenes attacked with his cavalry.

This drove the chariots back into the Seleucid cataphracts. Scythed chariots and heavily armoured cavalry do not mix well when the chariots are disorganized and moving in the opposite direction at speed. The cataphracts had not recovered from nearly being chopped up by their own chariots when the Pergamene and Roman cavalry fell upon them and chopped them up instead.

The battle now pivoted upon the two infantry blocks. The Seleucids on the river flank, under king Antiochus, had unsuccessfully attacked the Roman camp and were now attempting to attack the Roman rear. The phalanx had engaged with the legions and, because the phalanx was near invincible when coming forward in good formation, the legions were getting the worst of it. It became a question of whether Eumenes and his army could hammer through the Galatians guarding the flank of the Seleucid phalanx before that phalanx broke the *triarii*.

In the end, it was not even close. The legions hung on doggedly while the Galatians did not. The more flexible Roman legions were able to hold off Antiochus but, once the phalanx had its flank exposed, the entire formation was vulnerable and had to pull back. The Seleucids had learned from the Macedonian experience at Cynoscephalae, and the phalanx formed into individual blocks which retreated individually in a bristling mass of spear-points.

However, just as the scythe chariots had proven much worse than useless, so also proved the elephants. These were penned up within each block of pikemen but the pike blocks were small enough for the elephants to be well within missile range of their enemies. Eumenes had considerable experience of fighting with and against elephants and he now ordered his missile troops to concentrate their fire upon these large and vulnerable targets.

Bombarded by arrows and slingshots which did not kill them but caused them great pain and distress, the elephants reacted as Eumenes had expected – they tried to escape from their tormentors and the battlefield by the shortest route possible. This took them straight through the close-packed ranks of the phalangites.

It would be an understatement to say that being charged in the rear by their own elephants caused disruption in the ranks. Each phalangite had a long spear so deployed that even the spears of the third rank extended beyond the bodies of the first rank of spearmen. This presented a hedge of spears to the enemy, but it also meant that the men in the first two ranks were practically pinned into place by the spears of those behind. With elephants erupting from the rear and bloodthirsty Roman legionaries looking for the slightest opening, the phalangites blocks did not stand a chance. As each block collapsed, the massacre began. The only survivors of the phalanx were the lucky few whose surrender was accepted. The rest were slaughtered.

In all, Antiochus probably lost two-thirds of his army and most of those were his core troops, the phalangites. The Romans later claimed that they lost only 350 men. This is unlikely for troops which had been hard pressed by a phalanx pushing forward at full steam, let alone those broken in the initial cavalry charge by Antiochus. More probably, they lost several thousand men. Nevertheless, like Philip of Macedon,

Antiochus had been soundly defeated in a decisive battle and now had to seek whatever terms were on offer.

The Peace of Apameia

Despite the loss of his phalanx, Antiochus managed to pull back much of the remainder of his army intact, partly because the men he left to defend his camp did a sterling job of holding off the Romans while he backed out of the battlefield. Antiochus retreated towards Sardis while his son Seleucus gathered together what troops he could. Already messengers were fanning out across the kingdom to raise emergency levies.

Polyxenidas, the admiral in charge of the remnants of the northern Seleucid fleet, took advantage of the chaos following the battle to escape from harbour in Ephesus and break for the shores of the Levant. He escaped past Rhodes, probably because the Rhodians expected a ceasefire to have come into effect immediately after the Roman victory. However, when Polyxenidas got to his destination, Hannibal was no longer in charge of the southern fleet. As soon as he heard the result of the battle of Magnesia, the wily Carthaginian unilaterally resigned and escaped before the Romans could demand that he be handed over as part of any peace settlement.

While Antiochus made all necessary moves to continue the war, these were for the most part an attempt to persuade the Romans to offer peace terms as mild as possible. In a way, the king already knew what these peace terms would probably be. Scipio was not joking when he had said earlier that Antiochus might as well skip the battle and negotiate as if he had already lost. Now that Antiochus had indeed lost, what Scipio wanted remained the same. Unfortunately, Scipio was no longer in charge. With his consulship due to expire, the peace would be negotiated by his successor.

For a change, the Aetolians back in Greece were now being helpful. They knew that the bulk of the Roman army was now in Asia Minor and could not be withdrawn until a peace had been finalized. Therefore, they refused to accept the terms that the Roman senate offered them and announced themselves ready to resume the war. In fact, they had already taken advantage of the absence of the Roman army to retake some territory they had lost. It would take a brisk war before they once more agreed to Roman terms.

Manlius Vulso, the consul who replaced Scipio, came to Asia Minor with no intention of making peace. Rather, he intended to squeeze out whatever glory could be obtained from fighting a defeated enemy. With a fine Roman legalism that was barely distinguishable from hypocrisy – a distinguishing feature of Republican Romans after unsatisfactory peace talks – Vulso decided that though Antiochus had agreed a ceasefire, his Galatian allies had not. It did not matter that this was because Scipio, Antiochus and the Galatians had all assumed that Antiochus was negotiating for himself and his allies. Vulso had found someone he could legitimately fight, and he was eager to start.

Antiochus could not help the Galatians without breaking the ceasefire, and this he could not afford to do. Therefore, the Seleucids could only watch on as the Romans conducted a triumphal march across Asia Minor and then inflicted a painful defeat on the Galatians. The upshot of this was that Vulso, having gained his victory, was now prepared for peace talks with Antiochus to go ahead. Basically, the unimaginative Vulso re-presented Scipio's demands, thus showing again that his war in Asia Minor was largely unnecessary. The eventual terms agreed with the senate basically consisted of Antiochus agreeing to destroy his fleet, hand over his surviving elephants, and withdraw from Asia Minor (with most of the former Seleucid possessions going to the triumphant Eumenes of Pergamon).

To all this Antiochus agreed with hardly a murmur. For a start, the Seleucid hold on Asia Minor had never been more than tenuous, and after military defeat and Vulso's conduct thereafter, it would be fair to say the Seleucids had little authority remaining in the region in any case. Also, after Magnesia, there were few surviving elephants to be handed over and those were in Syria, safely out of Roman view and more likely to be even better hidden instead of surrendered.

With the fleet, Antiochus took a few pages from the Roman playbook and decided that only his own ships had been referred to. Most of his ships belonged to subject nations, and the Romans had apparently decided that allies were excluded from talks unless explicitly included. Therefore, the ships in the Seleucid fleet belonging to Greek and Phoenician subject cities remained unburned. Furthermore, with trained crews and timber on hand, Antiochus could quickly build more ships should the need arise. At present, the need was not apparent. Ptolemaic naval power was non-existent, and the Macedonian fleet had been knocked out by the Romans. Seleucia was basically a land empire so investment in a fleet was not currently required.

The Romans also demanded a substantial indemnity and – as expected – that Antiochus hand over Hannibal. Antiochus handed over the first instalment of the money but could honestly claim that Hannibal was no longer available to be handed over. With the indemnity, it is possible that Antiochus calculated that what he lost in paying the Romans, he would no longer have to pay in military campaigns to keep the contentious kingdoms of Anatolia under his control. Asia Minor had taken up a considerable amount of Antiochus' time and treasure since he had become king. It may have come as something of a relief to realise that now, rather like Greece once Macedonian power had been taken away, Anatolia was a Roman problem.

In any case, Antiochus could console himself that, over the past decade, he had gained Coele-Syria from Egypt and lost Anatolia to the Romans and this was a swap he would make any time. What he now needed to do was the same job that any Seleucid king had to do after a major setback – hold the rest of his fissiparous kingdom together.

Armenia and the east were particularly restive so Antiochus gathered his battered army and moved eastward. His problem was that the first installation of the war indemnity demanded by the Romans had been specifically designed to deplete his war chest. In doing this, the Romans intended to prevent the Seleucids from interfering with their settlement in Asia Minor. However, his present financial straits also severely hampered the efforts of Antiochus to maintain order elsewhere.

Therefore, when it came to the attention of Antiochus that he had camped near a potential source of revenue, the king was decidedly tempted. This was the temple of Bel-Elemais, where the people of the region had been depositing their treasure for generations. Antiochus mistakenly reckoned that the god would not mind that treasure being re-purposed for the cause of preserving the Seleucid empire. He accordingly set out with a group of retainers and workmen to claim the new-found bounty.

Whatever the opinion of the god on the matter, the locals were decidedly unimpressed. Quite correctly reckoning that what they were seeing was the blatant robbery of their savings (many locals would have their own valuables deposited at the temple for safe-keeping), the outraged locals rushed to the temple. The crowd became a mob which became violent. In a sudden and unexpected development, Antiochus III – the king who had fought the Egyptians, the Greeks and the Romans in battles involving tens of thousands of men – died in a sordid local squabble.

Chapter 9

The Fall of Greece

The Changing of the Guard

The decade of 185–175 BC saw a change of rulers across the Hellenistic world. This was important, not only because it brought kings with different characters and ability to power, but because agreements between the Hellenistic kings were personal rather than inter-state contracts. In other words, all deals were now off and the new kings had to set about negotiating a new balance of power.

Bactria

One king who had little to worry about when it came to the power of Rome was Euthydemus II of Bactria. Between him and Rome lay the Seleucid empire and Parthia (again asserting its independence after the death of Antiochus III). His father Demetrios I 'The Invincible' had extended Bactria's domains south into India and north-east into Afghanistan. While Demetrios' date of death is generally given as 180 BC, this is something of a flying guess based mainly on evidence from coinage. Demetrios was probably the most successful Hellenistic king of his generation, and the fact that we know so little about the man and his conquests is a telling indication of how far Bactria had drifted from western consciousness. In later years an increasingly isolated Bactria was to become almost a forgotten kingdom.

Euthydemus II appears not to have reigned for long. We know this because his coins show a lad even younger-looking than the twenty years which Euthydemus allegedly had behind him when he came to the throne. It is also not known whether he ascended to power on the death of his father or whether his father made him co-monarch in the last years of his reign, as was often done by Hellenistic kings to ease the transition of power. (A trick later adopted by the emperor Augustus of Rome to ensure the smooth succession of his successor Tiberius.)

Just to further confuse the situation in Bactria, one Agathocles was also minting coins as though he were king at the same time. Whether this man shared in the royal power, possibly as a regent, or whether he was a rebel relative who challenged the power of the young king is unknown. The latter is highly probable as it will be recalled that the Seleucids had (and were yet to have) considerable problems of this kind, as demonstrated by the two royal usurpers who at different times claimed control of Asia Minor.

In either case, a Bactrian general called Eukratides made the matter moot. Some time in the 170s Eukratides took power in Bactria, almost certainly by force. He was to rule for a generation and, under his command, Bactria beat off waves of barbarian invaders and became even more successful – not that anyone in the west took particular notice.

Macedon

There was a lot else going on – for example, the ructions surrounding the Macedonian succession. Philip V had ruled Macedon for almost forty years. In the decade following his clash with Rome, Philip had worked hard to re-make his kingdom. He had had to do this because, ever since the time of Philip II, the military and economic machinery of Macedon had been geared towards keeping control of Greece. Now that this task had been taken over by the Romans, Philip needed to set about consolidating his kingdom as it adapted to a more limited role.

The Pergamese had never been reconciled to the fact that, after their victory at Cynoscephalae, the Romans had left the Macedonian kingdom intact. They wanted the Macedonian threat gone once and for all and Macedonian military activity in the Balkans elicited loud squawks of protest from Pergamene ambassadors in Rome. These ambassadors made little headway because the Romans remained charmed by the diplomacy of Philip's son, Demetrios, the former hostage who was now friends with most of the Roman aristocracy.

Thus, despite protests from Pergamon about almost everything Philip did, the king was free to move populations of his citizens around the country, putting some in areas more secure from barbarian attack and others into lands which he reckoned more fertile and productive of tax revenues. For the latter purpose, Philip also reorganized the administration and the coinage. Eventually, even the smooth-talking Demetrios was unable to hide from the Romans the fact that Philip was rebuilding his kingdom in a manner that would allow his successor to stand off the Romans, should that successor have need to do so.

The Roman response was to hope that the successor to Philip would not need to do so, preferably because that successor would be the Romanophile Demetrios. The problem for Rome was that Demetrios was not the royal heir. That position was taken by Philip V's older son Perseus who regarded the growing ambition of Demetrios with ever-growing alarm. It definitely did not help his peace of mind that Demetrios had a legitimate claim to the throne. This was because Perseus was born not of a royal queen but from one Polycratia of Argos, whom Philip only married after the death of his first wife, the mother of Demetrios.

The Romans made no secret of the fact that they would prefer Philip's successor to be Demetrios and this drove Perseus to a series of ever more desperate steps to ensure his succession. It is worth noting that, in doing this, Perseus was fighting not just for his throne but his life. When a Hellenistic king had more than one viable heir, opposition to the regime tended to form around whichever heir was not in power. Therefore, as was almost traditional already among the Ptolemies, the first thing a new king did on taking the throne was to ensure that there were no more viable heirs left alive. The challenge facing Perseus was that he had to kill off the other heir before he came to the throne. Otherwise there was a good chance he would not become king at all – with fatal consequences to himself and his immediate family.

Perseus set about pushing Demetrios and Philip apart. This was not easy because father and son were on good terms. Thus, when Perseus came to his father claiming that Demetrios had engineered a plot on his life, Philip basically shrugged off the charge. Perseus retreated and sought advice from a fellow conspirator called Didas, a general of Philip who hoped to become even more powerful when the aged king passed away.

It may well have been Didas who noted that the growing distrust between Philip and the Romans could be leveraged to help Perseus. Since Demetrios was undoubtedly friendly with the Romans, it seemed a good idea to push the increasingly despotic and suspicious Philip into believing that this friendship was even deeper than it appeared. Although Philip had not accepted Perseus' charge of attempted murder by Demetrios, he had not completely disregarded it either. There was a consequent cooling in relations between father and son.

This made it much more credible when charges were laid that Demetrios was planning to flee from Macedon and join the Romans. They would then declare him king and replace the aged Philip. In fact, the conqueror of Greece, Flamininus, had even written to Demetrios endorsing this plan and offering his full support. The letter was a forgery, but Philip necessarily had to investigate the matter. He therefore had Demetrios arrested. Philip's general Didas volunteered to take custody of the young man. Then, claiming that he had misunderstood the royal intentions, he had Demetrios executed.

In due course, Philip's investigation revealed that the 'letter of Flamininus' was a forgery. One of the men who had presented the letter to Philip was executed on the spot – the other had already fled. Be that as it may, Philip had now the unenviable choice of leaving his kingdom rudderless without an heir – or allowing the man behind his son's murder to take over. Wracked by remorse for his part in the killing of his son, Philip did not last much longer. Before his death, he appears to have been seriously cultivating one Antigonus, son of Echecrates, as a possible replacement heir. Having sent Perseus off to campaign in Thrace, Philip was touring the kingdom with Antigonus when he died in Amphipolis in the summer of 179 BC.

The first two things Perseus did on claiming the throne were to execute Antigonus and send to the Roman senate offering to renew the friendship between their two nations. Rome did not take the loss of Demetrios well and relationships with Perseus never recovered from that rocky start. Despite increasingly frantic efforts by Perseus to placate the Romans, diplomatic relations steadily deteriorated over the next eight years.

The Seleucid Empire

On the other side of the Mediterranean Antiochus IV was struggling to fill the very substantial boots of his father Antiochus the Great. In part, he tried to do this by promoting himself to the status of a living god by taking the epithet *Epiphanes* ('God incarnate'). Apart from severely annoying his monotheistic Jewish subjects, this and the new god's decidedly eccentric character caused him to become known behind his divine back as Antiochus *Epimanes* ('Antiochus the Nutcase').

Like Perseus of Macedon, Antiochus' path to the throne was far from smooth. He was not even the designated heir. That was his brother Seleucus IV. When Seleucus came to power in 187 BC, following his father's unexpected death, he was already in his mid-forties. Seleucus inherited the challenge faced by his father of maintaining a bankrupt empire in which many powerful subjects had lost faith in their king.

Seleucus appears to have started by delaying payment of the second instalment of the indemnity demanded by Rome – quite legitimately in his eyes, as the treaty by which the indemnity was to be paid was owed by his now defunct father rather than by himself. Aware that the Romans might not see things that way, Seleucus sent his son to Rome as something between a hostage and an ambassador charged with explaining the Seleucid point of view.

Meanwhile, despite his father's clear demonstration that plundering temples was a very bad idea, Seleucus sent one of his chief ministers (plus a beefy military force) to seize the very substantial temple treasure stored in Jerusalem. This minister, a man called Heliodorus, succeeded in raising the money demanded. (It is uncertain whether he extorted this from the Jewish people or from their temple. According to the text of Maccabees 3.20 ff, Heliodorus was turned back from the sanctum by the force of divine power.)

Returning to Antioch, it occurred to Heliodorus that he now had the money to make himself king. He also had the military force, thanks to the army Seleucus had given him for his fund-raising mission. Accordingly, Heliodorus arranged the assassination of Seleucus and, in 175 BC, he set himself up in the former king's place.

It is uncertain whether Heliodorus intended to rule indirectly, with Antiochus IV as his puppet, or if the king managed to escape the usurper's grasp. In either case, Antiochus found an unlikely saviour in Eumenes of Pergamon. Evidently preferring the Seleucid devils he knew to Heliodorus, whom he didn't, Eumenes helped Antiochus to remove Heliodorus from the throne and become king in his own right.

Yet there was a flaw in the legitimacy of this arrangement also. Antiochus was not the true heir to the throne. That was the son of Seleucus IV, a man called Demetrios, whom Seleucus had dispatched to Rome early in his kingship. The Romans were well aware of the dynastic confusion that resulted from their being in possession of the true ruler of the Seleucid empire, and they wanted that confusion to last. The more chaotic things were in the east, the less of a threat the Seleucids would represent to their new settlement of matters in Asia Minor.

Thus, Antiochus IV was king of the Seleucid empire but the words 'for now' seemed permanently attached to his title. Needing to further legitimize his rule, Antiochus claimed to be co-ruler with the second son of Seleucus (yet another Antiochus). Since the newly designated co-monarch named by Antiochus was six or seven years old at this point, sharing the empire was not a major problem. It would certainly become more of a problem when the young Antiochus grew older and more assertive. Consequently, many cynical courtiers would doubtless have been prepared to wager large sums of money against the young king reaching adolescence. (And they would have won their bets. Young Antiochus died from unknown causes in 170 BC.)

Egypt

Most of the time during which Ptolemy V governed Egypt was taken up with the great rebellion in the south. It will be remembered that Ptolemy V did not govern Egypt for the early part of his reign, for he came to power at the ripe young age of five. The actual governing was done by, and for the benefit of, a succession of regents. Such governance as the kingdom did get occurred during breaks between the vicious intrigues, poisonings, executions and assassinations which made life as a royal courtier interesting, brief and deadly.

Only in 195 BC had Ptolemy V actually taken power for himself, to the general relief of a somewhat depleted royal court. Regrettably, Ptolemy's upbringing had rather soured him on the entire business of ruling. He preferred to pass his time with hunting, athletics and carousing while his appointees got on with running the country and ultimately suppressing the rebellion in the south. This revolt ended in 183 BC when Ptolemy proposed remarkably mild terms to the hard-pressed rebels. The rebels gratefully took the surrender terms and were then treacherously and barbarically slain. This may have been because Ptolemy was cruel and treacherous, but more probably it was because he simply did not have enough control over his generals (nor over his wife) to stop them from taking a long-delayed vengeance.

As had his father, Ptolemy V died young. He passed away in 181 BC, around the time of his twenty-ninth birthday. It remains uncertain whether he died from illness or whether his wife had something to do with it. That wife was Cleopatra, the first of a series of Cleopatrae who became queens of Egypt. Cleopatra I was a daughter of Antiochus III and she showed a greater talent for ruling than either of that great king's two hapless sons.

Even while her husband was alive, Cleopatra was the far from hidden power behind the throne, and with the death of Ptolemy V she began ruling the country in her own right – the first Hellenistic queen to do so (though even her reign was ostensibly in the name of her infant son). For the next five years, Egypt enjoyed a brief period of stability until Cleopatra also passed away, leaving the kingdom to yet another underage Ptolemy. This particular juvenile pharaoh was Ptolemy VI who took over from his mother in 176 BC at the age of ten.

Pergamon

Only in one Hellenistic kingdom was there a stable succession and a steady hand steering the ship of state. This was in Pergamon, the kingdom that had gone from an insignificant hilltop fortress in the time of Alexander the Great to the most powerful kingdom in Asia Minor two centuries later. Eumenes II had taken over from his father Attalus I in 197 BC in a smooth and uneventful transfer of power, and he was to rule Pergamon for just short of forty years.

Eumenes had the good sense to continue his father's strategy of siding with the Romans. The Roman senate at this point had little interest in taking over nations in the east, but senators were also very clear in their minds that they did not want anyone else in the east to be too powerful either. While Rome digested the conquests made after the Second Punic War – especially Spain which was proving quite a mouthful – what the

Romans wanted of the east was that it should remain weak, unthreatening and of little overall interest.

Since the Egyptians were very competently sabotaging themselves, the Romans remained on good terms with whoever was winning in the internal political struggles there at any given time. With the death of Antiochus III and the assassination of his eldest son, the Romans were happy to keep the next legitimate Seleucid king as a hostage in Rome while dynastic infighting kept their powerful rival from becoming a renewed menace.

Macedon had suddenly become a problem. Competently re-organized and rebuilt by Philip V in his declining years, the kingdom was quite capable of standing off the Romans indefinitely under a competent commander. It remained to be seen whether the newly enthroned Perseus was such a commander. Meanwhile, Eumenes was probably having difficulty in restraining himself from telling the Romans 'I told you so'. For over a decade, Eumenes had watched Philip at work and was well aware that, while Macedon might be able to withstand Rome, Pergamon might be hard put to withstand Macedon should the Roman alliance ever break down.

At least Eumenes could say he had done his best to ensure that would not happen. He had refused a marriage alliance offered by Antiochus III precisely because he had not wanted to alienate the Romans. He had succeeded all too well at the battle of Magnesia (the Romans were ever grudging in sharing the glory of victory) but had benefited vastly from the subsequent peace settlement.

Pergamon gained control of several minor kingdoms to the east, though regrettably not control of neighbouring Bithynia whose king Eumenes fought the Pergamese to a draw in 183 BC. Also, the Romans had also awarded a substantial chunk of south-eastern Anatolia to the Rhodians in recognition of the island state's contribution to the victory over Antiochus III. Consequently, Pergamon still faced substantial challenges before the kingdom could claim to be master of even western Anatolia, and this caused Eumenes some frustration. Indeed, the king may have been somewhat too vocal with this frustration, because at one point the Romans began to suspect that he and Perseus of Macedon might be scheming together to break the bonds of their Roman alliance.

Under Eumenes and his father Attalus, Pergamon had grown to become one of the great centres of Hellenistic culture, ranked just behind Alexandria and Antioch. Even today, many of the great surviving examples of Hellenistic art and sculpture come from Pergamum. This includes the Great Altar, an architectural and sculptural tour de force which was excavated in the 1880s and painstakingly reconstructed in Berlin, where it is now housed in a dedicated museum.

The Altar was originally on the acropolis of Pergamum and there Eumenes also commissioned a library designed to rival that of Alexandria. It is claimed that the jealous Egyptians made an effort to deny the Pergamenes the papyrus needed for copies of texts in the library. Rising to the challenge, the Pergamenes adopted the previously under-utilized technique of writing upon thinly-stretched animal skins. Indeed, so common was this material in the library of Pergamum that the Romans called such skins pergamenum, a word which has mutated in modern English to become 'parchment'.

At its peak, the library contained some 200,000 texts. It competed fiercely with the library at Alexandria for the finest scholars and the oldest extant copies of famous texts. In the reading room of the library stood a famous statue of Athena, goddess of wisdom and the sanctuary of the goddess was also located nearby.

A New Reality

When Philip V and Antiochus III had come to power, they and the other Hellenistic kings of the era regarded their power as supreme. Certainly, they and their kingdoms had problems but their kingdoms were richer, more cultured and militarily superior to any other nation in the known world. Yet all that had changed within a generation.

In 220 BC, Rome was a distant barbarian state that had been doing rather well in the western Mediterranean until Hannibal threatened to wipe it out in 218 BC. No-one in the east paid much attention to that event, and certainly no-one expected Rome to bounce back from near extinction, yet alone go on to comprehensively defeat Carthage and then crush Macedon with barely a pause between wars.

Even after this display of military potency, Antiochus had trouble taking Rome seriously. This is demonstrated by his attempt to step into what he regarded as a power vacuum in Greece. The Romans promptly demonstrated that they had already filled that vacuum to their own satisfaction and punished Antiochus for his presumption by defeating him in Asia Minor. By now, few doubted that the Romans could mete out similar treatment to Egypt if they really wanted to. It was at this point that Hellenistic diplomacy, not only in Egypt but also in Macedon and the Seleucid empire, began to revolve around the issue of persuading the Romans to not want to invade them.

The problem with this approach was that the Romans actually did want to invade people. The electoral system in Rome was based on how successful the military aristocracy of Rome were at such invasions. Every Roman aristocrat aimed at becoming consul. Not only did a successful consulship bring wealth and glory, but it also widened the network of influential friends and clients to whom an aristocrat had access, making it easier for a consul's heirs to emulate his feat. In the eyes of Roman voters, a successful consulship was measured by the success of the consul in war so every consul was ready to take Rome to war at the slightest pretext.

Even then, it seems not to have occurred to the Hellenistic kings to unite against the common threat. Instead, the Seleucids believed that their best bet for survival was to stand back while the Romans beat up the Macedonians and the Egyptians reckoned that they would be fine so long as they could persuade the Romans to take on the Seleucids instead of themselves. Indeed, this strategy even worked in the short term. The Seleucid empire did not fall because of Rome but because messy dynastic infighting between a series of ever-less competent kings and their equally vicious family members destroyed a state which was barely functional to begin with. With the Seleucids out of the way, nothing stood between Rome and Egypt.

First though, Rome needed to settle matters in Greece and Macedonia.

Preliminaries to the Third Macedonian War

As has been seen, Perseus of Macedon had started his reign on bad terms with the Romans. This was largely because Perseus was not Demetrios, the son of Philip V whom the Romans would much rather have seen on the throne. Not only that, but the pro-Roman Demetrios was dead largely as a result of insidious scheming by Perseus while his father was still alive.

So when Perseus sent ambassadors to Rome after he came to power, his envoys received a distinctly chilly reception. If they disliked someone, the Romans were inclined to declare war at the drop of a toga, so it was not surprising that Perseus started taking precautions lest that unwelcome event should come about. Equally predictably, the jaundiced Romans considered the preparations taken by Perseus as preparations for war, because that is exactly what they were. The Romans did not believe, or more probably did not want to believe, that the measures of Perseus were almost entirely defensive in nature.

Relationships between Rome and Macedon descended to a state of cold war with an increasing probability that the temperature would rise rapidly. For a start, there was the matter of a Thracian chieftain who, with the benevolent approval of the Romans, launched one of the traditional raids upon Macedon by which barbarians tested the mettle of a new king. Though the raid was devastating, Perseus beat it back. Then he went on the offensive to devastate the lands of the Thracian chieftain in return. When the Romans protested that this king was a Roman ally, Perseus ignored their complaints as the hypocritical cant that it was. To make things worse, Perseus then made alliances with other Thracian leaders impressed with the new king's military ability.

Even that did not alarm the Romans so much as the marriage alliance Perseus made with the Seleucids by marrying the daughter of Seleucus IV (a woman inevitably named Laodice). This alliance came to nothing because Seleucus IV was killed soon afterwards, but Perseus also arranged to marry one of his daughters to the king of Bithynia, despite vociferous protests from Pergamon.

All this Perseus might have got away with, but the new king also could not stop himself from interfering in affairs in Greece. It helped that this was laughably easy to do. Macedon was a well-organized, prosperous and politically unified state. The Greeks to the south were none of these things. The Greeks constantly fought between their different states and, within those states, between themselves. Macedonian agents were easily able to gain influence by offering to help one faction or another. It was not long before every city-state and confederation in Greece was defined by whether it was pro- or anti-Perseus, and even the anti-Perseus states were uneasily aware that Macedon was sponsoring pro-Perseus factions within their own governments.

With Greece on the verge of conflagration, the Romans sent envoys to calm the situation. A mixture of diplomacy and (very real) threats probably prevented civil war in the Aetolian League. The Romans were too late to prevent civil war which had already broken out in Thessaly, but they did at least manage to re-secure their alliance with the Achaeans. Ominously though, the Roman envoys and the Macedonian king did not meet and talk through their various issues.

Instead, Eumenes II of Pergamon took himself to Rome with the declared intention of getting Rome to invade Macedonia before Macedonia invaded Pergamon. In presenting his case, Eumenes was helped by the fact that the Rhodians and Pergamenes now shared a common and disputed border in Asia Minor, and Perseus was happily backing Rhodes.

Having delivered his bellicose exhortation, Eumenes made his way home, pausing along the way to visit the Oracle at Delphi. Greece was pervaded by the agents of Perseus, and the plans of Eumenes quickly became known. Delphi lies in highly mountainous country on roads accessible only on foot. At one point on a precipitous mountain path, the road was so narrow that only one person could pass at a time. It so happened that as Eumenes came to this point he was bombarded by large rocks from above. This may have been a co-incidental rockfall, but few believed that. The Romans later claimed that they even found a letter in which a wealthy woman at Delphi had acted as agent for a squad of Macedonian assassins ('men accustomed to this sort of work' says Livy, 42.15) led by a Cretan mercenary. Eumenes was injured, so severely that it was initially believed both in Rome and Pergamon, that he had died.

Even when word reached Rome that their ally had survived the attempt on his life, the Romans were not mollified. They were convinced that Perseus was behind the attack and declared him an enemy of Rome. There was no doubt that, once consular elections were completed, the Romans would take the final step and declare war upon Macedon. In a desperate attempt to avert hostilities, Perseus sent for Roman commissioners in Greece and tried hard to persuade them that he was not seeking war. Since the Romans wanted to launch their attack in the next campaigning season with a fresh army and new consuls, Perseus was invited to send an embassy to Rome to plead his case.

Meanwhile the Romans sent a force to take control of Thessaly and sent a fleet over the Adriatic to make advance preparations for the troopships. When the Macedonian ambassadors arrived in Rome, they were sent away without a hearing. Perseus could deceive himself no longer. In 171 BC the Romans confirmed what everyone already knew. Rome and Macedon were at war – again.

Chapter 10

Concurrent Wars

Most historians, knowing the outcome of events, are focused on developments in Macedonia for the next three years. So much so that many familiar with the Third Macedonian War are only dimly aware that, for most of that period, another was war also under way, a war which at the time most of those living outside of Rome and Macedon considered as much more significant.

Even as the Romans were readying their legions for war in Greece, the Egyptians – with the trauma of their southern rebellion finally behind them – were preparing to take up with Antiochus IV the question of ownership of Coele-Syria. It was the Egyptian opinion that Antiochus III had taken advantage of Egyptian internal problems to seize a large swathe of territory which was rightfully theirs. Now that the Seleucids had internal problems of their own, the regents of the boy-pharaoh Ptolemy VI decided it was time to redress the balance. Accordingly, they also began to prepare for war with the intention of invading the Seleucid empire in 170 BC, the year after the Romans attacked Macedonia.

Greece 171 BC

The previous invasion which kicked off the Second Macedonian War of 200–197 BC had been a thoroughly professional affair. By the time he came to bump heads with the Romans, Philip was a veteran campaigner with years of experience at fighting in Greece and Thrace. The Romans, fresh from their bruising war with Hannibal, were if anything more experienced. In comparison, the Third Macedonian War, fought a generation later, has a distinctly amateur flavour to it. One cannot help feeling that had either Macedon a commander of the calibre of Philip V or the Romans a general of Flamininus' ability, the war would have been a shorter affair.

The present Roman consul, Publius Licinius Crassus (an ancestor of Marcus Licinius Crassus the triumvir) set the tone of the war by marching through western Greece, careless of the potential for either ambush in the narrow mountain passes or of a Macedonian force waiting to crush the inexperienced and exhausted Roman levies as they finally reached central Greece. However, Perseus lacked the military intelligence (in every sense of the word) to do as his father would have done. Instead, he moved cautiously into northern Thessaly and consolidated his position there. As a result, he passed on the opportunity to separately defeat the small force of some 5,000 men which Eumenes of Pergamon had brought to Greece and which now joined the rest of the Roman force without hindrance.

This Roman force had a core of two legions, and in addition to this had some 16,000 allied and auxiliary troops. This, with the Pergamene reinforcements, brought the Roman strength to around 33,000 men. To withstand this invasion, Perseus had around 20,000 in the Macedonian phalanx, 3,000 cavalry and contingents from allies in Thrace, Greece and Crete. Overall, his army was around 40,000 strong. Philip's legacy stood the son in good stead.

The Macedonians were fighting on their home ground and, thanks to campaigns in Thrace, they were more experienced than their Roman adversaries. They could pick strong defensive positions and wait for the Romans to attack them. The objective of the war was for the Romans to fight their way into Macedonia. All Perseus needed for victory was to use the considerable advantages of the mountainous terrain to stop them. He could have made a start in Epirus as Philip had done with the army of Flamininus, but instead he chose to wait and let the Romans come to him in Thessaly.

When the Romans did arrive, Crassus was wary of committing his inexperienced troops to battle, though Perseus appeared ready and willing to get started. The first clash occurred near the city of Pherae in southern Thessaly. In the preceding days, Perseus had shadowed the Roman army offering battle which the cautious Crassus invariably declined. Finally, as the Romans prepared to move out from their camp near a hill called Callincus, Perseus attacked unexpectedly.

The resultant battle was a somewhat confused affair with the Romans having to form up their legionaries within the ramparts of their camp.

Perseus had mixed infantry in with his cavalry, and the Macedonian horse, which had once been the spear-tip of the army of Alexander, was far superior to the Roman offering. The addition of infantry to this already superior mix would have been disastrous had the sudden Macedonian attack not caught the Roman cavalry flat-footed. As it was, the infantry roamed among the near-stationary enemy riders stabbing at their horses even while those riders tried to fend off Macedonian lances. Only the arrival of the superb Thessalian cavalry supported by the Pergamene horse prevented disaster. Arriving just in time, the cavalry provided the Romans with an effective screen behind which their horsemen could rally.

Meanwhile the Macedonian allied infantry was chopping through the Greek allies of Rome arrayed against them. Panic spread through the Greek ranks as the Macedonian phalanx moved forward to finish the job. Again, the Thessalian cavalry deployed to cover the retreat, forcing the advancing Macedonian allies to close ranks and slow down in the face of this new threat. This delay allowed the Roman heavy infantry to complete getting its act together and join the battle. Perseus noted that his army was somewhat tired and out of position after the first round of the engagement. With the compact and disciplined legions now moving purposefully forward, it was time for him to cash in his winnings and withdraw. This he did, knowing that he had given the Roman force a significant mauling, killing around 2,500 of the invaders while suffering minimum casualties to his own force.

As head of the Roman state, a consul needed to get various legislative and administrative affairs of the nation in order before he began his campaigns. This, combined with the logistics of raising an army and getting it to Greece, meant that Crassus had launched the actual invasion of Macedonia late, and he had barely got it past the preliminary stage before the end of the campaigning season had begun to draw in.

This is observable in one of Perseus' initiatives as the Romans moved north. Their army had camped in a wheat field and literally harvested the wheat beneath them, before they pitched their tents. Observing the masses of straw carelessly deposited outside the ramparts, Perseus attempted a night raid on the Roman camp with the hope of setting the straw on fire and taking advantage of the resultant chaos. Sadly for Macedonian hopes, the same amateurism which had led the Romans to dump the straw just outside their walls also pervaded the night raiders and they were discovered before they could achieve their objective.

Nevertheless, amateur hour continued. The Romans continued stocking up for the coming winter and Perseus, who knew full well that adequate supplies awaited his army in Macedonia, shadowed them and waited for an opportunity. Sure enough, near the city of Phalanna, the Romans went out foraging without leaving an adequate force to guard their camp. Perseus pounced, capturing the camp and besieging the 800 men left as a garrison. These men retreated to a nearby hill and were able to hold off the light troops with which Perseus had attacked.

Both sides now needed the heavy infantry in a hurry. This was an eventuality which Perseus had somehow failed to anticipate and his infantry arrived late and in some disorder. After a confused action, the Macedonian infantry withdrew again as Crassus and his legionaries were advancing fast and in considerably better order. As the retreating Macedonians had to share the same narrow path as the captured Roman grain carts, the impatient infantry simply tossed the carts out of their way down a very precipitous slope. This did not destroy the grain as effectively as Perseus would have liked, but it certainly worked as an extempore job.

The Macedonians then rallied and prepared to take on the disorganized Roman pursuit, but Perseus again decided to cash in his winnings and pulled his men from the battle. As the Roman historian Livy (42,46) remarks, Perseus should either have completed his raid and pulled back immediately or have been ready to commit his heavy infantry on demand. As it was, he was caught between these two policies and turned what might have been a minor success into a drawn engagement. (Livy reckons that was the end of the matter, but he adds that 'some authorities' (ibid) make the improbable claim that the Romans followed up the retreating Macedonians and a battle followed in which some 12,000 men were slain in a bloody Roman victory.)

The raid on the Roman grain supplies wrapped up events in Thessaly for the year. Thereafter, Perseus took his army back to Macedonia. Crassus, lacking the supplies to remain in Thessaly, led the Romans south to winter in Boeotia. Before he departed, Crassus attempted to storm one of the fortresses guarding the passes into Macedonia on the basis that, if he captured the strong-point, the Macedonians would find it much harder to return to Thessaly the following year. As it was, the Romans failed to make even a significant dent in the fortress' defences – an indication of how difficult a time they would have getting into Macedonia if Perseus decided to simply retreat and hunker down behind his mountain ramparts.

The first year's campaigning showed again the magnitude of the task facing the Romans. In terms of military ability, Perseus was no Alexander the Great but he had managed to fight his equally inept opponents to a standstill. Crassus, who had hoped to get rich on booty from Macedonia, had to content himself with treating formerly friendly Boeotia as conquered territory. He plundered several cities which, until that moment, had rather considered themselves neutrals. The overall effect of such Roman misconduct was to push neighbouring Epirus into the Macedonian camp.

To make things worse, Perseus had noted the careless attitude of the Romans to their grain supply and he launched another surprise attack. This time his target was the Roman grain transports anchored at the island of Euboea, and again he was successful. He captured the grain – and five warships besides – sank everything else and returned to the north where he spent the winter assisting his Thracian allies. Meanwhile, the commanders of the Roman fleet were sanctioned in Rome for pillaging their supposed allies in Greece and the delinquent commanders ordered to free and return those innocent civilians whom they had enslaved.

In various engagements, Perseus had not followed up his initial successes against the Romans as well as he might have done. This may have been simple incompetence but it may also have been because he wanted to allow the Romans to be able to pull out of the war without losing too much face. Throughout the summer campaign, he had repeatedly sent envoys to Crassus offering to make peace. Knowing that the Roman commander was partly driven by a desire for booty, he added as incentive that he was prepared to pay a substantial indemnity and also a large private bribe to Crassus himself. (It should be noted that such was the Roman desire for glory and loot that the other Roman consul, who was meant to be campaigning in northern Italy, also wanted to launch his army in an impromptu invasion of Macedonia. He eventually had to be recalled by a sharp reminder from the senate that he was leaving Italy undefended.)

Greece and Syria 170 BC

While much of the Mediterranean world was at war in the new year of 170 BC, the actual fighting definitely lacked enthusiasm. In Spain, the Roman mistreatment of the Lusitanian people had sparked what was to become a drawn-out guerilla war. In north Italy and Illyria, the Romans struggled with recalcitrant barbarian tribes. In northern Greece, if the campaign of 171 BC had been uninspiring, the campaign of 170 BC set a new low.

Following the example of his predecessor Crassus, the Roman consul Aulus Hostilius again blundered his way in through Epirus and, again, Perseus blundered in not meeting the Romans as they arrived. In this case, he delayed in getting to Tempe when a speedier approach would have practically ensured a quick victory. Once safely arrived, Hostilius spent his time probing the passes into Macedonia in the unavailing hope of finding a chink in the Macedonian armour. He was rebuffed every time and, rather like Crassus the year before, he had to make what profits he could from plundering his 'allies'.

On the Adriatic side of Greece, matters were more lively and more deadly. With the passes into Thessaly secure against the marauding Hostilius, Perseus made a pre-emptive strike against the Dardanians and gave them a comprehensive beating. Further south, the Roman commander in Illyria was told that a town loyal to Perseus was ready to turn itself over to him. Cheerfully setting out to occupy his new possession, the Roman commander, an aristocrat of the Claudian family, allowed his army to approach in no particular order. His straggling troops arrived strung out along the road and walked right into a well-organized ambush. Of the 8,000 Romans and allies who had set out on the ill-fated venture, less than 2,000 made it back. More might have straggled in had Claudius not promptly abandoned his camp, gathered what men were with him and fled.

The result of a less-than-stellar year's operations led to an enquiry in Rome. 'The unsuccessful operations in Macedonia were ascertained [while]... commissioners described the gains made by Perseus and the consequent alarm of Rome's allies. ... The consul blamed the military tribunes, the tribunes threw the blame back at the consul.' (Livy 43,11 ff) It was an altogether unsatisfactory state of affairs.

Meanwhile, back in Syria, the Egyptian's planned campaign of reconquest had failed to even get started. The regents of the young pharaoh were too busy dealing with the political fall-out from the death of Cleopatra I and the subsequent realignment of power among the various palace factions. In the end, to appease everyone, the regents declared the younger siblings of Ptolemy VI to be his co-rulers. This left Egypt under the nominal rule of a kindergarten class consisting of Ptolemy VI, Ptolemy VIII and Cleopatra II. (That Ptolemy VII, who died sometime around 145 BC, comes after Ptolemy VIII is because the seventh Ptolemy's reign was so short and obscure that no-one outside Egypt noticed it until it was too late and historians trying to tidy up the succession of Ptolemies only succeeded in muddling the situation further.)

Antiochus IV had spent 170 BC waiting for an Egyptian invasion that never came. Deciding that he might wait indefinitely, he began to plan instead to take the battle to the Egyptians in the following year. Part of the funding for this came from Judea. The Jewish state had fallen into the hands of Antiochus III when he had successfully regained Coele-Syria in the previous Syrian war of 202–195 BC (the Fifth Syrian War). One of the reasons why Antiochus III is known as 'the Great' is because – apart from one fatal misjudgement – he knew when not to push his subjects too far. After careful contemplation of the potential disaster area that was Judea, he left the Jews well alone.

Not so his sons. Seleucus IV came to grief after his attempted seizure of the temple treasure in Jerusalem. Now Antiochus IV became involved in the politics of the temple itself. The question was whether Simon the Benjamite should be High Priest or the more Philhellene Yeshua (a name often Hellenized to 'Jason'). Antiochus was naturally inclined towards supporting Yeshua and once Yeshua threw in a substantial cash payment, the job was his for the asking. The new High Priest followed this up by building a Hellenistic-style gymnasium in Jerusalem – a measure which outraged conservative Jewish opinion.

With Antiochus building his war chest for the forthcoming Egyptian war, Yeshua sent a relative of Simon the Benjamite with the Jewish contribution. This relative – whose name is usually Hellenized to Menelaus – recognized the desperate need of Antiochus for cash. He therefore offered to supply much more of the same if he were made High Priest in place of Yeshua. Antiochus happily agreed and sent Menelaus home with a promotion and a substantial bodyguard. The latter proved necessary, not only because Yeshua was not at all happy about his demotion, but because the only way that Menelaus could get the funds he had promised Antiochus was by plundering temple treasure.

To add insult to injury, Menelaus was very well aware that he held his office at the pleasure of Antiochus and therefore he continued and accelerated the Hellenizing ways of his predecessor. This actually did Hellenization a disservice because Menelaus was massively unpopular with the common people for his desecration of the temple. His policy of Hellenization therefore became likewise unpopular by association with his odious self. In the end, the upshot of Antiochus' meddling was to turn Judea from a relatively placid subject state to a seething hotbed of discontent.

Of all Mediterranean leaders, Perseus alone was probably satisfied with the course of events in 170 BC. He had kept his kingdom intact and had inflicted a few stinging setbacks to Rome's allies. The Romans were deeply annoyed by their lack of anything resembling progress and looked likely to find a different victim to fight in the coming year. Egypt remained a political basket case incapable of harming anyone and Antiochus had been forced to remain on a war footing without an actual war to resolve matters. It is also probable, as will be recalled from earlier (p.118), that this was the moment when the usurper Eukratides seized power in Bactria. With the world mired in wars that were going nowhere, it seemed unlikely that the year 169 BC would produce many breakthroughs.

The year 169 BC

Rome prepared for the new campaign by selecting Quintus Marcius Philippus as consul in command of the Macedonian War. This was something of a break with tradition as the predecessors of Philippus had been mildly inept placemen. Philippus was a very different character – he possessed verve, imagination and total incompetence in equal abundance. He was the sort of commander under whom every regular soldier dreads serving – a committed glory-hound with the military ability of a seven-year-old child.

As mentioned above, consuls took the field relatively late in the campaigning year once they had settled other matters in Rome. In the context of the Macedonian wars, this did not really matter anyway. There was little chance that legionaries could force their way through the pikemen guarding the high mountain passes into Macedonia from Thessaly, and even less chance if those legionaries had to wade through deep snow to do so.

While waiting for the main act to begin, Perseus passed the time by making life miserable for Rome and Roman allies on the Adriatic coast. He attacked and plundered various cities and then campaigned in Epirus.

Conditions were too poor for any major campaigns but Perseus showed that he was prepared to fight and made some minor gains in the process. Among those gains was another success against that hapless Claudius who had previously bungled the capture of a city in Illyria. To redeem himself, Claudius had attacked Epirus but had the misfortune to arrive even as Perseus did, the latter with a much larger army. Claudius escaped with fewer casualties this time around but he still lost over a thousand men. Thereafter, he retired to Rome to seek success in other fields of endeavour.

There matters rested, until Philippus took charge of the army in Greece and made a determined effort to lose the war once and for all. This took careful planning, effort and dedication but the new consul was up to the task. He determined that the reason that his predecessors had failed to break into Macedonia was due to lack of imagination. Consequently, he planned a daring and heroic march through a pass called Octolophus. This was no easy journey and it involved several extempore detours to get around Macedonian garrisons which refused to budge from well-defended positions. In the end, the Romans ended up breaking their own trail, sometimes down hillsides so steep that pack animals fell to their deaths and the army's elephants slid down on their backsides.

Eventually, the exhausted Romans reached Macedonia by staggering into an enclosed valley through which ran the river Baphirus. A minor Macedonian city occupied the mouth of the pass, effectively preventing the Roman exit. The sides of the valley were too precipitous for anything but a fit young mountain goat to surmount and getting back the way they had come would have been just as difficult as getting in, except that it would also be uphill and the Macedonians had blocked off the route in any case.

Philippus had effectively led his army into a trap far more deadly than even the most skilled enemy commander could have prepared for him. The small enemy force now guarding the mountain pass was more than enough to prevent the Roman return to Thessaly and the same force prevented any supplies or reinforcements from reaching the trapped Romans. The approach to the town blocking the valley was steep and easily defended, and only a rudimentary rampart was needed to block it altogether. The stage was set for the biggest defeat since Hannibal had massacred the Roman army at Cannae in 216 BC.

Egypt

Since the time of Ptolemy I, Egypt had remained invulnerable between the desert and the Red Sea. All the nation needed was to concentrate its armies to defend the narrow strip of land along which now runs the Suez Canal. However, for all their bellicose threats, the regents for the clutch of infant pharaohs nominally ruling Egypt were unable to achieve even this.

An aggressive and well-prepared Antiochus IV swept aside their flimsy resistance and, after a brisk battle outside the walls, Ptolemy took the town of Per Amun (called 'Perusium' by Greek historians) at the edge of the Nile Delta. The changing coastal conditions were already choking off the small lake by which Per Amun had access to the sea, but at this time the town appears to have still been a serviceable port.

Every conqueror of Egypt from the Persians onward had started by taking Per Amun for once this city was secure, the way to the Nile delta was open. However, previous conquerors had not needed to reckon with the formidable city of Alexandria which the Macedonians, under Alexander, had planted at the north end of the delta. Antiochus accordingly went south and took instead the enduringly beautiful city at the apex of the delta. (In Egyptian 'Men-nefer' means 'enduringly beautiful' – though the city is better known by its Hellenized name of Memphis.) From there, Antiochus was well placed to fall upon Alexandria and end his brief war.

On the other hand, Antiochus must have asked himself, did he really want Egypt? Bactria had all but dropped out of Seleucid control and the Parthians were getting restive. There was a pending rebellion in Judea and no-one knew where the ambitions of Eumenes of Pergamon might take him. In other words, Antiochus had an empire's worth of problems facing him already and little desire to add to these the colossal headache that Egypt was certain to become. Easier by far to do as the Seleucids usually did with the other states of their ramshackle empire – that is, make himself suzerain of that state while leaving its administrative machinery intact. Accordingly, Antiochus offered to keep Ptolemy VI in power (the boy was after all, the nephew of Antiochus through his sister Cleopatra) as a subordinate king with 'advisors' appointed by Antiochus himself.

This settlement was satisfactory to Ptolemy VI and Antiochus, but not apparently to the people of Alexandria who were violently opposed to being a part of a Seleucid hegemony. (How the rest of Egypt felt was not under consideration – the outcome of the recent rebellion had left Thebes and southern Egypt totally subordinate to Alexandria.) Now the Alexandrians decided that if Ptolemy VI had gone over to the Seleucids, they would adopt Egypt's other two pharaohs as their joint rulers. Antiochus was happy with this outcome also. He pulled back and left Egypt on the brink of being crippled by a nicely prepared civil war between Ptolemy VI on the one side and Cleopatra II and Ptolemy VIII on the other. With Egypt out of the military picture, his southern flank was secure and Antiochus prepared to move on to his myriad of other problems.

Meanwhile, back in Macedon

It will be recalled that we left the Roman general Philippus up the proverbial creek (in this case the river Baphirus) without an exit for his trapped army. One can well imagine the cynical amusement with which Philip V would have greeted the news of the predicament into which his enemy had placed himself. Philip's son Perseus was a general of a very different calibre. A general inclined to panic, for a start.

When news reached him that the Roman army was ensconced in Macedonia, Perseus did not bother to check how the Romans had got there. Since no rational commander would have got his army into Macedon the way that Philippus had done, Perseus immediately jumped to the conclusion that the Romans had in fact done the logical thing and forced one of the passes. Operating from the false belief that the secure fortress of his kingdom had been breached, Perseus did the obvious thing. He pulled the remaining garrisons back from the passes, because if one pass had fallen, there was little point in guarding the others. He then mustered his army near his capital at Pydna and prepared to stake everything on a final battle. In other words, in his belief that the passes to Macedonia had been turned, Perseus did what the Romans could not and allowed them unfettered access to his heartlands.

As soon as he discovered that communications with Thessaly had re-opened, Philippus quickly sent scouts to secure his supply lines. Then he marched his army out of the now unguarded exit from the trap he had led it into. On the way, Philippus came to the sobering realization that, but for his supreme luck in having Perseus as his opponent, he would have doomed his army. Under those circumstances, Philippus wisely decided not to press his good fortune and spent the rest of the year consolidating the Roman bridgehead in Macedonia.

The senate was in agreement with Philippus' reassessment of his abilities. One would expect that the general who had managed the difficult feat of breaching the mountain walls of Macedonia could easily have had his command extended so that he could finish the job by defeating Perseus in battle. As it was, after an appalled review of Philippus' strategic choices, the senate removed him from command as swiftly as could decently be done. The senate replaced him with the experienced Aemilius Paulus, a general who actually knew what he was doing.

The Roman success in getting into Macedonia was not altogether welcome news to Macedonia's enemies. The Rhodians and Pergamenes abruptly realized that, instead of having a weakened Macedon on their doorstep, they would henceforth be exposed to the full power of a vigorously expansionist Rome. As the allies realized the implications of losing their Macedonian buffer, the senate was suddenly besieged with envoys from eastern states offering to negotiate on Macedon's behalf.

Perseus himself openly encouraged these manoeuvres but rather spoiled them by being tight-fisted. For example, he offered a Thracian king a large sum of money to declare war on the Romans but, having received that declaration and believing that this king was now committed to war, Perseus decided not to send payment after all.

In Pergamon, Eumenes offered to pull out of the war altogether in exchange for a modest payment for which he would also mediate with the Romans on Macedon's behalf. Again, Perseus could not bring himself to pay for a potential lifeline. In this latter case, he might have been right. The Romans had finally got the Macedonians where they wanted them and they were not going to pass up the chance to score a decisive victory. They, therefore, politely declined to take their foot off the Macedonian throat but instead, quietly took note of those whom they now considered fair-weather friends.

Decision in 168 BC

Just as 169 BC started with wars that seemed to be going nowhere, it suddenly looked as though 168 BC was going to see dramatic shifts in the geopolitics of the Hellenistic world. Antiochus started the year by re-instating Menelaus as High Priest in Judea after a popular uprising against that Philhellene leader. While the Seleucid king was doing this, he received the unsatisfactory news that instead of being at each other's throats, Egypt's pharaohs had come together in a rush of brotherly and sisterly harmony. The young pharaohs (or, in reality, their advisors) had seen the folly of fighting one another and Ptolemy VI had agreed to repudiate his Seleucid alliance.

An indignant Antiochus responded by capturing the Egyptian possession of Cyprus (which he did with the fleet that, according to the Romans, he was not supposed to have). Since Antiochus had never relinquished Per Amun, it was straightforward enough for him to load the army into his prohibited troopships and take up the war where he had left off.

The Egyptians appealed to Rome for help. The Romans still had their hands full in Macedonia but they rose to the challenge – by sending one man. This was Popillius Laenas. Laenas did not set off on his war-ending mission immediately. How he went about his business would depend on how the war played out in Macedon and there matters were rapidly coming to a climax.

The battle of Pydna

Though the Romans were now within Macedonia, they had still to beat the Macedonians. Perseus had a large, well-trained and well-equipped army and still had the advantage of the terrain. When Paulus came to assume command, the army of Perseus was dug into a near-impregnable position near the slopes of Mount Olympus. It took an elaborate military exercise, complete with feints and night marches, for the Romans to turn the Macedonian flank, but the experienced Paulus was as capable of managing the manoeuvre as the inexperienced Perseus was incapable of preventing it. Once the Romans were in a position to cut his lines of communication, Perseus had no choice but to abandon his position and fall back towards Pydna, a major coastal city.

We know the date of the battle with certainty, because our sources are unanimous that there was a lunar eclipse the night before. Though by now it was well known that eclipses were caused by astronomical interactions, both sides felt it was necessary to sacrifice to propitiate the gods, just in case. Perhaps as a result of these extended preliminaries, the battle itself did not start until the afternoon of 22 June.

The outcome of such a long-expected battle had been keenly debated by military experts around the Mediterranean. Supporters of the Macedonian phalanx felt that, on the broken and sloping ground of Cynoscephalae, the formation had not been allowed to perform at its best. There was still a school of thought which maintained that, in the right conditions, the phalanx was invincible. At Pydna, the phalanx was in near-ideal conditions on a battlefield of Perseus' own choosing. The Macedonians had the edge in numbers but everyone knew that to some degree this was irrelevant. The battle would be won or lost with the confrontation between some 30,000 pikemen and 20,000 Roman legionaries supported by the heavy infantry of their allies.

The pike phalanx did what it did best by rolling down on the Romans with levelled pikes – a sight which was to populate the nightmares of Aemilius Paulus for decades afterwards. The Romans had no defence against a well-formed and unbroken phalanx and began to give ground.

One commander tried the desperate expedient of hurling his unit's standards into the Macedonian ranks and challenging his men to retrieve them. The unit tried and was wiped out. On a more personal level, a young man dropped his sword while fending off the advancing enemy. Rather than report the disgraceful loss to his formidable father, Cato the Censor, the young man plunged into the enemy ranks to retrieve the lost weapon. Remarkably he did, and lived to tell the tale.

Despite this promising start, once again the Macedonians were let down by Perseus' generalship – or rather by his lack of it. It had not occurred to Perseus that the disciplined Romans would be able to fight hard while retreating, and the Romans reached the edge of the battlefield with their army still a going concern, even if the going was backwards. Once off the smooth level ground upon which it fought best, the phalanx began to develop cracks in its orderly lines.

The phalangites on level patches pressed forward, while their fellows were slowed by rougher terrain. The Romans, with their more flexible formations, were able to tear off units from their main battle line and charge these into the breaks in the enemy line. Once the legions got to close quarters within a part of the phalanx, a local collapse followed. These patches of chaos within the Macedonian formation spread until the phalanx fell apart.

A much-disputed question was what the superior Macedonian cavalry were doing while all this was going on. It might be assumed that a Roman army going in reverse would have done so much less successfully had there been cavalry harassing the flanks and rear. It is possible that the Macedonian nobility who commanded the cavalry abandoned their commander at the critical moment and simply refused to take part in the battle. More probably, Perseus dithered about playing his final card until it was too late to do so anyway. Either way, the cavalry were largely passive bystanders until the phalanx collapsed. Thereafter, they fled the battlefield with Perseus leading the way.

After this less-than-heroic performance by their king, the Macedonian army not unexpectedly lost its will to fight. Not that there were many Macedonians left to do the fighting – the Romans were again merciless towards their defeated opponents. About half the army was cut down on the battlefield before the Romans started accepting surrenders and a further 10,000 Macedonians were captured and imprisoned. Paulus had Macedonia at his mercy and, as a Roman of the old school, mercy was not among his redeeming qualities.

Decision in Egypt

The result of the battle of Pydna made the task of the Roman envoy Popillius Laenas much easier. He and Antiochus IV knew each other personally as the result of a sojourn Antiochus made in Rome before he became king. Now he prepared to renew that acquaintanceship under less amicable circumstances.

Laenas found Antiochus encamped with his army at Eleusis, a small settlement very close to Alexandria. It is significant that Antiochus could have stormed Alexandria at any time in the preceding month but had held off attacking. In fact, it is quite possible that Antiochus also was waiting to see how things played out in Macedon. There is certainly no way that Antiochus could have believed that the Romans would be happy with a Seleucid conquest of Egypt. This would create a super-state on Rome's new eastern frontier which, if its component parts ever got their act together, could easily outmatch Rome in money, technology and manpower.

It is also quite probable that Antiochus also was not too happy with the prospect of conquering Egypt. The reasons that he had not done so the previous year were still valid, and that was before the Romans could dispute that conquest with the large battle-hardened army now available after the resolution of the Macedonian war. In consequence, Antiochus was in the position of being all too successful. All he had wanted was a brisk and successful war that beat off the Egyptian threat to his southern border. This would have increased his popular standing with the people and impressed restive subject rulers to the east. There might have been booty involved.

Instead, Antiochus was in imminent danger of becoming a reluctant pharaoh and enemy of Rome, and he could not really avoid becoming either without alienating those among his followers who saw only the chance of finishing off the Egyptian threat once and for all. Under the circumstances, the arrival of Laenas was possibly something of a relief.

This meeting became the stuff of legend. Rather than greet Antiochus warmly and retire to his tent for negotiations, Laenas came straight to the point and opened the conversation by demanding that the Seleucids leave Egypt immediately or consider themselves at war with Rome. Somewhat taken aback, Antiochus asked for time to consider his options. Laenas told Antiochus to take all the time he needed. Then the envoy walked around Antiochus while dragging his staff in the dirt. He announced that Antiochus was not to leave the circle just created around him until he had made his decision.

Literally put upon the spot, Antiochus caved, and probably did so with some relief at having had matters taken out of his hands. He could now claim that, rather as with Asia Minor, any issues with Egypt were a Roman problem. The Seleucid king had plenty of other problems of his own awaiting him back home and, humiliating as the brutal show of force by Laenas had been, it offered him a clear line of escape from the Egyptian quagmire.

Thus, by the end of 168 BC, both the third Macedonian War and the Sixth Syrian War had ended. In effect, the victor in both wars was Rome.

Chapter 11

The Decline of the Seleucids and the Fall of Greece

Top of the list of issues with which Antiochus had to deal after the abrupt end to his Egyptian campaign was the problematic situation in Judea – a situation which he had done much to exacerbate. However, aside from Antiochus' clumsy mishandling of appointments to the High Priesthood, there were more fundamental issues in play. The basic problem was the attraction of Hellenistic culture. As we have seen, the Seleucids did not press Greek ways upon unwilling subjects, but they also had no objection if those subjects voluntarily adopted their customs.

So it was in Jerusalem, where the upper classes found that the easiest way to curry favour with their Hellenic overlords was to become Hellenized themselves. The more conservative element among the Jewish people were outraged by the sight of uncircumcised Jews participating naked in events staged in Greek-style gymnasia in the Holy City. They were also none too impressed with what they saw as corruption extending upwards through the priesthood to the very top. Gradually, the Jewish people became polarized between a group who saw the conservative element as rustic, backward and ignorant, and a group who saw the Philhellenes as apostates who were betraying traditions which had kept the Jews united for thousands of years.

Conflict between the two different factions steadily escalated until it became indistinguishable from a civil war. At this point Antiochus intervened. In a matter calling for the uttermost delicacy, he adopted a sledgehammer approach. Given the situation in Judea he was forced to do something but, in a major policy misstep, he picked a side (which he did not have to do). Naturally enough, the side he picked was that of the Philhellenes.

It has to be admitted that Antiochus' opponents took a sledgehammer approach of their own. Indeed, the name adopted by the rebels – Maccabees – means 'hammer' and this was symbolic of their approach. The original victims of the hammer of religious orthodoxy were Hellenistic Jews who were ostracised, forcibly circumcised and had their places of worship demolished. In at least one instance, a Jew who sacrificed to the Greek gods was killed for doing so. This is reliably, indeed proudly, reported in the Jewish text of Maccabees. Less reliable, however, are the reports of the reaction of Antiochus, which response, according to the text of Maccabees, was basically to ban the practice of Judaism and to set up worship of the Greek gods in its place.

This is dubious, not least because we have no other example of the Seleucids banning entirely the religion of a subject people. Also, there can be no doubt that the text of Maccabees, as we have it today, is not an objective history but propaganda specifically written to promote the conservative ideology. As a result, in both Maccabees and also in the relevant texts in the Bible, Antiochus appears as the blackest of villains, for example ordering the deaths of mothers who circumcised their children, along with the execution of the babes themselves. Insofar as Antiochus did implement harsh measures, these seemed aimed at the people of Judea. There is no record of any attempts to suppress traditional Jewish practices in any of the very substantial Jewish communities elsewhere in the empire.

No matter how hard or restrained Antiochus was in Judea, this hardly mattered. His intervention on the Philhellenic side changed what was essentially an internal conflict into a struggle between the Seleucid government and the Jewish people – and by 265 BC the Jewish people had had hundreds of years of practice at opposing oppressive foreign governments. The Seleucids found their garrisons in Judea mired in an ever-escalating guerilla war that was gradually shaping up to be a successful war of independence. One reminder of that war is still seen today in the mid-winter Jewish celebration of Hanukkah, where the lighting of candles commemorates the taking of the temple in Jerusalem by the rebels.

Eventually, the exasperated Antiochus decided to send a major military force into Judea in a surge of manpower that would overwhelm the

Maccabees. The king was not able to lead the force himself because he had pressing business in the east. The Parthians were ostensibly a subject people of the Seleucid empire and, for most of the reign of Phraates I (176–171 BC) and his predecessors, the rulers of Parthia were happy to give lip service to this idea.

Not so Mithridates I of Parthia, who took over from his brother around 170 BC. Mithridates was the brother of Phaates and, as a ruler, Mithridates combined an expansionist approach with a cautious nature. Thus, news of the coup of Eukratides in Bactria (p.118) immediately attracted the new king's attention, but it appears that he instead sent spies to establish the exact situation. It would have been good to know what that situation was, because by now reports reaching western historians about the situation in Bactria were vague, confused and contradictory.

A second-century AD epitomater called Justin summarized the very extensive history of the earlier historian Gnaeus Trogus, and this condensed source tells us that Eukratides fought wars against practically everyone but the Parthians almost as soon as he came to power. This is probably because the civil unrest following the coup signalled weakness to Bactria's predatory neighbours and, as soon as one neighbour took the chance and invaded, all the others piled in. By all accounts, Eukratides was an excellent general who managed to fight off the various assaults on his kingdom and he even expanded Bactria's borders in the process.

Inevitably though, war on multiple fronts weakened the kingdom. Once Mithridates had determined that Bactria was both vulnerable and unlikely to get any weaker, he struck. Justin assures us that Parthia usually was the weaker nation but the timing of Mithridates more than made up for the difference in strength. Eukratides was eventually forced to make peace at the cost of losing two of Bactria's western provinces.

It may seem that the transfer of ownership of two provinces in a kingdom barely connected to the Seleucid Empire would not be enough to draw Antiochus from a major rebellion in Judea. However, larger issues were at play. Firstly, Antiochus needed to stamp his authority on the east where the minor kingdoms had last formally offered fealty to Antiochus III. Secondly, both Parthia and Bactria were acting like the independent kingdoms they actually were instead of the subordinate states that the Seleucid kings wanted them to be. Finally, and most importantly, it is very probable that Mithridates' capture of the western Bactrian provinces disrupted the highly profitable trade route to the east, which today is known as the Silk Road.

Just as the Parthians had been able to take advantage of Bactria's military engagements elsewhere, so Antiochus was able to exploit the fact that Mithridates was busy with other commitments. After a successful show of force against the Armenians, it seems that Antiochus also secured the submission of Eukratides, probably because the Bactrian ruler was desperate for allies. It is also significant that, at this time, mints in northern Mesopotamia started issuing a series of new coinages, possibly after a stern royal reminder that the region was still under Seleucid control.

How successful Antiochus was against the Parthians depends on which of the conflicting sources one follows. What we know for certain is that in November 164 BC Antiochus died (or was smitten by the Lord, according to a triumphant gloat in Maccabees), possibly from appendicitis. In the short term, Antiochus, despite an undoubtedly erratic personality, had done well to keep his kingdom together, partially repair its crippled finances and restore a degree of order in the east. His major shortcoming was entirely involuntary, for he did his kingdom no favours in dying prematurely while his son and heir was all of nine years old.

The Judean campaign against the Maccabees was conducted with considerable success by a commander called Lysias. Lysias was a man of considerable diplomatic skill because he was able to negotiate a tenuous peace between the Seleucids and the warring Jewish factions. This could have happened at one of three points – before Antiochus set off on his final expedition against Parthia (as some historians claim), when news of the death of Antiochus reached the west and Lysias set up the nine-year-old son as Antiochus V, or when Lysias had to hurry to Syria to deal with another rebellion once news of Antiochus IV's death became public (as other sources maintain).

The Romans decided that the removal of Antiochus IV represented an opportunity to make the Seleucids actually stick to the terms of the treaty agreed to by Antiochus III after his defeat at Magnesia. They sent an envoy to Syria who high-handedly ordered the killing of the elephants and burning of the ships which the Romans reckoned that the Seleucids should not have had. Thereafter, relations with Rome took a nosedive because the outraged Syrians responded by killing the envoy. Lysias insisted that his government had nothing to do with the killing to which the Romans replied, probably just as disingenuously, that they had nothing to do with the escape of Demetrios, the hostage Seleucid heir who now took ship for his homeland.

Either Lysias had managed to make himself very unpopular already, or Demetrios had been preparing the ground well in advance of his return. In either case, the result was the same – the empire fell to Demetrios with hardly a struggle and Lysias and his boy-king were executed.

160–150 BC: An (almost) stable decade

Greece

For the next ten years the Hellenistic kingdoms were able to keep business going almost as usual, though Macedon was no longer a kingdom. In fact, Macedon as such no longer existed. After his defeat at Pydna, Perseus attempted to flee to parts unknown. He was captured and taken to Rome where he appeared in the triumphal parade of Aemilius Paulus. In Roman tradition, a captive king was executed immediately after the celebration of a triumph but in this case the Romans chose to keep the king in captivity in Italy. (There he had a miserable time being bullied unceasingly by his guards. His son, meanwhile, found employment as a clerk in Rome and thereafter the Macedonian royal line vanished into the general population of the capital.)

The Romans had one final act of revenge before their army left Greece. Epirus had sided with Perseus and now the Romans repaid the invasion of Pyrrhus two generations before by destroying that state. Even though the Epirots had surrendered as soon as it was clear that Macedon had been defeated, this did not stop the Romans from making a co-ordinated attack on every Epirot city. These cities were systematically pillaged and the inhabitants enslaved. Overall, some 150,000 Epirots were taken as slaves to Italy by the returning legions, leaving the region devastated for generations to come.

Macedon was divided into four 'independent' Republics. These were very much puppet governments with economies crippled by the need to pay tribute to Rome, even though most formerly profitable enterprises of the Macedonian state were now run directly by Romans for Roman benefit. The Romans closed the gold and silver mines which were the basis of Macedonian wealth and allowed only copper and iron to be mined. Ostensibly this was to demonstrate that the Romans had no interest in extracting Macedonia's resources. More probably, it was because the Romans realized that an operating mine could easily be taken over by rebels and thereafter used to fund a war of independence.

A war of independence was highly likely. The Romans attempted to make the four republics separate and rival (for instance, they forbade intermarriage between citizens of each republic or ownership of property in more than one republic). Despite this, nationalist sentiment remained strong.

In the Greek mainland further south, the Achaean League was now the dominant force in the Peloponnese. The Romans were wary of this league, rather as they also now regarded with suspicion their former allies of Rhodes and Pergamon. In an attempt to keep the league under control, the Romans demanded, and received, family members of prominent League leaders as hostages.

Among those hostages kept in gilded captivity in Rome was a young soldier and diplomat called Polybius. Deftly switching careers to match his changed circumstances, Polybius became a historian. His history of recent events quickly became indispensable to later historians in both the ancient and modern eras. 'For who can be so idle and indifferent as not to care how ... almost the entire inhabited world was ... brought under the domination of the single city of Rome, and that also in less than two generations?' So Polybius opens his narrative, and his question remains just as provocative today.

Egypt

In Egypt, the pharonic triumvirate of two Ptolemies (VI and VIII) and a Cleopatra was growing towards adulthood. Cleopatra simplified matters (and also her family tree) by marrying her older brother Ptolemy VI. This alliance left Ptolemy VIII (known as Physcon or 'pot-belly') as the outsider who was left in charge of a smaller part of the kingdom mostly consisting of Cyrenaica. The young pharaoh tried to extend his rule by making himself virtually a client of the Romans. He went to the Romans in the mid-150s, claiming that his brother and sister had tried to assassinate him and, while he was there, asking for Roman aid in reconquering Cyprus which had once been a Ptolemaic domain.

The Romans, in similar mind as the Seleucids, were happy to see the Egyptian kingdom divided and rudderless. The guiding force in Egyptian affairs, insofar as there was one, was provided by the diplomatic skill of Cleopatra who persuaded her husband to release Physcon when he was captured after his unsuccessful campaign in Cyprus. Eventually, peace was restored between the brothers when Cleopatra betrothed her daughter (another Cleopatra, usually called Cleopatra Thea) to her uncle Physcon, who retired – for the moment – to Cyrenaica.

The Seleucid Empire

Rather to general surprise, Demetrios proved to be an effective king. In a way he had to be, because his overall reputation was to be forever sullied by his blatant execution of his relative, the previous king. This was later to become almost the standard Seleucid means of succession, and henceforth the slowly crumbling empire was to be in an almost constant state of civil war between various claimants to the throne.

As was usual when a new Seleucid king took over, the first order of business for Demetrios was to suppress a wave of rebellions. The first of these was against the Maccabees in Judea who were deeply miffed by the execution of Lysias, of whom they had grown rather fond. The other more serious affair was in Mesopotamia, where the governor decided that he had done so well in standing off the aggressive Parthian king Mithridates that he was entitled to rule Mesopotamia as a king in his own right.

Demetrios demonstrated to the Maccabees in no uncertain terms that they were incapable of withstanding the Seleucid army in the field. Then, having blooded his army in successful combat, he moved east and re-took Mesopotamia. The tradition of the Hellenistic kings marrying their female relatives to one another had by now broken down, as the Macedonian line was as good as extinct, and the Egyptians were apparently set upon marrying each other. This left the sister of Demetrios (another Laodice, naturally) as a serious liability, since whoever married her had a serious claim to the throne. In the end, Demetrios adopted the pharonic solution and married his sister himself.

Demetrios then antagonized his Roman patrons by interfering in Anatolia, where he dethroned the current king and set up a puppet in his place. With Mesopotamia under control, Bactria offering nominal submission, and Coele-Syria firmly in Seleucid hands, the empire seemed almost secure. It was a superficial security, which masked deep and irreparable flaws but for the rest of the decade things were stable.

Pergamon

Eumenes II had been ailing for several years and, in 159 BC, he died. By then, his brother had been co-ruler for several years and the succession passed smoothly to Attalus II who was to rule for the next two decades. The opening decade of Attalus' reign saw him fight two wars against Pergamon's perennial rival Bithynia and bump heads with Demetrios over the kingship of Cappadocia. By and large, Attalus was successful in his primary mission as king – to repair relations with Rome, which had become strained under Eumenes.

In all, the 150s BC were a period of relative calm which ended explosively when war broke out simultaneously in Seleucia and Macedonia.

The fall of Demetrios

While he enjoyed military success, Demetrios was a poor politician. As a result, he was unable to make himself fully accepted even in the kingdom's heartlands of Syria. The Mesopotamians tolerated him while the Bactrians resented him. Attalus of Pergamon openly longed for regime change and the Romans, upset with Demetrios' interference in Cappadocia, were in full agreement with Attalus. The Jews and Parthians were naturally even more vigorously anti-Demetrios and the Cappadocians and Egyptians soon came on to the bandwagon.

Perhaps the deadliest of this assortment of powerful enemies was, naturally, a member of Demetrios' own family. This was a daughter of the deceased Antiochus IV, a Laodice called (for those who are keeping count) Laodice the sixth. In 152 BC, she threw her support behind one Alexander Balas. Balas was an adventurer who claimed to be the son of Antiochus IV despite, in reality, having no relationship whatsoever to the deceased king. Nevertheless, with Laodice (the sixth) vouching for his legitimacy, Balas was able to make himself the preferred ruler of the Seleucid empire in the eyes of the many groups who wanted Demetrios removed from that post as soon as possible.

When Alexander landed in Syria with a strong force, Demetrios came to engage him in the field. For once, Seleucia's warrior king was unsuccessful, probably because his generals betrayed him. It is highly suggestive that, immediately after the battle (in which Demetrios probably perished), one of Demetrios' former generals became a trusted advisor of the new king.

Thereafter, the Egyptians took a hand and, as often happened when the Egyptians joined in, things got really complicated. For a start, Ptolemy VI broke off his daughter's engagement with his brother Ptolemy VIII and married Cleopatra Thea to the new king, an arrangement which meant that thereafter Balas' reign was heavily dependent on Ptolemaic support. Balas managed to father a child with Cleopatra between bouts of increasingly unrestrained debauchery which strained the patience of his subjects and the royal court.

At some point Ptolemy VI must have decided that his Seleucid client king was not going to last much longer. Popular support was swinging behind yet another claimant to the throne, a son of Demetrios who bore the same name as his father. Consequently, Ptolemy arranged to depose Balas with help from the Maccabees while Balas was distracted by yet another rebellion. With Jewish support Ptolemy sneaked a small army through Judea, and with this he captured the city of Seleucia. He also recaptured his daughter Cleopatra Thea in that city and unilaterally divorced her from Balas. Since Ptolemy's new choice of Seleucid client king was Demetrios the younger, son of Demetrios I, the by now somewhat confused Cleopatra Thea was promptly remarried to him.

When Balas came storming back with his army, Ptolemy met him head-on and was successful in the subsequent battle. Balas fled south, while Ptolemy collapsed on to what would be his deathbed, probably from wounds sustained when he fell from his horse in that battle. Ptolemy had the pleasure of seeing Balas once more before he died, for the minor king to whom Balas fled for shelter wanted nothing to do with the dangerous fugitive. He kept the body but returned Balas' head to Ptolemy.

This left Demetrios II in charge of the Seleucid Empire. His was to be a relatively long and storied reign which began badly when the mercenary force he had brought with him began plundering indiscriminately. Immediately, the people of Antioch adopted a new king, the infant son of Balas and Cleopatra Thea, which left Demetrios II at war with his stepson.

Egypt

With the death of Ptolemy VI in Syria, Cleopatra II (Thea's mother) promptly declared her son to be the replacement Pharaoh. At that point, it seems that Cleopatra II received a better offer from her brother Physcon (Ptolemy VIII). She married Physcon and, as a wedding gift, had her son assassinated at the nuptial feast.

Physcon had long been an outsider and felt himself despised by the Alexandrian elite. Once he came to power, he began by taking revenge on all whom he felt had mocked or insulted him. Suddenly, the universities of Athens, Seleucia and Pergamon had a massive influx of scholars fleeing for their lives (several did not make it) or who had been expelled from the Library of Alexandria and other Egyptian places of learning. Meanwhile, Ptolemy Physcon's relationship with Cleopatra II took a sharp turn for the worse when the pharaoh took an additional wife – who was also his stepdaughter, Cleopatra II's daughter and a sister of Cleopatra Thea. Even by the remarkably elastic standards of Hellenistic kingship, a brother married simultaneously to his sister and her daughter (his niece) raised a few eyebrows.

The Fourth (and final) Macedonian War

Alexander Balas was not the only royal pretender of his era. Macedon had Andriscus, the son of a fuller in the city of Adramyttium, which was not even in Macedonia but in western Anatolia. Despite the handicaps of birth and location, Andriscus decided to promote himself to become Philip, the son of Perseus, heir presumptive to the kingdom of Macedon. (For which reason some older texts refer to him as Pseudophilip).

Andriscus took advantage of simmering Macedonian resentment towards Rome and used a mixture of fiery nationalism and savage murder to appoint himself king. Nevertheless, Andriscus still needed an army to remove the Roman garrison from 'his' kingdom, and Macedon no longer had an army. Therefore, Andriscus attempted to raise one with the help of the Seleucids. The Seleucids had no interest in adding a war with Rome to their already extensive list of problems. They handed the man who would be king over to the Roman authorities, who failed to take the threat seriously. Andriscus was placed in loose custody while the Romans decided what to do with him and Andriscus temporarily resolved the question for them by escaping.

Passing through Thrace on his way home, Andriscus gathered an army of Thracians. Some were interested in plunder and others joined his cause because they had fond memories of Perseus, who had supported several local kings. This makeshift army fell upon Macedon in 149 BC and took the outnumbered Roman praetor in charge by surprise. With the Romans forced out, for a year, Macedon was a kingdom once again. The shocking news inspired Greeks to the south, where the Achaean League – also disillusioned with Rome – began to put itself on to a war footing while Thessaly returned to its long-standing subordination to the Macedonians.

The entire Macedonian revival was to be ephemeral. It was very much a fantasy to assume that a rag-tag Macedonian army of untrained conscripts and Thracian irregulars would succeed where the battle-hardened armies of Philip V and Perseus had not. Nor were the Romans prepared to tolerate a united Macedonian kingdom for longer than it took to gather an army to put a stop to the whole business. In 148 BC, that Roman army commanded by a Metellus of Rome's rising Caecilius family, was ready to go. Attacking from the south, the legions steam-rollered over the Macedonians in a one-sided massacre politely known as The Second Battle of Pydna. Thereafter, all pretence of Macedonian independence came to an end as the exasperated Romans formally made the nation into a Roman province.

Roman exasperation was felt even more keenly further south. The Greeks of the Achaean league had felt that they were a free people. The Romans reckoned they were more in the position of Roman freedmen who still owed a duty of obedience to their emancipator. Since the Greeks had clearly failed in that obligation, the Romans demonstrated their displeasure by destroying the ancient city of Corinth after another one-sided war, which ended in 146 BC. The Romans sacked Corinth of its ancient treasures before destroying the city.

A telling anecdote has the Roman general Lucius Memmius telling workmen packing priceless Praxilates statues (the equivalent of Bernini or Michaelangelo sculptures) that anything they broke would come out of their wages. The Romans may have conquered the Greeks, but sophisticated Greeks still regarded their conquerors – with some justification – as oafishly uncultured barbarians. It would take centuries before Corinth would rise again but, with typical Greek resilience, it did. Another city demolished by the Romans at the same time was the 4000-year-old city of Patras. This also made a recovery in the Roman era and has survived until today. (In 2006, it was declared European Capital of Culture by the European Union.)

Going ... going

With Syracuse absorbed into Rome's growing empire in 212 BC and Macedon and Greece made into Roman provinces in 148 BC, the surviving western Hellenistic kingdoms were those of Pergamon, the Seleucids and the Ptolemies.

Bactria in the far east looked as though it might go under at any time, as the once-dominant kingdom battled waves of barbarian invasions. After getting beaten by the Saka people, the Bactrians lost much of their northern lands and found it of little consolation when the Yuezhi people took those lands from the Saka.

On a more positive note, the Greek peoples of southern Bactria had been expanding into India and a strange fusion of cultures had developed into the oddly-named Indo-Greek kingdom. This was to endure for another century and a half after the fall of Hellenistic Bactria itself. Exactly when that fall occurred is uncertain. The last evidence we have from Hellenistic

Bactria is in the form of coins with the names of otherwise unknown kings – and a slightly confused report from a traveller who, significantly, came from China rather than the west.

While Rome may have accounted for the fall of Macedon, the troubles of the Seleucids were largely of their own making. The empire was always a thin web of Hellenism holding together a mass of nations which had very little in common with one another. The population of Greeks within the empire remains frustratingly hard to quantify though the Seleucid kings would have emphatically claimed that it was nowhere near enough, even as they frittered away that manpower in pointless and damaging civil wars.

Meanwhile, the predatory Mithridates I of Parthia was right next door to Mesopotamia. It was only a matter of time before the Parthians decided that political turmoil in Syria meant that Mesopotamia was Parthia's for the taking. While the Romans were removing Greece and Macedon from the Hellenistic orbit, the Parthians did the same with Mesopotamia. Babylon, Seleucia-on-the-Tigris and the former Persian capital of Ecbatana all became Parthian in the decade of the 140s BC.

Demetrios II did his best to rectify the situation. His stepson had died (or had been killed by the general who was using him as a puppet king) so the empire was temporarily reunited. This left Demetrios free to march east to take on the Parthians. A capable commander, Demetrios managed several initial successes. Nevertheless, in 138 BC, as the Seleucid force penetrated deeper into the Parthian heartlands, it was ambushed in the mountain passes and Demetrios was taken prisoner.

Mithridates treated his royal captive with great consideration, marrying him to a royal wife and allowing him to live in gilded exile. He looked indulgently upon the king's occasionally frantic efforts to escape, once with a friend who travelled anonymously right across the Parthian kingdom to effect a rescue. The two escaped together but were speedily recaptured. Mithridates did not punish the friend of Demetrios but instead commended him on his loyalty.

When news of the capture of Demetrios reached Syria, this was regarded as a sort of abdication. While a prisoner in Parthia, Demetrios was unable to rule an empire on the brink of chaos so his younger brother became king Antiochus VII by default. Since it was by now obligatory that whoever ruled the Seleucid empire had to marry Cleopatra Thea, the queen was promptly divorced from Demetrios and remarried to the new monarch.

Egypt was unable to take advantage of Seleucid problems and recapture Coele-Syria in the same way that the Parthians had taken Mesopotamia, because Egypt had political problems of its own. Ptolemy VIII Physcon was not a popular ruler, and Cleopatra II was busily plotting to take advantage of that weakness to ensure that her husband-brother was replaced by her son (known to posterity as Ptolemy Memphites). Consequently, Ptolemy Physcon barely had the political strength to keep his throne, let alone embark on potentially risky foreign adventures against the Seleucids.

The year 133 BC saw Pergamon fall under Roman control. This happened in a somewhat bizarre fashion. Attalus II died in 138 BC after ruling the city-state for two decades. Power passed to his nephew Attalus III who did not really want it. The new ruler of Pergamon was a reclusive, studious type who was much more interested in medicine and botany than in politics. He had a close relationship with his mother but, perhaps unsurprisingly, had no offspring. (It is uncertain whether he even married.)

The problem facing a ruler with no obvious heir was that every ambitious noble in the country considered himself eligible to take over when the current incumbent died. Furthermore, whoever was the front-runner to succeed at any given time might decide that, rather than hang on to his leading position, perhaps for decades (Attalus III was still young), it might be better for the current ruler to die immediately. Attalus might have been an unenthusiastic ruler, but he was not a stupid one. He resolved the problem by making the Roman Republic his heir.

No-one wanted Rome to take over Pergamon, so suddenly those aspiring to rule the place developed a deep concern that Attalus should remain a healthy ruler for a long time while they worked to change his mind about the succession. In due course, Attalus might have picked a successor, groomed him to take his place, and politely disinherited Rome. It was a cunning plan with one – literally fatal – flaw. In an uncertain world, no-one could tell when death might strike through illness and Attalus died soon after making his will. Thus, with the stroke of a ruler's pen, Pergamon became a Roman possession.

Chapter 12

Things Fall Apart

The century 132–32 BC is generally seen as a period of decline and decay in the remnants of Alexander's once-mighty empire. The kingdom which once stretched unbroken from the mountains of Afghanistan to the shores of the Adriatic Sea had shrunk to Egypt, Syria, and a hybrid Indo-Greek kingdom that had as much lost interest in affairs in the west as the west had forgotten that it existed.

For much of the period, the Seleucids and Ptolemies were too engaged in internecine palace politics and civil war to care much about the crumbling borders of a shrinking Hellenistic world. Yet to concentrate on their decadent palace politics is to overlook that most people in Alexander's former empire were neither kings nor politicians. By and large, the common people of the region did not really care who was in charge so long as their rulers kept the peace intact and taxes low. By their standards, things in the century before Roman rule could have been worse – except in Asia Minor where people were already under Roman rule and things became about as bad as they could get.

Certainly, for the Greeks in Mesopotamia, the change from Seleucid to Parthian rulers meant mostly that, instead of a distant king in Syria, they had more local rulers who were prepared to put their backs into defending the place. This was necessary too because the same barbarian tribes which had taken down Bactria had no intention of stopping there. The Parthians had to fight hard for Mesopotamia and not just against the Seleucids.

However, the Seleucids were the first of the Parthian problems because Antiochus VII (known as Sidetes because he originated from the Anatolian city of Side) was determined to continue where his brother had left off. First, naturally, he had to suppress the rebellions which generally occurred whenever the Seleucid empire changed rulers, even though the empire was running out of territory in which to have those rebellions.

The decisive approach of Antiochus VII was first felt by the Maccabees, though unfortunately the text relating their deeds runs out before the ascent of the new Seleucid monarch.

While our sources do not give much detail, we know that Antiochus VII attacked Judea, besieged Jerusalem and captured the city. Yet what broke the back of the rebellion was that Antiochus thereafter acted almost as if the Jews had won and arranged a peace settlement which offered the greatest respect to Jewish tradition and religion. This act of statesmanship lanced a festering boil on the western flank of the empire and left Antiochus VII free of distractions and able to march east in his brother's footsteps.

In his Parthian campaign, Antiochus imitated his brother all too closely. He started his campaign with even greater success than Demetrios II had enjoyed. The elderly Mithridates I was unable to prevent the Seleucids from recapturing all of Mesopotamia and indeed, when Mithridates made a final desperate effort to do so, he was defeated and killed in battle.

The campaign of Antiochus VII shows yet again that the failure of the Seleucid empire was, above all, a political failure. Properly led and organized, the Seleucid army was as capable of enforcing the royal will as it had ever been. However, as the following decades were to show, the royal family was simply not up to the challenge of leadership. Demetrios II and his brother Antiochus VII were the last effective rulers of the empire.

The new Parthian king was Phraates II. He also was a capable ruler, and he took immediate steps to contain the Seleucid threat. Firstly, he released Demetrios from captivity. The motive was anything but charitable, since Phraates intended that once the Seleucids had two kings, the result would be a civil war which could only be to his advantage. Even as Demetrios made his way westwards, Phraates did the same, taking with him a compact but highly mobile army. This army entered Seleucid-occupied territory without Antiochus even knowing it was there.

Consequently, when unrest broke out in a part of his newly recaptured domains, Antiochus did not bother to muster all of his army (which was currently stood down after the end of the campaigning season). Instead, he took only a small force for what was intended to be little more than a police action rather than a pitched battle against a Parthian army. The result was that Antiochus' tiny force ended up fighting a very one-sided battle in which the king perished.

The Seleucid empire was down to just one king again and Demetrios had to run hard for the border in order to avoid recapture by Phraates, who immediately realized that he had made a mistake in releasing him. It would be fair to say that the Syrian people were less than impressed by Demetrios' return. They had seen the highly competent and statesmanlike Antiochus march off to the east and had seen the unloved Demetrios return in his place, followed by whatever dribs and drabs of the army that had managed to fight its way out of Mesopotamia, which was now permanently a Parthian possession. Fortunately for the Seleucids, Phraates was unable to follow up his success by invading Syria because he had now to turn to deal with the same wave of barbarian invaders which had already wiped out Bactria. However, as the children of Antiochus had joined their father in the supposedly pacified east, Phraates decided to marry the daughter – a Laodice, of course – and keep the son (a Seleucus) for release in Syria when this might cause maximum disruption. (At least this can be inferred from Justin 38.10. Other sources have the children as the offspring of Demetrios II, whom Antiochus was keeping with him to prevent them from causing trouble in Syria during his absence.)

Also unimpressed by the return of Demetrios was Cleopatra Thea who discovered first that she was a widow and second that she was about to be married once again to Demetrios as her former husband took over the kingdom once more. The palpable lack of enthusiasm for Demetrios by both his former wife and his former kingdom inspired yet another rebellion.

The weakened Seleucid empire was now dragged into a proxy war between Cleopatra II and Ptolemy Physcon of Egypt. Cleopatra came to Syria to join Demetrios and finance his military campaigns, whereupon Ptolemy sponsored the usurper who is known today as Alexander Zabinas. Lacking political support, Demetrios struggled on with his unenthusiastic army until he suffered a minor defeat near Damascus. He retreated to the city of Ptolemais and discovered that Cleopatra Thea had got there before him.

Cleopatra's dislike of Demetrios had only increased since his return to Syria and she was further angered because her husband had not only taken a Parthian bride during his enforced absence but also had children by her. Also, she was probably sick of her status as the automatic wife of whoever was ruling the Seleucid empire at a given time. In his turn, Demetrios was probably outraged to find that, in his hour of need, his wife had no intention of standing by her man (she closed the gates of Ptolemais against him) but, instead, actively wanted him dead. Demetrios attempted to escape by sea to Tyre but the ship's crew killed him for reasons which remain unclear.

Cleopatra Thea did not have to marry the next ruler of the Seleucid empire because she herself was in effect that ruler, though ostensibly the regent for her sons. By now, in 126 BC, the empire consisted only of Syria and parts of pirate-infested Cilicia, for Judea had become largely autonomous and many Phoenician cities on the Levant had quietly evicted their Seleucid governors to become independent.

Even as one of the last two remaining Hellenistic kingdoms, the Seleucid 'empire' was fast becoming irrelevant in international affairs. As a result of this, the attention of historians in the ancient era largely moved away from Seleucid affairs to the more portentous growth of Rome's empire and the ever-entertaining soap-opera of the Egyptian royal family. Our sources for the Seleucids now become steadily more degraded, out-of-date and contradictory, even as palace politics became more obscure and complicated. Therefore, much of what is given as fact in this chapter is largely the common consensus among modern historians, with many dissenters offering other opinions in an ongoing academic debate of immense complexity.

Egypt

If politics in the Seleucid empire were dysfunctional, this was but a minor spat compared with the three-ring circus going on in Egypt. Here, the relationship between Ptolemy Physcon and his sister/wife Cleopatra II had broken down completely, mainly due to ferocious rivalry between Cleopatra II and her daughter, who was Ptolemy's other wife, Cleopatra III (the sister of Cleopatra Thea).

Cleopatra II had a son with Ptolemy VII Physcon, which strengthened her position in court, but Cleopatra was further angered by Ptolemy's fecundity with his legion of royal mistresses. These produced an apparently never-ending stream of children who had to be found positions at court as they came of age.

In 132 BC, Cleopatra II had decided enough was enough and staged a palace coup. She failed to capture her brother who escaped to Cyprus with the rest of the royal family. This included the joint son of Ptolemy Physcon and Cleopatra and, in a ghastly act if disinheritance, Ptolemy had the son killed and dismembered. He sent the pieces to Cleopatra II as a birthday gift. In 127 BC, Ptolemy had strengthened his position to the point where he could force his return to the Egyptian mainland and Cleopatra II was in turn driven out. She took shelter with Demetrios in Syria, as described above.

Cleopatra II was able to finance the military campaigns of Demetrios because she had taken the royal treasury with her as she departed from Egypt. Ptolemy Physcon may not have missed his sister/wife at all but he certainly missed the treasury. Also, Cleopatra II was popular in upper Egypt. This mattered because, although the Egyptian people had to date been remarkably tolerant of the shenanigans of their royal family, no-one wanted a repeat of the devastating civil war of a generation before which had pitched nationalist upper Egypt against the more Hellenized north.

Consequently, Cleopatra Thea was able to negotiate the reconciliation of her mother with Ptolemy Physcon and her sister. Cleopatra II (and the treasury) eventually returned from exile in a carefully staged reconciliation. Thereafter, the three rulers of Egypt worked together and appeared at least to tolerate one another.

A joint edict re-codifying and reforming Egyptian law was issued in 118 BC which represented the first serious effort at government by the royal family in decades. Fortunately for the Ptolemaic dynasty, most of the actual administration of Egypt was done by a relatively competent class of civil servants who worked closely with the country's priesthood. In most of Egypt, and especially in the rural areas, the system itself had very much stood the test of time. Most Egyptians lived rather as their ancestors had done for centuries and the government was stabilized by the weight of long tradition.

Cleopatra II had the satisfaction of outliving all her rivals and contemporaries apart from her despised daughter. In Syria, the Parthian king Phraates released his brother-in-law Seleucus who promptly set about deposing Cleopatra Thea and establishing himself as Seleucus V. Cleopatra Thea proved unexpectedly capable at mustering a defence for a situation she had probably anticipated. Seleucus ended up being put to death at the hands of his mother after a brief and remarkably unsuccessful military campaign.

Regrettably, while the Egyptians were used to periods of queenly rule, there was no precedent for a woman ruling the Seleucid empire, especially since Cleopatra Thea had other sons who could do the job (apart from the now deceased Seleucus V). While these sons were minors, Cleopatra Thea ruled her diminished empire competently. Under the nominal command of her son Antiochus VIII, the usurper Alexander Zabinas was finally captured and executed.

As it happened, this success was to be the death of Cleopatra Thea. Antiochus VIII felt that he was now quite capable of ruling and he chafed under the overbearing hand of his mother. The mother in turn reflected upon the fact that she had another son in reserve and the one she had raised to the throne was acting uncomfortably too much like a king. Mother-son relations became strained. So strained in fact that, when Cleopatra Thea offered her son a beaker of wine one day, her son was immediately suspicious of this uncharacteristic behaviour. Antiochus demanded that his mother drink the wine herself and was neither surprised nor disappointed when the draught proved fatal. (At least this was Antiochus' version and there were no survivors to dispute it.)

Thus in 121 BC Cleopatra Thea died in Syria. In 116 BC, Ptolemy VIII died in Egypt at the age of sixty-six. This was a relatively ripe old age, given that the other Pharaohs in the half-century before him had all died young. It also meant that he died on the verge of celebrating the thirtieth anniversary of the most turbulent marriage in Hellenistic history and – given the state of marriage among Hellenistic monarchs – this is quite a claim. Cleopatra II herself died a few months later. This may have been because she was in poor health and had been hanging on for the pleasure of outlasting her husband or because (by some other suggestions) Cleopatra III now saw the chance to dispose of the last obstacle to her sole rule and enthusiastically took it.

If Cleopatra III expected things to go smoothly thereafter, she could not have been following Egyptian politics. Cleopatra had five children with Ptolemy Physcon. Three were daughters, two of whom were called Cleopatra and one was called Tryphaenea. Tryphaenea left Egyptian politics early for the equally dangerous job of becoming wife to the Seleucid king Antiochus VIII. This left the two Cleopatras available as wives for their brothers, if so required. These two brothers were Ptolemy IX and Ptolemy X and they did not get along.

In part, this was because Cleopatra III deliberately cultivated the rivalry between her sons and because the people of Alexandria (for the most part a cosmopolitan mix of Greeks, Jews and native Egyptians) were often out of step with the rest of the country in their choice of ruler. Therefore, a deposed Pharaoh always had the option of either appealing to the Alexandrian mob or taking sanctuary in Cyprus.

In a tragi-comic farce, the rule of Egypt went first, in 116 BC, to Ptolemy IX. Then, when Cleopatra III decided that her son was becoming dangerously independent, she had him deposed in 110 BC and replaced with Ptolemy X. Then, in 109 BC, Ptolemy IX came storming back again and deposed his brother. Cleopatra III intervened and defeated Ptolemy IX in battle near Pelusium. In 107 BC, Ptolemy X was back on the throne with his mother now officially his co-ruler. Ptolemy X liked being ruled by his mother no more than had his older brother and, after six difficult years, he had her executed.

The problem with this matricide was that Cleopatra III was popular and competent while Ptolemy X was not. After a politically rough decade, Ptolemy was forced from the throne by his outraged citizenry and exiled in Syria. As a further display of his political ineptitude, Ptolemy X recruited a mercenary army he could not afford and re-took Alexandria. Then he outraged the entire Hellenistic world (or what was left of it) by melting down the golden sarcophagus of Alexander the Great to pay his army. The furious Alexandrians again rose in rebellion and Ptolemy X fled to Cyprus. There he was killed by a rogue general called Chaereas. Ptolemy IX took over Egypt again.

The shambolic state of Ptolemaic rule in Egypt was completely self-inflicted. Under competent rulers, there was nothing to prevent Egypt from being a well-organized and prosperous kingdom, just as it had been under the earlier Ptolemies. As it was, Ptolemy X demonstrated that the whole country was in so shambolic a state that it could be taken by a rag-tag mercenary army. Egypt was very fortunate that at this time there was no other threat to the kingdom, for even a well-organized bandit chief was probably capable of conquering the place by playing the various factions off against one another.

However, the Seleucids were in no shape to attack anything, and indeed their empire was struggling for survival amid its own political crises. To the south, the once-threatening Numidian and Kushite kingdoms had problems of their own. (Modern research has linked to the increasing desertification of the south. This, combined with over-use of timber and degradation of the soil, meant that the south was in a state of chaos from which it would not emerge for generations). To the east and west, Egypt was protected by desert and sea – natural barriers which defended the kingdom far better than its inept rulers could do. In the absence of external threat, a moderately competent and highly experienced lower tier of government was able to keep the country functioning despite the best efforts of its rulers to ruin it.

Rome Distracted

The obvious predator to take down the dysfunctional kingdoms of the Seleucids and Ptolemies was Rome – the warrior Republic which had already absorbed the Phoenician-ruled domains of Carthage and the Hellenistic states of Sicily, Greece and Macedon. Yet, in the period of 130–60 BC, Rome played remarkably little part in the implosion of the last two Hellenistic kingdoms.

This was because the Romans had problems of their own, and these were also largely self-inflicted. First, the Romans got into a damaging war with the Numidians in north Africa – a war they had trouble getting out of because of the incompetence and venality of the generals who fought it. (The Numidian king Jugurtha seems several times to have simply bribed the Roman commanders to go away.)

Bracketing the Jugurthine War of 112–106 BC was a threat for which the Romans were certainly not responsible – a massive wave of Germanic warriors called the Cimbri who swept down from the north and threatened the very existence of Rome. Indeed, Rome might have fallen after the battle of Arousio in 105 BC which cost the Romans some 80,000 lives. Italy was saved when the barbarians chose instead to pillage Spain. When the Cimbri did return in 102 BC, the Romans were ready for them.

A titanic series of battles followed, culminating in a decisive encounter in northern Italy at Vercellae in 101 BC. Here, the Cimbri were virtually wiped out. They lost (at a very rough estimate) 160,000 men with another 50,000 captured and enslaved, figures which amounted to the loss of the entire male population of the nation.

Yet, before Rome could return its attention to the east, there followed a rebellion of Rome's allies – a revolt which had been long brewing. Once so generous with their citizenship that they literally forced it upon conquered communities, the Romans after the Punic wars had limited the citizenship and the privileges it bestowed. This would have been acceptable to the people of Italy if the Roman aristocracy did not abuse the power of Rome in Italy to seize land and property. Roman citizens had legal protection from such abuse and, having failed to get that protection, Rome's Italian allies revolted.

At this point, in 88 BC, Rome's catastrophic mismanagement of the former kingdom of Pergamon led to yet more difficulties. The Romans had never before had a province as profitable as the former kingdom, which they renamed the province of Asia. At this time, Roman politicians had great need of money. Not only was their nation fighting a series of very expensive wars but the Roman state was crippled by corruption.

The Roman voters expected to be paid for their vote by lavish public services or even direct bribes from a successful candidate and the amount of money needed for a successful electoral campaign rose exponentially. Roman aristocrats often invested everything they had in a bid to get elected and then borrowed more. Then, once elected to a foreign command, they would do their very best to recoup their expenses from the provincials they were sent to govern. It was said that a Roman aristocrat needed to make three fortunes for each office held. One to get elected to a lucrative foreign command in the first place, one to bribe juries for the inevitable (and usually justified) charges of extortion and corruption while in office and one to finance the next electoral campaign.

The people who paid for all this were largely the unfortunate citizens of Asia Minor. Taxes rose inexorably while governors and their staff also employed a raft of revenue-raising devices of dubious legality. (All of these are described in detail in one of the few successful indictments of a corrupt governor. This was the prosecution of one Verres by an up-and-coming lawyer called Marcus Cicero. Cicero delivered his indictment in 70 BC but the same abuses in Asia had gone unpunished for decades.)

By 90 BC, Rome had justifiably earned the bitter hatred of the Italians and the people of Asia Minor. They were to pay terribly.

By 88 BC, Rome had not one but two major wars on its hands. In 90 BC, the Italian allies of Rome had united in rebellion. (Allies are 'Socii' in Latin which is why this is usually called the 'Social War'.) Fighting against the state's own allies was a very different task to fighting Hellenistic armies. For a start, the allies used the same formations, tactics and equipment as the Romans and they were every bit as stubborn and bloody-minded. Secondly, they knew the countryside and their enemies intimately – in fact, many rebel generals were personal friends with their opposite numbers on the Roman side. By 89 BC, Rome was fighting for its very existence.

At this point, an opportunistic and greedy official called Aquillius led a Roman delegation to Asia Minor to confront the king of the expansionist kingdom of Pontus. This was Mithridates VI, sometimes called 'The Great'. It was no part of the delegation's official brief to provoke a war between Pontus and Rome, yet this is exactly what Aquillius set out to do. Possibly he was prompted by political masters back in Rome who had their own agenda or perhaps he simply saw the opportunity for vast profits and took it.

Pontus was a kingdom to the east of Pergamon and Bithynia, on the northern shore of what is today Turkey. A series of capable rulers (mostly called Mithridates) had used the decline of Seleucid influence to build themselves a tidy kingdom which Mithridates VI substantially increased when he came to power. Conquering and looting such a kingdom would be a very profitable enterprise. Many Roman aristocrats were looking forward to the chance and, though the timing was not ideal, Aquillius had his chance in 88 BC – an opportunity he would not get again.

Clearly, he believed that the Roman troops already in Asia Minor were sufficient for the task, especially as these were backed up by those of the king of Bithynia. The Bithynian king was totally subordinate to Rome and, when Aquillius told him to provoke a war with Pontus, the king had no choice but to obey. In short, the plan of Aquillius worked perfectly, right up to the outbreak of war. Then it was discovered that Mithridates was a highly competent general with an excellent army. In a matter of months, the attacking Romans were driven out of Pontus, out of Bithynia and out of their new province of Asia. Aquillius was captured and killed in a manner suited to his motives for starting the war. Molten gold was poured down his throat.

The way that the peoples of Asia Minor reacted to this barbaric execution was telling. They were ecstatic that a corrupt Roman official had finally gotten his comeuppance. When Mithridates thereafter ordered the cities under his control to kill every Roman or Italian they could find, the order was enthusiastically obeyed. Some 80,000 men, women and children were slaughtered in a gory demonstration of exactly how much the Romans and Italians had made themselves hated in their efforts to extract profits from their eastern possessions.

Family life with the Seleucids

The Seleucids were unable to exploit Rome's distractions and the turmoil in Asia Minor because they had enough chaos and distractions to immobilize the kingdom at home. A whirlwind summary of the situation follows, though the point to bear in mind through the storm of Antiochuses, Seleucuses and Cleopatras is that the Seleucids were far too busy fighting, assassinating and otherwise doing away with one another to have much interest in even governing their crumbling empire, let alone expanding it.

Antiochus VIII spent most of his reign of 121–96 BC fighting a relative and rival, Antiochus IX, for what was left of the empire. As mentioned above, he had married Cleopatra III's daughter Tryphaenea. Meanwhile, Antiochus IX had married another Ptolemaic princess, Cleopatra IV, who was Tryphaenea's sister.

Cleopatra IV had been briefly married to her brother Ptolemy IX until her mother Cleopatra III ordered the couple to divorce as she now favoured Ptolemy X. Once Cleopatra IV had remarried and come to Syria, she and her sister were on opposite sides in that nation's civil war. Tryphaenea proved herself a true Ptolemy when her sister was captured in Antioch. Although Cleopatra IV sought sanctuary in a temple, Tryphaenea sent troops who executed her sister. This happened despite the protestations of Antiochus VIII. The king felt no love for his sister-in-law but feared the wrath of the gods. And indeed, the gods duly smote the unfortunate Antiochus VIII who was assassinated in 96 BC.

By then, Tryphaenea had been dead for over a decade. Whether accidentally, or accidentally on purpose, Antiochus VIII had allowed her to be captured as he retreated after an unsuccessful clash with his rival Antiochus IX. Antiochus IX avenged the death of Cleopatra IV by having Tryphaenea sacrificed to the spirit of his dead wife. Antiochus IX was killed in the same year as Antiochus VIII by Seleucus VI, the son of Tryphaenea who defeated Antiochus IX in battle and took over the empire. Seleucus lasted for around two years before a mob, exasperated by his tyrannical misrule and the imposition of high taxes, staged a riot in which he perished.

Seleucus was replaced by Demetrios III who was actually a competent ruler. Demetrios followed in the footsteps of most competent Seleucid rulers of his era. That is, he suppressed local rebellions with a degree of success, campaigned successfully in Judea, and then turned his attention to the Parthians. He was captured by a Parthian ally and taken to Parthia where he lived a comfortable life as a Parthian hostage until he died of illness (possible) or was killed when he outlived his usefulness (probable). Rule of the Seleucid empire fell to Philip Philadelphus, another son of Antiochus VIII and Tryphaenea, though naturally his rule was immediately challenged in yet another rebellion and civil war.

The Fall of the Seleucid Empire

While various Seleucid monarchs were usurping, assassinating and warring with one another, large parts of their empire were falling away. Judea was largely autonomous despite spasmodic attempts by the

Seleucids to restore their authority there. Phoenician cities of the Levant such as Byblos and Tyre remained nominally Seleucid but, in fact, politely ignored their so-called rulers, kept tax revenues for themselves and chose their own governments, in the full knowledge that the Seleucids could do nothing about it.

Mesopotamia and everything east of the Euphrates river were now Parthian possessions and, in the north-east, the Armenians had thrown off any pretence of being Seleucid vassals. Under their king Tigranes, the Armenians had expanded into Asia Minor and added to their nascent empire by snapping up whatever former Seleucid possessions the tides of civil war left unguarded. In short, if histories of the later Seleucid empire seem scant, it is because the empire which once stretched from the Mediterranean coast to Afghanistan now consisted of a few cities in northern Syria which were in a semi-permanent state of civil war. Contemporary historians had better things to do than record who was currently on top in a never-ending dogfight.

By 83 BC, even the cities of Syria had become war-weary and disillusioned with the current dynasty and its feuding family members. They decided that a complete change of ruler was the only solution and they took the unprecedented step of inviting Tigranes of Armenia to take over the remnants of the empire. Tigranes was confident enough to accept the challenge and his troops took over Syria with little opposition.

At the time, Syria's unending civil war was a contest between another daughter of Cleopatra III known today as Cleopatra Selene, and Philip Philadelphus. Philip vanishes without trace, after Tigranes' invasion, while Cleopatra was captured and executed. Armenia, for years a vassal state of the Seleucid empire, was now master of the Seleucid heartlands.

Armenia's nascent empire now stretched from the south-east shore of the Black Sea to the Caspian Sea in the east and to the Mediterranean coast to the west. Southward expansion past the headwaters of the Tigris and Euphrates was checked by the Parthians who had, by now, inherited much of the former empire of the Persians who had preceded Alexander. Nevertheless, Tigranes was able to stretch his empire further by subjugating Cappadocia into a client state and conquering some Phoenician cities.

The problem with the creation of such an empire was that it was certain to attract the predatory interest of Rome as soon as Rome recovered from its current difficulties. Recover Rome did, though not without much pain, bloodshed, and damage to its Republican constitution. The Italian rebels were either defeated on the battlefield or reconciled with Rome by a promise to give the citizenship to anyone who was not at the time trying to kill them to get it. This left the Romans free to raise an army to take on Mithridates of Pontus, although a squabble over who should get the potentially profitable command degenerated into a full-blown civil war.

The winner of that civil war was Cornelius Sulla who started by taking his army east, despite recall orders issued by an opposing faction who had staged a counter-coup in Rome. By that time, Mithridates had expanded his empire into Greece, and had to be summarily ejected by Sulla's legions. Needing to sort out his enemies in Italy, Sulla made a peace with Mithridates which basically involved Mithridates returning his kingdom to its pre-war borders.

Mithridates suffered no punishment for the tens of thousands of Romans and Italians massacred on his orders. Instead the cities of Roman Asia Minor paid – literally – in crippling taxes and fines levied as punishment for their behaviour and because Sulla urgently needed money. Thousands of Greeks from Asia Minor were forced by poverty to emigrate to Roman territories in the west. Thousands more went to Italy involuntarily as slaves – former citizens of Rome's eastern allies who now paid for their debts with the loss of their freedom. Tragic as this was for the individuals concerned, it led to a huge influx of often educated and skilled Greeks into the Roman west. Greek teachers and doctors became standard for the upper classes, and Greek became the second language of the Roman aristocracy.

With order restored in Italy, a former subordinate of Sulla, Lucullus, was sent to wind up the unfinished business with Mithridates. Instead, he chose the more lucrative target of Armenia and comprehensively defeated Tigranes in battle. However, although Lucullus became one of the wealthiest men in Rome as a result of his victories, he did not share the wealth with his troops and they mutinied. In 67 BC, Lucullus was replaced by another former Sullan supporter, Gnaeus Pompeius Magnus, known today as Pompey the Great.

Pompey was a master of logistics and he quickly boxed Mithridates into one of his northern castles, where the king committed suicide. Tigranes of Armenia found himself caught in a three-way war between Pompey, his rebellious son and the Parthians who invaded from the south. Realizing that he was trapped, the wily monarch threw himself on Pompey's mercy. He was allowed to keep his kingdom (restored to its original borders) for the payment of a huge fine. However, he was forced to give up his possession of Syria and other parts of the Seleucid empire which he had seized.

These Seleucid possessions now became part of the new Roman province of Syria. Other formerly Seleucid cities were granted autonomy under Roman protection, and Judea became a subordinate kingdom of Syria (though not without protest – Pompey had to fight a brisk military campaign and storm the temple in Jerusalem before the Jews agreed to accept their new status). The last of the Seleucids was probably a young man called Philip II, who may have reigned briefly as a client king of Pompey.

Plans were afoot to marry the shadow king to Berenice VI of Egypt but either the Roman authorities or Berenice disapproved of the match and Philip was quietly murdered. In this at least, Philip followed the example of his royal predecessors. Kingship of the Seleucid empire was a dangerous business. From the assassination of the founder Seleucus I in 281 BC to the murder of his last successor around 250 years later, ruling the empire was one of the most dangerous jobs on earth. Of the thirty-plus monarchs and pretenders to the Seleucid throne since Antiochus the Great in 187 BC, only one may have died naturally (and Antiochus the Great and his two predecessors also died violently).

In the north, Pontus and Bithynia became a merged Roman province, and other kingdoms in the region continued as subject states subordinate to Rome. Thus by 63 BC, the Seleucid empire, once the largest empire in the known world, had completely vanished and the Roman era of the Middle East had begun.

Chapter 13

Sleeping with the Enemy – Cleopatra VII and the Fall of Egypt

Despite his irregular career, Ptolemy IX could count his reign as a personal success which we shall summarize again here. Actually, he had two reigns – the first from 116 BC until 107 BC, when he was very much junior Pharaoh to his pushy mother Cleopatra III. Following mother's orders, Ptolemy IX had divorced his sister Cleopatra IV and married another sibling, today known as Cleopatra Selene. (It will be remembered that Cleopatra IV went on to marry the Seleucid Antiochus IX and came to a sticky end in that country's unending civil wars.)

Despite (or because of) this divorce, relations between Ptolemy IX and his mother did not improve and Cleopatra III eventually forced Ptolemy IX from the throne. Ptolemy's sister/wife did not follow him into exile, and instead married Ptolemy X, the son whom Cleopatra III had chosen to replace him. When Ptolemy X's misrule led to his death, Cleopatra Selene went to Syria and was killed by Tigranes of Armenia, while Ptolemy IX returned to become Pharaoh of Egypt.

This second reign was from 88–81 BC. During this time, Ptolemy IX restored a modicum of order in the country which included putting down a nascent rebellion in the southern interior. There are also signs that, at this period, there was further temple-building and restoration – always a sign that the pharaoh was trying to play nicely with the country's priestly administrators. This was particularly necessary at this time as Alexandria was becoming definitely unruly, to the point of being ungovernable, and the Ptolemies needed the support of the rest of Egypt to stay in power.

When Ptolemy IX died, this left his daughter Berenice III (who was possibly also his wife) in nominal charge of the country. Berenice was well aware that powerful factions in the court were manoeuvring to replace her and worked hard to counter their intrigues by building herself a strong popular base among the people, especially with the Alexandrians.

Here she both failed and succeeded. She failed in that palace courtiers forced her to marry her half-brother Ptolemy XI, who promptly had his new wife killed nineteen days later. She succeeded in that her courtiers quickly realized that they should not have done this because the outraged Alexandrians subsequently rose in rebellion and lynched Ptolemy XI and his backers at court.

The higher than usual rate of attrition among the Ptolemies meant that the kingdom's stock of family members had run low. However, Egypt had now become so accustomed to rule by the Ptolemies that there was little serious effort to establish another dynasty. Instead a – possibly illegitimate – son of Ptolemy IX was fished out of exile from Pontus in Asia Minor and informed that he was now Ptolemy XII.

This Ptolemy is often called Ptolemy Auletes from his fondness for playing the flute at religious festivals. No-one had ever expected that he would ascend to the throne so accounts of his origins are somewhat sketchy. Many contend that he was born of a concubine of Ptolemy IX while the latter was exiled in Cyprus. Others point out that he has a strong claim to the ill-fated Cleopatra IV as his mother. It does not help that, by now, even contemporary historians were getting tangled in the intermarried web of Cleopatras and Ptolemies.

For example, it is known that on his arrival in Egypt, Ptolemy married Cleopatra V who was either his sister, half-sister or cousin. She may well also have been Cleopatra VI because by now historians were losing track. It may be that Cleopatra V died in childbirth and was replaced by Cleopatra VI without most of the Mediterranean world paying attention for, by now, Egypt was something of a backwater in a world dominated by Rome and the struggles of its dynasts and failing republican system.

The most significant fact about Cleopatra V(I) is that she was probably the mother of Cleopatra VII whom, to most people of later eras, is the only Cleopatra that matters.

The main challenge facing Ptolemy Auletes was not keeping track of his wives but fending off the increasingly predatory advances of Rome. The cost of maintaining status in the dysfunctional Roman political system had produced increasing numbers of Roman aristocrats desperate for cash and Egypt was relatively rich. This was largely due to the fact that Egypt's own politics had been too dysfunctional for the kingdom to be organized enough to go to war with anyone. To generalize heroically, the Egyptian economy had originally been set up by the first Ptolemies with the assumption that the nation would need a large military budget. Much of that budget was currently unused so Egypt currently had a financial surplus, helped by the fact that crops had recently been better than average.

It was not long before factions of the Roman senate made their first play for the wealth of Egypt. They produced a 'will' of very dubious provenance, by which Ptolemy XI had allegedly left his kingdom to the Romans rather as Attalus III had done with Pergamon. Facing the annexation of his country, Ptolemy Auletes demonstrated that he understood well what was happening. If the problem was Roman greed, he was happy to bribe the most influential Romans. One bribe, in the form of money and military support, went to Pompey who was currently in the Levant tidying up the remnants of the Seleucid empire. Pompey was already vastly wealthy from his conquests but he appreciated not having to spend his own money anyway. He was also grateful for the military support as the sudden expansion of Rome's domains had left his army somewhat over-stretched.

Another judicious bribe went to one of the Roman consuls of that year – an ambitious but cash-strapped rising political star called Caius Julius Caesar. Caesar passed legislation that recognized Ptolemy Auletes as the legitimate king of Egypt. He compensated the faction seeking annexation by stripping Egypt of its last overseas possession of Cyprus and passing the island over to the Roman state to be plundered.

Ptolemy Auletes' totally submissive attitude to Rome secured him the title of 'Friend of the Roman People', a status less flatteringly known to modern historians as 'client king'. This outraged the volatile Alexandrians, who remembered the days when Egypt was part of an empire that spanned all of central Asia, and one of the dominant kingdoms when that empire broke up. Within a few months, while Rome continued to recognize Ptolemy Auletes as king of Egypt, it was very easy for prominent Romans to recognize him in person – he was a permanent guest at Pompey's villa just outside the Rome itself as he tried to persuade the Egyptian people not to lynch him should he return. Meanwhile, the administration of Egypt was handled in his absence by Ptolemy's wife and eldest daughter Berenice IV.

Thus matters rested until 57 BC, when Ptolemy Auletes' wife died, leaving Berenice IV in sole charge. Berenice rather liked her job and sent an embassy to Rome asking that she be confirmed as Egypt's ruler. Borrowing heavily against his future return and access to the Egyptian treasury, Ptolemy Auletes managed to bribe enough senators to keep open the question of who ruled Egypt. A further dive into near-bankruptcy arranged for the assassination of the Egyptian delegation. Further monies were distributed to the Roman authorities to ensure that no-one investigated too closely the very convenient deaths of several Romans who were vocal supporters of Berenice.

Then, deciding that a more proactive approach was needed, Ptolemy Auletes took himself east. While he was unable to get to Egypt himself, he was able to get into the retinue of the Roman governor of Syria. At the time, Rome's interest had shifted to Caesar's war in Gaul and the efforts of the senate to impeach him for war crimes committed in that country. The Roman governor of Syria gambled that he would be able to bribe his way out of trouble if he allowed Ptolemy Auletes to pay him a massive sum in return for restoring him to the throne. In 56 BC, a triumphant Ptolemy Auletes was carried back to power by the Roman legions. The first thing he did on retaking the throne of his now bankrupt country was to execute his ungrateful daughter.

In 51 BC, Ptolemy Auletes passed away. By then he had made his surviving daughter Cleopatra VII his co-regent and expected that she would marry her brother Ptolemy XIII as a co-regent. However, the reality was that the Egyptian kingdom was no longer his to dispose of – the final decision now rested with Rome.

As to the Cleopatra in question, the biographer Plutarch says this of her:

> It is not that in itself her beauty was incomparable nor (so they say) was it the first thing that struck one about her. But when she talked, her conversation was persuasive – partly because this was combined by her sheer presence and irresistible charm. There was something

stimulating about the way she interacted with others and the mellow tones of her voice, while her tongue was like a many-stringed instrument which she could use in whatever language she wanted.

Plutarch *Antony* 27.2

Indeed, coins depicting Cleopatra show a young woman with her hair in a severe bun. She has a viciously hooked nose and a prominent chin. Doubtless this charmless image was designed purposely by Cleopatra's coiners who wanted to show her subjects a competent ruler rather than the alluring sexpot of later legend. It is also claimed that Cleopatra was the first of her line to be fluent in Egyptian a fact that, if true, tells us much about the relationships of the Ptolemies with their subjects.

Cleopatra was eighteen when she came to the throne. This was young, but better than her co-ruler Ptolemy XIII who was just ten years old. Cleopatra was thus the dominant member of the ruling couple, a fact which did not sit well with some members of the court. Even while her father was alive, Cleopatra had shown herself as strong-willed and competent while those wanting to be the power behind the throne wanted a weak and compliant ruler. Consequently, in 49 BC, these courtiers staged a palace coup and evicted Cleopatra from the throne, leaving Ptolemy XIII as a puppet ruler.

The rest of the world paid little attention for in that same year, Julius Caesar returned from Gaul, marched his armies across the little river Rubicon and, in the process, declared war on the Roman senate. The Mediterranean world was immediately convulsed with war. Caesar and his veteran army quickly took charge of Italy, for Pompey – whom the senate appointed as their commander-in-chief – was unable to raise the troops to prevent this. Instead, Pompey (with much of the senate in tow) retreated to Greece while Caesar went on to fight the senate's supporters in Spain.

In Africa, west of Egypt, another lively war was being fought between Caesarian and senatorial proxies while the client states in the former Seleucid empire desperately tried to work out which side they should take in the struggle. Because Pompey had been recently campaigning in that region, many of the rulers owed him allegiance. For example, Antipater the Idumaean, who at that time was an important official in Judea, initially threw his weight behind Pompey. (The political alignments and re-alignments of Judea are both well documented and typical of the experience of other former Seleucid Mediterranean states and Judea can thus serve as an exemplar for the rest.)

By the end of the year, Caesar was installed as dictator in Rome and Cleopatra was an exile in Syria. The year 48 BC was a decisive year for both because, after narrowly avoiding catastrophe when he followed Pompey to Greece, Caesar defeated Pompey's less experienced army at Pharsalus and then followed the beaten Pompey as he fled to Egypt.

By now, Egypt was the only part of the Mediterranean world not under Caesar's direct power, though it says something for the degree to which Pompey's hopes had been crushed that he needed to find sanctuary there. It had been decades since Egypt was truly independent of Rome. The advisors of young Ptolemy XIII were horrified by the arrival of their unwelcome visitor and had him murdered even before he set foot on Egyptian soil. When Caesar arrived a month later, the Egyptians presented him with promises of their complete allegiance – and the head of Pompey.

Caesar claimed to have been appalled by this treatment of his rival. Of course, he could afford to profess shock at Pompey's end now that the man was safely dead, but his anger at the Egyptians appears to have been genuine. Caesar and Pompey had got along well as individuals (Pompey had even been Caesar's son-in-law until the death of his wife) and the whole civil war had been a political rather than personal feud.

Therefore, when Cleopatra had herself smuggled into Caesar's presence – in a Persian rug, according to legend – Caesar was ready to undertake serious talks about regime change in Egypt. The supporters of Ptolemy XIII objected vehemently to this proposition and Caesar was not able to immediately enforce his will. This was because he had not come to Egypt expecting to fight a war and much of his army was elsewhere. Nevertheless, Caesar did have the loyal and highly experienced Legio VI Ferrata with him. Though Caesar's men were outnumbered, they were veterans while the more numerous followers of the young Ptolemy were both inexperienced and unenthusiastic about dying for their pharaoh.

Caesar – or more probably one of his legionary commanders – wrote a detailed account of the struggle for Egypt in *The Alexandrine War*, a text which still survives today. Alexandria suffered in the fighting and the famous Library of Alexandria was partly burned. Caesar gained some relief with the arrival of fresh troops. These were led by Antipater the Idumaean of Judea who had seen the chance to redeem himself for his earlier support of Pompey and had adroitly switched sides. In the end, matters were decided in a battle alongside the Nile. Afterwards, Ptolemy XIII was drowned while fleeing the battlefield with the remnants of his defeated army.

Even after victory, Caesar and Cleopatra continued to work closely together – so closely, in fact, that in 47 BC Cleopatra gave birth to Caesar's son, known today as Caesarion. The pair did a sort of royal tour through Egypt and then together returned to Rome. Royalty were by tradition forbidden to enter the city of Rome itself so Cleopatra was installed in Caesar's trans-Tibertine villa. (This was fortunate as Caesar already had a wife living in Rome, an unhappy lady called Calpurnia.) In theory, Cleopatra was also married, her current husband being her youngest brother – a nonentity called Ptolemy XIV. This brother remained in Egypt as the figurehead of the administration headed by the country's absent queen.

It was fortunate that the Egyptian administration was largely autonomous, for Cleopatra remained in Rome until 44 BC as a general embarrassment to the senate. Cleopatra's presence was added to a list of senatorial grudges which grew until Caesar was assassinated by his senators on the infamous Ides of March. On news of the assassination, Cleopatra took her son (and Caesar's) and fled to Egypt to await the outcome of subsequent developments. One of the first events following her arrival in Alexandria was the suspiciously convenient death of her husband. Thereafter, Cleopatra ruled in conjunction with her son, who officially became Ptolemy XV Caesarion.

It would not be fair to say that Cleopatra spent until 41 BC sitting on the sidelines of the war between the assassins and Caesar's successors because, over recent years, the huge disbursements to Romans from the Egyptian treasury had left the country on the verge of ruin. Cleopatra spent the time working hard to stave off financial collapse. The assassins of Caesar, like Pompey before them, withdrew eastwards to Greece and demanded the allegiance of eastern kingdoms – including Judea.

Cleopatra had no intention of committing herself until the struggle had played out but she gave lip service to the assassins.

For this she had to answer when the victors in this latest bout of Rome's civil wars turned out to be Caesar's adopted heir Octavian and his second-in-command Mark Antony. Rome's new rulers were a triumvirate – the three men who now ruled the empire were a Roman aristocrat called Lepidus (who took control of Africa), Octavian (who took Italy and the rest of the west), and Antony (who got the east). Because Antony commanded the east, Egypt fell under his purview as a Roman client kingdom.

While she had to obey Antony's summons, Cleopatra was still queen of a supposedly independent nation and, to prove it, she took her time about showing up. The pair met in the city of Tarsus in Cilicia, in a scene which has become legendary.

> She arrived in a barge with a golden stern and purple sail. Oars of silver beat the water to the tune of flutes and harps. Dressed as Aphrodite, Cleopatra lay under a canopy of cloth-of-gold with young boys in attendance dressed as cupids. Maids dressed as nymphs worked the ropes and took the tiller, and clouds of perfume wafted ashore to the multitude gathered on the river bank.
>
> Plutarch *Antony 7*

It would be fair to say that Antony never knew what hit him. Though, to be fair, a close alliance with Egypt suited him politically as well as personally. The alliance was cemented by Antony ordering the killing of Cleopatra's younger sister Arsinoe, the last of her rivals for the throne of Egypt. Thereafter, Cleopatra and Antony became lovers.

This was a bad move, both politically and personally. Personally, because Antony had a wife and that wife was the sister of Octavian. Though yet a young man, Octavian had a reputation for taking that sort of insult very personally – generally with fatal consequences for those who had offended him. Politically, Antony's Egyptian alliance allowed Octavian to claim that his fellow triumvir had been seduced away from his loyalty to Rome by the Egyptian queen, in whose interests he was now acting. Eventually, Antony formally divorced Octavia and appears to have taken Cleopatra as his wife. Cleopatra gave birth to twins – Cleopatra Selene and Alexander Helios. (Selene being the goddess of the moon and Helios was god of the sun.) This pair were later joined by a younger brother Ptolemy Philadelphos.

With Antony protecting Egypt from further Roman extortion and the economy under Cleopatra's careful administration, Egypt grew prosperous once more. Antony even restored to Egypt some of its traditional Ptolemaic possessions including Crete, Cyrenaica, Cyprus and that long-disputed battleground with the Seleucids, Coele-Syria. Cleopatra also had designs upon Judea which made her an enemy of the current ruler of that country. This was the son of Antipater the Idumaean, a man today called Herod the Great. Herod's rule was highly insecure because his clan had deposed a long-ruling former dynasty whose claims to power Cleopatra now supported.

Though nominally subject to Antony, Herod kept a precarious grip on power through the personal support of Octavian and by ruthlessly executing and assassinating any internal threats to his rule. He also built lavishly and one of his surviving edifices – part of a larger, now-destroyed complex on the Temple Mount in Jerusalem – is today known as the Wailing Wall.

Antony may have been aware that popular support was fast draining away in Rome where Octavian skilfully manipulated public opinion against him. Consequently, he decided to campaign against the Parthians. A victory over Parthia would be excellent propaganda, for the Parthians had not only destroyed a Roman army that went against them in 53 BC but they had captured that army's standards. Rome was desperate to avenge this humiliation, and Caesar had been about to campaign against the Parthians when he was killed.

Also, if Antony could defeat or at least drive back the Parthians, he could legitimately claim to have restored the Seleucid empire. With himself at the head of that empire and Cleopatra ruling Egypt, the glory of Hellenistic rule in the east would be well on the way to being restored. Therefore, Antony felt that it was well worth the attempt.

While Antony's eastern campaign was not the catastrophic debacle that supporters of Octavian were later to claim it had been, it certainly failed in its main objective of defeating the Parthians. Antony was initially successful and he managed the traditional first step of any Seleucid campaigning in the east, which was to subdue Armenia. The Parthians were another matter. Not only was Antony unable to defeat them, he was barely able to extricate his army intact after a series of setbacks.

Cleopatra was waiting for her husband on his return and had brought with her substantial aid with which to resupply his battered army. In return, Antony announced a major resettlement of the east in which, basically, the dreams of every Ptolemaic pharaoh were realized. Alexander Helios became king of Armenia and Parthia (the latter rule to take effect once the Parthians had been conquered). Cleopatra Selene became ruler of Cyrenaica and Libya. Ptolemy Philadelphos got most of the rest of the former Seleucid empire, apart from Asia Minor (though he was awarded Cilicia).

This was less a slap in the face for the Romans than a *de facto* declaration of war. For the past two hundred years, the main thrust of Roman policy in the east had been to weaken the Seleucid empire and to prevent an alliance with Egypt. Now at a stroke, Antony had effectively reversed that policy and restored the Seleucid empire under Egyptian control. Powerful as Rome was, the combined resources of the east were nevertheless a substantial threat. Under the command of a ruler as competent as Cleopatra undoubtedly was, and with a general as capable as Antony in command of its military, the new eastern empire might well overshadow even Rome itself within a decade.

As if his actions were not provocative enough, Antony went on to threaten Octavian's legitimacy directly by acknowledging Caesarion as Caesar's son and heir. Though Caesar had made Octavian his heir, the young man was only a distant relative (he was a great nephew who, in fact, was almost as closely related to Mark Antony as to Caesar). Caesarion was Caesar's actual son.

It is uncertain what Antony and Cleopatra expected Octavian to do about their restoration of the Hellenistic east. Perhaps their elevation of Caesarion was a bargaining chip which they felt they could negotiate away in exchange of Octavian accepting the rest. After all, Octavian's grip on Italy was none too secure and the country had been devastated by over a generation of civil wars. Add that Spain and Gaul were newly conquered and restive and perhaps Octavian might settle for what he had, rather than risk a war against a well-financed and militarily powerful enemy. (At a very rough count, both sides could muster some thirty legions apiece – more men than the Roman empire had under arms ever before or since.)

Even at this point, Antony had enough support in the senate to prevent Octavian from persuading its war-weary members to declare war on him – outraged as those senators were when Octavian released the contents of Antony's will which declared his intention to be buried not in Rome but in Egypt. However, war on Egypt was another matter. Octavian was able to force a declaration of war against Cleopatra in the certain knowledge that Antony would stand by his wife. In 32 BC, the final confrontation between Rome and the Hellenistic east began.

Yet again, Greece had the misfortune to be the battleground between east and west, just as it had been when Pompey and his client kings had faced Caesar at Pharsalus, and Octavian and Antony had taken on Caesar's assassins at Philippi. The world now awaited yet another battle on a scale even greater than these world-changing confrontations.

It was not to be. In the end, and despite the later efforts of Octavian's regime to talk up the final confrontation as a true clash of the titans, the truth is that the battle which decided the fate of the Mediterranean world for the next five centuries was a definite anti-climax. Also, partly because of later propaganda surrounding the event, it is hard to be certain exactly what happened – in fact, even the people who were there at the time were confused by how events unfolded.

For a start, the gigantic armies – almost half a million men by some counts – were mostly spectators. This was because the climactic battle was fought at sea off the promontory of Actium in Epirus. It is not even certain that the battle, fought on 2 September 31 BC, was intended as the decisive battle of the war. Some modern historians reckon the battle was intended as a withdrawal that went disastrously wrong.

By this argument, Antony's intention was to pull out of a stalemate which had resulted from the two armies each holding a strong position and refusing to engage the enemy on theirs. As the days went by without a battle, morale on Antony's side began to slip – as demonstrated by several high-ranking senators who defected to Octavian. Eventually, Antony may have decided to pull his army back to Asia Minor. Cleopatra had accompanied Antony to war and had brought with her a useful contingent of sixty ships. While both Antony and Octavian had around the same number of warships, those of Antony were larger but Octavian had more experienced crews and he had delegated command to the highly competent Marcus Agrippa. (If Antony's later scornful comments are to be believed, delegating command was necessary because Octavian spent most of the battle flat on his back, prostrated by seasickness.)

By this reading of events, the plan was for Antony to use his heavier ships to breach Agrippa's line. Then Cleopatra and her ships would escape to Egypt where the queen would be more useful than in a long retreat to Asia Minor. Certainly, we know at least that Cleopatra's ships took sails aboard as they set out for battle. Usually, before a naval engagement, such encumbrances were left ashore to allow oar-powered warships to better manoeuvre. Once Cleopatra had broken out, Antony's men would run their ships aground, disembark and the army would begin pulling back. Antony would lose some ships but extricate his army from a difficult position.

Things went exactly according to plan with but one exception. After a heated sea battle, Cleopatra and her fleet broke out successfully and headed for the horizon. However, the roughening weather and the fortunes of battle pulled Antony's flagship out of position. He was caught between the open sea and Agrippa's fleet, and eventually had no choice but to transfer to a swift galley which caught up with Cleopatra. As soon as he was able, Antony sent frantic messages ordering Canidus, his second-in-command, to proceed with the withdrawal to Asia Minor, but he was probably aware that the damage had been done.

Octavian's heralds quickly spread out, asking Antony's men what they were fighting for, now that their commander had abandoned them. As Plutarch remarks, at first the men simply did not believe that this was what had happened. Antony had still a huge, undefeated army and he was no stranger to adversity. There was simply no reason why he should not keep on fighting. Yet, day after day, Octavian kept pushing the same message – Cleopatra, a weak woman and a cowardly oriental, had simply lost her stomach for the fight and had fled. The lovesick Antony had chosen to abandon his men rather than abandon his lover and he had left the battlefield to remain with her.

Incredibly, this narrative (despite its obvious appeal to bias and long-discarded stereotypes) is still the generally accepted story of events, mainly because that is how Plutarch reports it, apparently with a straight face. Certainly, Antony's army were persuaded, especially when Canidus decided that there were better ways to die than leading the army on a doomed retreat. He deserted his men in the night, leaving them leaderless. Promised generous treatment by Octavian, Antony's army surrendered without a fight.

With the loss of this army, the dream of a Hellenistic revival in the east died also. And, as Antony and Cleopatra were gloomily aware, it would not be long before they too might be dead.

The final act

Cleopatra was at first defiant, believing the situation might yet be salvaged. According to Plutarch, she made plans to move her fleet overland with the idea of finding safety across the Arabian Gulf. (The plan was abandoned when rebels attacked some of the ships.) Her lover Antony had meanwhile secluded himself at Pharos where depressing news arrived almost daily. The former Seleucid and Ptolemaic possessions in the east hastily transferred their allegiance to Octavian, with Herod of Judea at the forefront. (Herod could legitimately claim to have been a none-too-secret supporter of Octavian all along, since Cleopatra's plans to take over his kingdom were common knowledge.)

There remained hope that Octavian might yet consider that the new eastern realm which had already fallen under his control was enough for him to handle for the present, especially as the west of the Roman empire remained bankrupt and restless. Indeed, Agrippa was at that time writing to Octavian with increasing urgency telling him that he was desperately needed at home to pick up the reins of government in Rome. There was a chance, albeit slender, that Octavian might content himself with Egypt's unconditional surrender instead of personally conquering the country. Accordingly, Cleopatra sent ambassadors to Octavian promising to abdicate her throne and asking if one of her children could rule in her place while Antony offered to live in exile as a private citizen.

Octavian's response was to continue his relentless march through the Middle East towards Egypt. Cleopatra was informed that, if she wanted reasonable treatment, she should either kill Antony or cast him out of Egypt. (Octavian did not specify what would constitute 'reasonable' treatment once Cleopatra had done this.) Realizing that negotiations were pointless, Cleopatra vindictively killed all surviving members of the Seleucid family who were still sheltering in Egypt, presumably so that Octavian would not be able to set them up as client rulers in his new eastern possessions. (This vindictiveness was to prove useful to her offspring. Lacking any other Hellenistic family to set up as puppet rulers, Octavian felt the Ptolemies might be useful. Cleopatra Selene (Jnr.) was later married to Juba who became king of Mauritania. Ptolemy Philadelphos and Alexander Helios were reared in Octavian's household but died before they became adults.)

Determined to resist Octavian to the last, Antony sent his (well, probably Cleopatra's) fleet to oppose the landing of his enemy on Egyptian shores. That fleet reached the invaders, promptly deserted and joined the attacking force. Antony then threw his cavalry against Octavian's troops in the hope of preventing them from gaining a beachhead. The cavalry deserted also. Since Antony was largely using Egyptian troops at this point, he could not help suspecting that they had betrayed him on Cleopatra's orders so that the queen might curry favour with Octavian.

Antony came storming back to the palace for a confrontation but was stymied by attendants who informed him that Cleopatra was already dead. Either in grief for the death of his beloved (as Plutarch, Shakespeare and others would have us believe) or in the sure and certain knowledge that Cleopatra's successor would, as the first act of his reign, hand him over to Octavian, Antony stabbed himself. Allegedly, he lived long enough to discover that Cleopatra was in fact alive and well and the pair made up their disagreements in a touching deathbed scene.

On hearing of his rival's demise, Octavian showed the same remorse that Caesar had shown at the equally convenient death of Pompey, remarking how he had been denied the opportunity to show mercy to his beaten opponent. As to what mercy Antony might realistically have expected had he surrendered, one has only to consider the fate of Caesarion, Julius Caesar's son – and technically Octavian's stepbrother. When asked what should be done with the lad, Octavian mused that 'One could have too many Caesars' (Plutarch *Antony* 81). His subordinates took the hint and Caesarion was quietly put to death.

However, Octavian was determined to have Cleopatra alive. Not only would she be a prime decoration for a Roman triumph but displaying her as a captive to the Roman people would further Octavian's propaganda claim that the war had never been about destroying Antony but was directed against Egypt, the last Hellenistic kingdom and the only Mediterranean power even close to being able to challenge Rome. Ironically, it was partly Cleopatra's careful stewardship of her kingdom that had led to her downfall. Octavian wanted the wealth of Egypt to stabilize the precarious situation in the west. He had a massive army to demobilize, and a bankrupt Italian economy to re-finance. The wealth so carefully accrued by Cleopatra would do the job nicely. Octavian intended to take Egypt, not for Rome but as a personal possession with himself as the new (absentee) pharaoh and open the country's treasury for his political benefit.

Cleopatra had lost her kingdom to Octavian, but she was determined that he would not also take her person. Legend has it that she had an asp smuggled into her rooms, concealed in a basket of figs. Baring her breast, she encouraged the snake to bite her bosom and quickly perished from the venom.

This legend is highly improbable. Firstly, there was no-one to tell the story, for all of the witnesses to Cleopatra's suicide killed themselves also. They died by poison so either they had asps of their own or access to other poison. And if they had access to other poisons, Cleopatra would have taken that. For all that the asp is a highly venomous type of cobra, death by its neurotoxins is a very unpleasant way to go – assuming that one dies at all, for cobras do not necessarily release their venom when they bite. Rather than take a chance on dying horribly, it is more probable that Cleopatra imbibed a pre-prepared mixture of wolfsbane and opium that eased her painlessly into the afterlife.

When Octavian was alerted that Cleopatra had done something drastic, he rushed to her rooms. There he found Cleopatra's corpse neatly laid out (with none of the signs of convulsions, vomiting and diarrhoea that accompany death by asp-bite). It remains for Plutarch to describe the final scene:

> When the doors were opened, Cleopatra was found dead on a golden couch. Of her two female attendants, the one called Iras lay dying at her feet. The other, Charmion, was staggering as she fumbled with the diadem that she was trying to arrange on the queen's brow.
>
> Someone said angrily, 'Charmion, was this well done?'
>
> She replied, 'It was indeed well done, and a suitable end for one who was the descendant of so many kings.'
>
> With that Charmion died.
>
> (Plutarch *Antony* 85)

That day, the last of the Hellenistic kingdoms passed away also.

Epilogue

Recently, Sony Pictures announced that a film of Cleopatra would feature a well-known film star. There was an immediate online backlash because the proposed actress was white and many insisted that Cleopatra should instead be played by a black actress, 'because Cleopatra was an African' (*The Independent* Biba Kang Tuesday 15 January 2019)

The debate later became a lot more complex but this initial reaction underlies how little is known about the Hellenistic period in the Middle East and Egypt. For the average person today, the idea that Syria was once the heartland of a Greek empire is as confusing as the suggestion that Cyprus and Crete were once Egyptian, and at the time Egypt's rulers were Greek.

It is also true that many of the lands conquered by Alexander were only briefly under Greek control and the Greek presence barely registered on the genetic make-up of the lands where they lived.

So how are we to think of Hellenism and the Hellenic kingdoms? Was the Greek conquest historically nothing but a bizarre flash in the pan, to be forgotten within a generation or two after it ended? After all, there is not much about the Middle East today that reminds one of classical Greece. Yet the legacy of the Hellenistic era is one that we still live with today.

For all its many drawbacks and its short-sighted, squabbling monarchs with their petty politics and pointless wars, the Hellenistic era was one of great progress. For a start, like the Persian empire which it preceded, the Seleucid empire was a political entity which transcended nationalism. Greeks, Armenians, Parthians and Phoenicians lived, if not in harmony, at least without tearing each other's throats out, all the while under a government and a set of laws largely common to all.

Science made epic strides. Even as the custodians of the Library at Alexandria reckoned theirs was a dark age because no-one was producing good epic poetry or decent plays, discoveries in mathematics, astronomy, botany and mechanical engineering were powering the human race forward.

Once the bloody conquests of Alexander were done, even the perpetual warfare of the period, while never less than nasty and brutal, was a relatively civilized affair largely fought between consenting adults. The losers were generally recruited into the winner's army. Damage to infrastructure and the civilian population was avoided because these were exactly the prizes that the Hellenistic kings were fighting for, and they wanted their gains to be as intact as possible. It was because the Romans seemed not to have grasped this concept that they appeared to the Hellenistic Greeks as uncivilized and bloodthirsty brutes.

We also forget that the glory days of ancient Greece were long gone before the Romans took over. While the Roman Empire became so pervaded with Greek culture that today historians refer to a Graeco-Roman civilization, this culture was imported wholesale, not from Greece but from Syracuse, Asia Minor and Alexandria. If, as the poet Horace remarked, 'Greece conquered her rough conqueror' (*Epistles* 2.1.156) the arts of civilization were learned from the Hellenistic world rather than from just Greece itself.

Yet, it was after the fall of Rome's empire in the west that the effects of Hellenism were most profound. The rulers of the Byzantine Empire called themselves 'Romans' but in language and culture they were Greek and in many ways their empire was the last of the Hellenistic kingdoms. In many places in the east, there was a seamless transition from Greek to Roman and back again which resulted in over fifteen hundred years of stable government.

Even in places further east which were among the first to shrug off Hellenistic rule, the implications of that brief occupation were profound. The Parthians did not destroy the Greek communities which they conquered – rather these were valued for the economic benefits they brought the Parthian empire and Greek civilization continued to influence these eastern lands. When the head of the defeated Roman general Crassus was brought to the Parthian king after his troops were victorious at Carrhae in 53 BC, the king was at the time watching a play by Euripides.

Eastern civilizations valued and preserved Hellenistic culture through the dark ages of the west after the fall of Rome, for Muslim scholars valued classical knowledge in a way that Christian ones did not. It was the rediscovery of Hellenistic texts from the east that helped to spark the Renaissance and when the great thinkers of the Enlightenment turned away from conventional wisdom, it was to Hellenistic values and thought that they turned. Had Hellenistic culture remained only in the west, rather than being taken east by Alexander, it might have vanished altogether.

Yet unlike many followers of ideologies and belief systems of later ages, the Greeks of the Hellenistic era did not force their philosophy or way of life on anyone. On the other hand, they did not exclude others either. Anyone who wanted to have a try at being a Hellene was welcome to give it a go, and if that person mastered the language and culture to a sufficient degree, that person was for all practical purposes considered 'Greek'.

Certainly, the Romans who defeated the Hellenistic kingdoms had nothing to offer in competition to Greek philosophy, theatre, architecture or science. If these ornaments of civilization were enough for conquest, Italians would be speaking Greek today. Yet, as Alexander once proved to the Persians, in the end civilization and sophistication were no match for brute force.

FINIS

Select Further Reading

Ashton, S., *Ptolemaic Royal Sculpture from Egypt: the interaction between Greek and Egyptian Traditions*, Oxford, 2001.

Austin, M., *The Hellenistic World from Alexander to the Roman Conquest*, Cambridge, 1982.

Bar-Kochva, B., *The Seleucid Army: Organization and Tactics in the Great Campaigns*, Cambridge, 1976.

Bugh, G. (ed.), *The Cambridge Companion to the Hellenistic World*, Cambridge, 2006.

Chaniotis, A., *War in the Hellenistic World: A Social and Cultural History*, Blackwell, 2005.

Fischer-Bovet, C., *Army and Society in Ptolemaic Egypt*, Cambridge, 2014.

Grainger, J., *The Roman War of Antiochus the Great*, Leiden, 2002.

——, *The Fall of the Seleukid Empire*, 187–75 BC, Pen & Sword, 2016.

——, *Kings and Kingship in the Hellenistic World*, 350–30 BC, Pen & Sword, 2017.

Green, P., *Alexander to Actium: The Historical Evolution of the Hellenistic Age*, Berkeley, 1990.

Macurdy, G., *Hellenistic Queens*, Baltimore, 1932.

Matyszak, P., *Roman Conquests: Macedonia and Greece*, Pen & Sword, 2010.

Momigliano, A., *Alien Wisdom: The Limits of Hellenization*, Cambridge, 1975.

Pollitt, J., *Art in the Hellenistic Age*, Cambridge, 1986.

Walbank, F., *The Hellenistic World* (Revised ed.), Cambridge, MA, 1993.

Index

Ancient and modern authors cited in the text